Theology of Anticipation

Princeton Theological Monograph Series

Series Editor, K. C. Hanson

Recent volumes in the series:

Caryn Riswold
Coram Deo: Human Life in the Vision of God

Paul O. Ingram, editor
Constructing a Relational Cosmology

Richard Valantasis et al., editors
The Subjective Eye: Essays in Honor of Margaret Miles

Stephen Finlan and Vladimir Kharlamov, editors
Theosis: Deification in Christian Theology

John A. Vissers
The Neo-Orthodox Theology of W. W. Bryden

Byron C. Bangert
Consenting to God and Nature

Sam Hamstra, editor
The Reformed Pastor by John Williamson Nevin

David A. Ackerman
Lo, I Tell You a Mystery

Mark A. Ellis, editor and translator
The Arminian Confession of 1621

Theology of Anticipation
A Constructive Study of C. S. Peirce

ANETTE EJSING

Pickwick *Publications*
An imprint of *Wipf and Stock Publishers*
199 West 8th Avenue • Eugene OR 97401

THEOLOGY OF ANTICIPATION
A Constructive Study of C. S. Peirce
Princeton Theological Monograph Series 66

Copyright © 2007 Anette Ejsing. All rights reserved. Except for brief quotations in critical publications or reviews, no part of this book may be reproduced in any manner without prior written permission from the publisher. Write: Permissions, Wipf & Stock, 199 W. 8th Ave., Eugene, OR 97401.

ISBN 10: 1-59752-518-9
ISBN 13: 978-1-59752-518-3

Cataloging-in-publication data:

Ejsing, Anette.
        Theology of anticipation: a constructive study of C. S. Peirce / Anette Ejsing.

xii + 178 p.; 23 cm.
Includes bibliographical references, p. 169–178

Princeton Theological Monograph Series 66

ISBN 10: 1-59752-518-9
ISBN 13: 978-1-59752-518-3
(alk. paper)

1. Peirce, C. S. (Charles Sanders), 1834–1914. 2. Hope. 3. Hope—Religious aspects—Christianity. 4. Pannenberg, Wolfhart, 1912–. 5. Philosophy, German—19th century. I. Title. II. Series.

BR118 E8 2007

Manufactured in the U.S.A.

*"Return to your fortress,
O prisoners of hope."*
Zech 9:12

Contents

Preface and Acknowledgments / ix

Abbreviations / xi

1 Introduction: Anticipation in Context / 1

2 C. S. Peirce: Regulative Hopes and Metaphysics / 15

3 Peirce's Theory of Abduction / 74

4 A Peircean Theology of Anticipation / 112

5 Conclusion / 163

Bibliography / 169

Abbreviations

CP   *Collected Papers of Charles Sanders Peirce.* Edited by Charles Hartshorne, Paul Weiss, and Arthur Burks. Cambridge: Harvard University Press, 1935, 1958. Followed by volume and paragraph number: CP 6.38, for example, refers to volume 6, paragraph 38.

EP   *The Essential Peirce.* Edited by Nathan Houser and Christian Kloesel. Bloomington and Indianapolis: Indiana University Press, 1992. Followed by volume and page number.

MS   *The Charles S. Peirce Papers.* Microfilm edition. Harvard University Library, Photographic Service, 1966. Followed by catalogue manuscript number and page.

NEM *The New Elements of Mathematics by Charles S. Peirce.* Vols. 1-4. Edited by Carolyn Eisele. The Hague: Mouton, 1976. Followed by volume and page number.

PS   *Peirce on Signs: Writings on Semiotic by Charles Sanders Peirce.* Edited by James Hoopes. Chapel Hill: University of North Carolina Press, 1991. Followed by page number.

SS   *Semiotic and Significs: The Correspondence between Charles S. Peirce and Victoria Lady Welby.* Edited by Charles S. Hardwick. Bloomington: Indiana University Press, 1977. Followed by page number.

Trans. Transactions of the C. S. Peirce Society: A Quarterly Journal in American Philosophy

xii *Abbreviations*

W *Writings of Charles S. Peirce: A Chronological Edition.* Edited by Max Fisch et al. Projected in 30 vols. Bloomington: Indiana University Press, 1982–), followed by volume and page number: *W*2 731, for example, refers to volume 2, page 731.

The author has translated foreign texts where English translations were not available. In those cases the original text is provided in the footnotes.

1

Introduction: Anticipation in Context

A theology of anticipation is about endurance through suffering. Not suffering under the weight of imposed and destructive evil, but suffering under the weight of imposed promise. Abraham—the biblical character and father of faith in God's promise—conceals the meaning of this claim. More than being the admirable character of a spiritually devout man, Abraham's life of faith is conditioned by suffering personal defeat before God.

For Abraham to live a good fourteen years with God's promise of a son, without seeing this promise fulfilled, but trying to convince himself and everybody else that it is already fulfilled in Ishmael—*this* is to endure a suffering no less real and no less imposed than the suffering he faces through God's command that he must sacrifice his other son, Isaac, the way he would sacrifice an animal. In fact, might not Abraham's prompt willingness to go through with this sacrifice reflect the severity of the prolonged suffering he had already endured because of the promise? The severely delayed event of Isaac's birth simply overrules Abraham's many years of commitment to God's promise being fulfilled in Ishmael, who then turns into a painful and constant reminder that Abraham invested his faith, and his love, in the wrong place. It is improbable that Abraham should lose his right mind instantaneously when God asks him to sacrifice Isaac, but quite probable that he could act in such swift and almost blind obedience because he had already lost it. It is not the senseless command to sacrifice his son that causes Abraham's back to break. Rather, it is the unusual nature of the suffering that is bound to a promise he never asked for, but which he is nevertheless compelled to pursue, through means unavailable to him. But why must Abraham suffer this way?

This question is not foreign to another, but much more famous, question: Why must Job suffer? Far beyond the circles of Judeo-Christian theology, Job has turned into something like an icon of the suffering innocent who believes that God provides, protects, and knows what is best. And

1

then God suddenly allows the stripping of this man's life to the bare bones, for no apparent reason at all. Obviously, that evil has God's permission to bring inflictions on Job puts God's good reputation solidly at stake.

So, leveled by the burden of divinely ordained suffering, Abraham and Job pose the same question: I have not asked for this, or deserved it. Then why does God let me suffer? Still, an important factor separates them. Job's suffering originates with a destructive source of evil whose intensions are purely negative, Abraham's with a source of goodness whose intentions are purely positive. Because of this difference, Abraham's suffering makes much less sense than Job's suffering. That is, from the moment Abraham receives and believes God's promise, he is a hostage of this promise and his own anticipation of its fulfillment. The promise takes on a life of its own, and by believing it, Abraham becomes its prisoner. The fact that his anticipation becomes a more and more confining place for him to live only makes it even more difficult for him to abandon hope in the very thing that weighs him down.

A narrative like this makes it exceedingly difficult to comprehend the reality of suffering. Why must God's good gifts be wrapped in suffering? Moreover, it intensifies the traditional problem of evil and makes it acutely important for theological reflection to dwell on the nature of anticipatory and believing hope.

Approaching Peirce's Philosophy

How does the philosophy of C. S. Peirce relate to suffering and anticipatory, believing hope? Answering this question begins with the fact that Peirce gave his readers little more than indicators of the complete form of two important portions of his thought, namely his theory of abduction and his philosophy of religion. This situation leaves us with the need to pursue not only a constructive completion of these two portions but also the need to determine how such a construction relates to the other elements of his philosophical system. In response to this need, and based on the material Peirce did provide, one can make the case for a reading of his piece on religion—*The Neglected Argument for the Reality of God*, or the N.A., as Peirce preferred calling it—which, in turn, provides argumentative background for a theology of anticipation. Implicit in this reading is the thesis that Peirce's theory of abduction is a function of the principle of anticipation, that it is an intricate part of his philosophy of religion, and that it plays a determining role in his philosophy as a whole.

Introduction: Anticipation in Context 3

Arguing for this reading, I say it all began on Friday, June 20, 1879, when Peirce experienced his own guessing instincts overwhelmingly effective in solving a theft case. That is, this experience quite simply marks the birth of Peirce's theory of abduction as he began to contemplate the wider scientific and philosophical significance of the detective's method. Although his account of what happened is fascinating, perhaps even a tad fantastic, Peirce assures us that his story "is sober truth, sedulously freed from all exaggeration and colour."[1] Be that as it may, Peirce was on a coastal steamer from Boston to New York and at one point left his stateroom of the boat to get some fresh air on land. He took a cab to a location where he was later to attend a conference. Upon arrival, he realized he did not wear his Tiffany watch. This watch was worth more to him than its actual $350 price because of his work with the U. S. Coast Survey's chronometers and the fact that he could rely on its precision. Hence, Peirce rushed back to his room on the boat, only to find the watch (and his overcoat) missing. Commanding all possible suspects to line up, he talked to each of them but no one confessed to the theft, and they left him with absolutely no helpful clues. He turned away for a moment, made a little loop in his walk, and literally commanded himself to point out the thief—which he then turned around to do. He walked straight up to the man and commanded that he bring back the watch. The man denied knowledge of anything related to the accusation. After a while, however, Peirce decided on going to this man's home in person and pick up the watch. Once inside the suspect's house, Peirce steered directly to a trunk on the floor beside the bed, and dived down under a pile of clothes to pull out the very same watch he had lost only a few hours earlier. He also reclaimed his overcoat in the same manner.

Reflecting on this astonishing experience, Peirce concludes that it was the method of abductive reasoning that led him to choose the one real suspect among the many hypothetical ones. The detective relies on a logic of discovery, or a logic of guessing, he reasoned, which must be fundamental to the acquisition of knowledge about all of reality, not just the reality of crimes. Interestingly, twenty-two years later Peirce seems to have changed his mind very little on the matter of abduction and quite simply states that "abduction is, after all, nothing but guessing" (*CP* 7.219). In fact, before the end of his life, his reflections on this rather simple, but astonishing, experience of finding a lost watch had become part of his am-

---

[1] Charles S. Peirce, "Guessing," *Hound and Horn: A Harvard Miscellany* 2 (1928) 277.

bitious projection of a comprehensive philosophical system of Aristotelian rank. Most intriguing about Peirce's systematic ambitions is his intention to span theoretical knowledge and religious experience by the link of an epistemology of abduction and the claim that experiential knowledge of God is the most significant instance of abduction.

Pursuing this driving vision behind Peirce's work leads to an interpretation of Peirce's theory of abduction that holds the potentially theological argument that both knowledge and experience of God's reality are functions of anticipation. Therefore, this study approaches Peirce's work with two analytical foci. First, the manner in which Peirce's thinking is a particularly creative response to the tradition of 19th century European philosophy, especially Immanuel Kant and F. W. J. Schelling. Second, the structural likeness of Peirce's theory of abduction and Wolfhart Pannenberg's theory of anticipation. This approach branches into a number of related arguments that eventually also come to a halt at the need for a theologically constructive study of Peirce's philosophy of religion.

Reconciling Philosophy and Theology

One argument is that Peirce offers a very strong and uniquely American contribution to the theoretical project of reconciling the disciplines of philosophy and theology. This project is, of course, not new, and especially the thought and legacy of the German idealists make it a recurring challenge in theoretical discourse. Hence the need to explore why Peirce keeps returning to both Kant's critical philosophy and also to Schelling's speculative metaphysics. In broad terms, these are the two outer post figures that frame the intellectually intense epoch of German idealism. Kant opens it by a critical separation of the faculties of reason and faith (and, by implication, the disciplines of philosophy and theology), creating completely new conditions for his successors to establish, or re-establish, their unity. At the other end, the later Schelling has earned the reputation of bringing the German idealist project to a closure—or rather collapse—by questioning its most important categories of synthesis and unification. That is, with Schelling's unique ability to critique the idealist tradition from within, especially the idealism of G. W. F. Hegel, a realization of the idealist vision was no longer possible. In light of Peirce's many, but often imprecise, references to Hegelian idealism, it is interesting to explore his ambivalent fascination not only with Hegel's work but also with Schelling's. In Peirce's attempts to tackle the theoretical expanse between Kant and Schelling

Introduction: Anticipation in Context   5

it might just be that he was steeped much deeper in the complexity of German idealist thought than most commonly recognized.

Considering the likelihood of this possibility brings out the fact that Peirce's work is a unique attempt to close the gap between the two disciplines of philosophy and theology. Obviously, it is the fact that Peirce's theory of abduction is of both philosophical and theological significance that establishes the importance of this argument. But what is more, if the theory of abduction is elaborated more completely than Peirce managed to do, then it can also help alleviate the unfortunate tendency to write off Peirce's religious writing as an obscure and bewildering appendix to an otherwise genius philosophical system. That is, the gap that threatens to split Peirce's work in two can be lessened also.

Abduction and Volition in Peirce's Philosophy of Religion

A second argument relates to a more specific implication of the fact that Peirce did not provide a complete and exhaustive description of the theory of abduction. Apart from the fact that he simply did not have time and resources to finish this theory, a more important reason for its incompletion is the extremely complex nature of the issue he struggled to clarify. In its most naked form, this issue concerns the definition of the process of human perception as an activity of self-controlled initiation *and* a disposition of receptive submission. For Peirce, this relates directly to the difficult question of rational self-control in the reasoning process: what it is, and the details of its functions. It is commonly agreed that Peirce's work with the theory of abduction continues to gravitate toward this question, but he is particularly sparse regarding a prospective and substantive answer to it. This is regrettable, of course, because it pertains to Peirce's philosophy as a whole.

With this in mind, it is interesting to notice how Peirce's problem with the theory of abduction is reflected on the grander scale of his cosmology, most particularly in the tension between his two cosmological doctrines of tychism and synechism. It appears that the difficulty Peirce has with reconciling the active and receptive faculties of human perception is reflected in the difficulty he has reconciling tychism (the doctrine of absolute chance) and synechism (the doctrine of continuity). Even more interestingly, a similar reflection is detectable in Schelling's philosophy. That is, both his epistemology and his speculative metaphysics center on the challenge of trying to reconcile the active and the receptive, or in Schelling's language: disruption and synthesis, freedom and necessity, *Real und Ideal* (real and ideal). In a word, there are important systematic similarities in the works of Schelling and Peirce, which suggests a closer relatedness of the two than Peirce's scattered references to Schelling indicate.

A close consideration of these systematic similarities yields insights about the principle of volition, will, and choice that converge in what can be termed metaphysical voluntarism. Applied to the context of Peirce's theory of abduction, these insights are significant for a deeper understanding of the interplay of the active and the receptive in Peirce's epistemology. Most important is the insight that volition is more than the crude and overruling activity of initiation; it is also the *receptive activity of holding initiation back*. The active and the receptive are not each other's incompatible counterparts.

In turn, this insight is particularly important for the argument that there is compatibility and structural likeness between Peirce's theory of abduction and Pannenberg's theory of anticipation. To summarize the argument of the analytical part of this study: first positioning Peirce's work in the context of the German idealist project, then looking at volition in the context of systematic similarities between Schelling and Peirce, and then applying the resulting insights to Peirce's theory of abduction, the argument can leave the philosophy of Schelling and turn to a discussion of abduction in the context of Pannenberg's theory of anticipation. The scope of this argument is that in Peirce's way of appropriating metaphysical voluntarism there is the glimpse of a commitment to volition and the faculty of choice as operative at both the human and the divine levels, and that this makes it relevant to explore the theological potentials of Peirce's philosophy.

Peirce's philosophy is an architectonic system where phenomenology, the theory of the three universal categories, semiotic, metaphysics, and cosmology are closely intertwined, and it is necessary to map the details of this systematic architecture. Analytical details aside for now, it is important to notice that Peirce holds his system together by what he terms *regulative hopes*. Peirce consistently invokes regulative hopes at critical philosophical junctions where it is necessary to make assumptions in order to guarantee the growth of knowledge, maintain the process of inquiry, and simply hold the system together. These regulative hopes are best understood against the background of his appropriation of a metaphysical voluntarism built on the kind of hope that involves the anticipatory activity of volition, will, and choice. This kind of hope is anticipatory in so far as it involves both active initiation and active holding initiation back. In other words, the structural and systematic challenges of Peirce's system direct an interpretive and constructive approach to Peirce's philosophy, in the direction of applying the notion of anticipatory hope to it. One could also say that Peirce's regulative hopes are anticipatory in nature because they establish qualified reasons to believe that what is hoped for will actually turn out to be real. They are more than empty assumptions, or wishful hopes, but still never more than hopes.

Introducing Pannenberg's Theory of Anticipation

A third argument is that Pannenberg's theory of anticipation is particularly well suited to help unlock the conceptual quandary that formulating the theory of abduction had created for Peirce, including its connection to his philosophy of religion. These two parts of Peirce's work can come significantly closer to completion by reliance on Pannenberg's most convincing insights about anticipation. In its simplest form, Pannenberg's argument is that the concept, in and of itself, is anticipation, and so is God's revelation in Christ. *Therefore,* we can gather epistemology, metaphysics, philosophy, and theology under the methodological principle of anticipation. Having argued that anticipation is the most basic and fundamental element of both philosophy and theology, Pannenberg then proposes a comprehensive *ontology of anticipation*. This leads him on to the proposal of a positive theological metaphysics employing conjectures, hypotheses, and anticipations in a way that establishes qualified reasons to believe that hopes of truly hypothetical and anticipatory nature—philosophical and theological—are not unfounded, or just wishful.

Pannenberg's ambitions on behalf of the notion of anticipation are grand and not without problems. One problem is his prompt and bold conclusion that all questions (regardless of origin, context, and nature) express a longing for the hope of Christianity, i.e. the revelation of God in Christ. Another, not unrelated, problem is the systematic command by virtue of which Pannenberg ends up creating something like an unfortunate metaphysical closure that exiles all forms of non-fulfillment, disruption, and even the intentionally novel. This is unfortunate because it betrays the core principle of his own metaphysical enterprise, anticipation, which can never exceed the anticipatory precisely because it must endure hope in a promised fulfillment that either is not coming or, if it does come, can overrule any specific expectations of what it would be like in its fulfilled form.

Still, applying Pannenberg's insights to Peirce's theory of abduction gives interpretive confidence to argue that Peirce's theory of abduction is in fact already a function of anticipation, although in a way that allows and accounts for what Pannenberg does not. Pannenberg's theological metaphysics emphasizes anticipation's involvement in the activity of the choice that takes the fulfillment of God's promise for real in the present although it still belongs to the future. That volition and choice play an important role for Peirce's epistemology of abduction is already established, but that this importance also carries potential importance of religious and theological nature is what Pannenberg's theory of anticipation helps uncover.

Next is now the need to address the theological potential of Peirce's work directly, and to move into the constructive part of this study. Here the argument is that a theology of anticipation implements the philosophical, epistemological, and religious significance of abduction and the question of self-control in the process of human perception in a manner that also begins to develop a theological answer to it. It employs the methodological strength of abduction as anticipation in order to unfold what remained for Peirce only a *vision*, but which has the potential of providing the theoretical support of a complete theological position.

A Peircean Theology of Anticipatory Hope

Most agree that Peirce's religious writing places him in the company of traditional theism. But, given the tentative nature of Peirce's philosophy of religion, what exact shade of theism does it entail? And to what extent is Peirce's neglected argument for God's reality, the N.A., supportive of a theist theology?

Currently, there are two important responses to this question. Michael L. Raposa's proposal of a Peircean theosemiotic that draws significantly on the theology of John Duns Scotus, and Robert S. Corrington's proposal of a Peircean theology of divine potentialities that has very strong parallels to the speculative metaphysics of the later Schelling. My proposal of a Peircean theology of anticipation is an alternative to both. It does not lean on medieval scholasticism and it does not espouse speculative religion. As attractive as both of these approaches are, and as insightful as their resulting works also are, a theology of anticipation approaches Peirce's philosophy of religion on the basis of experiential and believing encounters with the Judeo-Christian God of promises. It argues that Peirce's N.A. describes relatedness of God and human beings as structurally anticipatory. The principle of anticipation is not only played out in the process of abductive reasoning (i.e. in the perceptive relatedness of human beings to the phaneron), but it is also the inner dynamics of how we encounter and relate to God.

The reality of God exists as a promise we experience only by anticipation of it, and engaging the playful discipline of what Peirce calls Musement places a person where he or she needs to be in order to experience God's reality. And Musement is exactly a mixed attitude of active self-control, or deliberate orientation toward God, and receptive expectation of a revelation of God's reality, whatever form it will turn out to have. So, when this God makes more specific promises, these too are accessible by anticipation only—nothing more (one can never do more than *hope* in their fulfillment), and nothing less (one can never avoid taking their future fulfillment for real in the present). This is the argument from Peirce's philosophy of religion that supports a theology of anticipation, or of anticipatory hope.

Where does a Peircean theology of anticipatory hope belong in the tradition of philosophical theology? An answer to this question must start with the general observation that, historically, both anticipation and hope have proven very attractive ideas.[2] Anticipation mainly because of its conceptual and systematic potentials; hope because of its practical applicability; and both because they share an obvious concern with the future. From the very outset, therefore, the notion of *anticipatory hope* has both conceptual and practical appeal, and is attractive to anyone who desires to reflect on what is popularly called *the human condition*. In so far as human experiences can not be confined to the present moment (because they always connect the present to the past and the future) the notion of anticipation and hope provides something like a structural skeleton for descriptions of the human condition.

The Hope Movement and Its Legacy

Discussing anticipatory hope, it is impossible to ignore the hope movement of the late 1960's, which was particularly interested in issues relating to hope in the future and, like Peirce, was provoked by the challenges of Kant's critical philosophy. Hence, many of the hope movement writers referred to Kant's famous claim that the interests of reason are contained in three questions: What can I know? What ought I to do? What may I

---

[2] Both anticipation and hope are rooted in the Greek and Latin languages. Anticipation in the Greek word πρόληψις and the Latin *anticipatio*. Hope in the Greek ἐλπίς and the Latin *spes*. In the English language, prolepsis is often used synonymously with anticipation. Only very rarely is *elpis* used in lieu of hope.

10   THEOLOGY OF ANTICIPATION

hope?[3] Their intellectual attitude, however, was one of deep tiredness with post-Kantian thinking and its inordinate and exhaustively methodological preoccupation with Kant's first question of knowledge. When this problem assumed overwhelming dimensions, they said, post-Kantian thinkers had tended to become just as inordinately preoccupied with Kant's second question of ethics. Consequently, the hope movement writers made a passionate commitment to Kant's third question of hope and offered an infusion of fresh energy into a tradition that had been almost paralyzed by preoccupation with Kant's first two questions.

With its dedicated return to matters of broad and existential concern, the hope movement had substantial influence on political theory, philosophy, and theological reflection at the time. Because of this obvious strength, it still echoes in the discourse of contemporary philosophical and practical theology. It is also the case, however, that, in its intellectual wake, some of its weaknesses continue to plague other and new theories of hope. One particularly troublesome weakness is a lack of systematic ideals. That is, reacting to a climate of excessive theorization, the early hope proponents swung the pendulum to the other extreme, hunting for any good arguments that would do the job of critiquing the current intellectual situation. But in this way they also surrendered to the rule of arbitrariness and lost a sense of systematic direction. Oddly enough, where Pannenberg's systematic command creates an impasse of metaphysical necessity, the hope movement is in fundamental agreement with Pannenberg's original commitment to the category of an open ended attitude about the future, but then ends up surrendering to the arbitrary. Again, paying focused attention to the *anticipatory* quality of hope is a way of offering an alternative to the conclusions of the hope movement. Because a theology of anticipation is also a critical response not only to Pannenberg but to the hope movement and its legacy as well, it is appropriate to throw a quick glance at the history of this movement.

Politically, the 1960's were marked by a sense of living, for the first time in history, in a unified, but therefore also more vulnerable, world. The cold war and the threat of nuclear disasters had helped create this situation, but also resulted in a growing atmosphere of claiming the future more actively. Engaged in optimistic speculations about the future, the hope movement rose alongside Marxist and anti-bourgeois factions in post-war Europe. Ernst Bloch was a strong, contributing voice here, espe-

---

[3] See Immanuel Kant, *Critique of Pure Reason*, trans. Norman Kemp Smith (New York: Macmillan, 1929) A805–806/B833–834.

sad reverberation of desperation because the respect and help that so many people need has not developed as deep a root system as it should. In this sense, the tradition of liberation theology embodies the remains of what is still left of the hope movement, as also Moltmann's affinity with its fighting message of hope indicates. What is more, it points to the inescapable conclusion that we need a new kind of theological reflection on hope.

Theology of Anticipation

A theology of anticipation replies to this need. It argues that hope's relatedness to the future must be *more* than futuristic optimism, even optimism in its revolutionary and angry form. It also argues that hope's relatedness to the future must be *less* than a spiritual presumption of laying claim to a reality that remains unavailable in its complete form. We must ask for our hopes to give permisison to anticipate fulfillment, not only to fight optimistically for it. At the same time, we must be ready to endure and suffer the absence of this very same fulfillment.

We must accept, and even embrace, the life of prisoners of hope. Only the knowledge that our hopes are rooted in something greater than any set of circumstances—including our reactions to them—is able to survive the repeated pattern of hope and disappointment that follows in the wake of receiving God's promise without immediate access to its fulfillment. Without the reality of promise behind our hopes, we have no reason to anticipate their fulfillment, and without this anticipation we have no promised reality to hold us captive in the only suffering worth enduring. Only by enduring the imprisonment of anticipatory hope are we even in a position to ask for the meaning of suffering. This is what a theology of anticipation argues, and the philosophical background it needs is exactly what Peirce initiated but left incomplete. The logical argument of Peirce's N.A. proves this by not compromising the experiential reality of anticipation and endurance through suffering.

I come to Peirce's work already believing in a theology of anticipation and therefore find his religious writings appealing because they affirm what some may call preconceived notions about his work. Still, I consider it a permissible experiment to approach Peirce this way and even more so if it leads Peirce readers back to some level of renewed engagement with his own writings. Therefore, whether or not this study and its conclusion convince my readers, it is still a way to, if nothing else, exercise the skills of constructive interpretation in a manner reflective of a principle to which Peirce showed noteworthy commitment, namely anticipation. This study is, in other words, an invitation to engage a constructive experiment intended to be precisely that: an experiment in how to finish the job Peirce was unable to finish—if the job can be finished at all.

C. S. Peirce: Regulative Hopes and Metaphysics

UNDERSTANDING Peirce's metaphysics requires reading it against the European philosophical tradition of the nineteenth century. This chapter pursues such a reading by first looking at the way Kant's critical philosophy launches Peirce into phenomenology, semiotic, his own theory of the three categories and, finally, a triadic cosmology. Central to this reading is Peirce's strong, albeit not explicit, dependence on Schelling's metaphysics and the collapse of the German idealist tradition he effected by critiquing Hegel.

As Christopher Hookway emphasizes, Peirce consistently invokes regulative hopes at critical philosophical junctions in his thought when it is necessary to make assumptions in order to guarantee the growth of knowledge and maintain the process of inquiry. Without hoping that questions have answers, and without reliance on the reality of these answers, our rational undertakings would never succeed. In this sense, regulative hopes are "adopted because they are necessary for achieving rational self-control."[1] They are invoked as instruments of control in order to regulate and secure a specific course of any given rational activity. Hence, regulative hopes demonstrate that rationality is indeed *activity* because it involves a choice of belief to introduce a postulate prior to establishing its truth value. For hope to be regulative, it must be established as more than an attitude of openness toward the *not yet*, for hope must be *willed* in a specific form and directed toward a specific goal as a matter of action.

Peirce's regulative hopes function akin to Kant's regulative ideas, providing optimism and confidence to the process of rational inquiry and it is tempting to expand this correlate to understand Kant's hope as perhaps the greatest of his regulative ideas. This, in any case, is what Susan Neiman

---

[1] Christopher Hookway, *Peirce*, Arguments of the Philosophers (London: Routledge & Kegan Paul, 1985) 76.

suggests: "Understood as regulative, it is an unshakable demand that the world come to meet the claims that reason advances, *permitting the hope that sustains all our efforts to make this so.*"[2] It is questionable, however, whether such a conclusion addresses the issue of rational control as it is exercised by the inquirer, for how can hope, as a prompting influence of optimism and confidence, be more than a certain kind of attitude? It is, after all, the very specific character of two persistently rational ideas (immortality and God's existence) that makes it necessary for Kant to include the question of hope as significant for rational inquiry. May this not indicate that the inquirer's control is guided not only by a need to regulate the course of reason but also by the reality that is to be unveiled as inquiry progresses? For hope to be a reliable instrument of rational control, and not just an attitude of optimistic openness toward the future, it must be anticipatory, for it must have qualified reasons to perceive as real in the present what still is a reality that belongs to the future.

It is well known that Peirce aspires to "outline a theory so comprehensive that, for a long time to come, the entire work of human reason, in philosophy of every school and kind, in mathematics, in psychology, in physical science, in history, in sociology, and in whatever other department there may be, shall appear as the filling up of its details" (*CP* 1.1). As impressive as this theory would be, had Peirce finished it, an alternative way of accounting for the coherency of his system is to consider "the role he comes to assign . . . to rationally adopted regulative hopes."[3] The predominance and universal applicability of regulative hopes, *not* their specific contents, increase the sense of their systematic importance, and rather than focusing on Peirce's architectonic vision itself, it is even more appealing that the principle of hope weaves itself in and out of Peirce's writings, regardless of the special science in question.

The universal applicability of regulative hopes has direct bearing on Peirce's metaphysics, for although there are different approaches to Peirce's metaphysics, a first point of reference is that his metaphysics "provides a specification of how reality must be if the various regulative hopes that are introduced at different stages of the investigations are all to be fulfilled."[4] Adopting regulative hopes necessitates a metaphysics because the rational inquirer has taken out a number of loans in reality that now need to be

---

[2] Susan Neiman, *The Unity of Reason: Rereading Kant* (New York: Oxford, 1994) 181; italics mine.

[3] Hookway, *Peirce*, 115.

[4] Ibid., 79.

justified: "it will not suffice for the regulative loans to be repaid through a scientific investigation. There must be a metaphysics, prior to all the special sciences . . . which will ground all the regulative hopes."[5] Most prominently, a metaphysics must provide some objective criteria for the assessment of rational claims, and, with the contention that metaphysics provides a description of the most general character of reality, it is to phenomenology that Peirce turns first.

On a more general note, it is Peirce's opinion that metaphysics consists of largely three divisions: ontology, religious metaphysics, and physical metaphysics. Although he allows for significant overlaps of these divisions, their existence still indicates Peirce's desire to hold together ontology, metaphysics and religion in the philosophical discourse. It also indicates the problematic nature of large parts of his cosmo-metaphysical reflections, which are often grouped with his religious writings and considered at cross purposes with the main corpus of his philosophical writings. Indeed, these parts of his work are not without difficulties, especially if one takes an epistemological or a logical approach to Peirce's work. High expectations for logical clarity and strictness of thought in the fields of religion and metaphysics are fostered by Peirce's argument for an application of logic in areas beyond what is normally regarded as obvious candidates for logical analysis, namely cosmology and religion, but these expectations are easily disappointed when one actually delves into them. In response, this chapter attempts to propose a constructive assessment of Peirce's metaphysics with the goal of lessening the conflict between his philosophical writings and the parts that address religion and scientific cosmology.

Phenomenology

Because precise terminology is important for Peirce, it is no surprise that for the discipline of phenomenology he claims *phaneroscopy* a better term for the prevention of unfortunate connotations. Perhaps he does this to stress the point that phenomenology is not a normative science but functions as the *basis* for the normative sciences, logic, ethics, and aesthetics. Whereas the normative sciences concern the standards of good and bad, be it in the areas of thought, moral action or aesthetic form, phenomenology is a preliminary discipline that "does not draw any distinction of good and bad in any sense whatever, but just contemplates phenomena as they are, simply opens its eyes and describes what it sees . . . stating what it finds in all phenomena alike" (*CP* 5.37). Phenomenology must, in other words,

---

[5] Ibid., 282.

operate in complete detachment from any kind of assumptions and suppositions; disinterest must always be its primary and most important qualification. Peirce intends to emphasize that phenomenology must be void of all prejudices, or pre-judgments. A truly phenomenological attitude is therefore very adequately compared to what "the world was to Adam on the day he opened his eyes to it, before he had drawn any distinctions, or had become conscious of his own existence" (*CP* 1.357). The moment a purely contemplative posture turns reflective and the contemplating mind becomes conscious of itself and its surroundings, it involves some measure of judgment and its activity is no longer just phenomenological observation.

It is important to note that for something to be a phenomenon, it does not need to have real existence. Peirce considers imaginations, potential inventions and possible conceptions phenomena too. Hence, phenomenology is not only about the character of all *actual* reality but of all *possible* reality. This claim is directly related to Peirce's contention that phenomenology is logically inseparable from the theory of the three ontological categories (i.e. the theory that nothing in the universe, actual as well as possible, can escape falling under the category of either Firstness, Secondness, or Thirdness). Exactly how Peirce defines these three categories is discussed later. Here it suffices to note that it is hard to determine whether Peirce argues that the reality of the three categories is proven by phenomenological investigations, or whether the result of phenomenology is the appearance of the three categories. Clearly, however, because he argues that the three categories are the absolutely most fundamental elements of everything, they must be found in both actual and possible phenomena, which therefore include what *may* be. Only so will there truly be nothing that escapes characterization by the three categories.

Phenomenology is not the first preliminary discipline but is itself based on another non-normative discipline, pure mathematics. Or rather, the discipline of phenomenology is an expression of the purely mathematical forms and thereby it confirms, "*Pure Mathematics*, whose only aim is to discover not how things actually are, but how they might be supposed to be, if not in our universe, then in some other" (*CP* 5.40). Mathematics operates within the realm of necessity, not actuality. If there is the requirement upon phenomenology to be completely detached from predetermined expectations and judgments, pure mathematics is in its very essence free from any and every kind of predetermination. With the discipline of pure mathematics Peirce is of course working to establish the reliability of his philosophical project as such; because pure mathematics is concerned solely with hypothetical truth and the necessary patterns of all possible reality, it has no need for logical justification. Therefore, observations based on pure mathematics are incontestably reliable and provides material for subsequent, trustworthy philosophical reflection. Hence, it is the role of phenomenology to link the purely non-normative disciplines with the normative, but itself being non-normative, it can not cross the boundary between the two and needs assistance. Furthermore, it is only if the art of phenomenology is possible in the first place that Peirce can document his theory of the three categories. If not, this theory does, at best, lack support. Because it is unable to employ judgments and reasoned conclusions, the phenomenological investigation does not yield the three categories automatically. So, in order both to link the non-normative with the normative and subsequently to release knowledge of the three categories, phenomenology needs the assistance of experimental or applied mathematics, Peirce holds, for only by using the inductive methods of experimental testing can phenomenology complete the task of transitioning from purely contemplative to reflective reasoning.

The use of inductive methods is problematic, however, because its results are subject to fallibility. The way Peirce solves this problem is by contending that although mathematical reasoning is fallible, when it employs inductive reasoning, it has a claim to an *a priori* certainty that other inductive forms of scientific reasoning do not. Because the inductive method of the natural sciences relies on actual reality only, Peirce says, its results are more liable to error than it would be, did it rely on all *possible* reality. The raw material of the natural sciences simply does not represent reality sufficiently, whereas that of phenomenology does. Relying on all possible reality, phenomenology's investigations are not delayed in the pursuit of reliable results by the long process of having to wait for empirical investigations to prove wrong and then redo the tests, a process that may need repetition numerous times. It is because phenomenology and mathematics rely on the imaginary faculty of the mind *also* (which is to say that they give the broadest possible, or imaginable, picture of reality) that their inductive methods are more certain than the inductive methods of the natural sciences. Using all possible reality as its experimental field, phenomenology and applied mathematics are the joined forces that can operate with inductive tests involving all possible counterexamples to any hypothesis, not only those who actually manifest. With the assistance of applied mathematics, Peirce has now linked the non-normative and the normative, and can confidently proceed to an unfolding of the theory of the three categories and argue that it has pre-logical status and is a product of knowledge *also*.

A final note before following Peirce to the theory of the categories relates to the critique that he does not explain why the imaginative faculty can be trusted to add the possible to what is given, phenomenological raw material. Repeating this critique in different terms, one could ask why Peirce relies on the *a priori* certainty of mathematical reasoning but not on Kant's proof of synthetic *a priori* judgments. What is the difference between Kant's *transcendental I* (which synthesizes object and predicate) and Peirce's imaginative faculty of phenomenology and mathematical reasoning? How can a person's imaginative claim to reality be universally applicable? It might simply be wrong. Hookway responds to this question by saying that here Peirce retreats to his familiar argumentative strategy of employing regulative hopes. The discipline of phenomenology and its ability to unveil the purest and most fundamental elements of all possible reality must be an assumption and it is only because of its foundational importance that "Peirce can claim that it is rational to adopt the ungrounded *hope* that phenomenology is possible."[6] Thomas A. Goudge's response is that Peirce's "basic naturalism involves certain 'metaphysical assumptions,'"[7] and therefore can not claim complete neutrality. The *a priori* certainty of phenomenology, he argues, is linked to Peirce's speculative cosmology and therefore gives phenomenology a flavor which is far from naturalistic and objective. This point relates to Peirce's contention that there is affinity of mind and matter and that therefore human imagination and speculative reasoning are reliable faculties. A third response to our question comes from Murray G. Murphey who first observes that "the problem confronting Peirce is accordingly the same as that which Kant attempted to solve in the *Critique of Pure Reason*."[8] He then continues to say that although one would expect Peirce to adopt Kant's proof, this is not what he does. "Not only does Peirce reject the Kantian argument but he declares that the truth of the 'primal truths' cannot be demonstrated—they must be accepted on faith."[9] These different responses have in common that they point to the necessity of formulating a kind of metaphysics

---

[6] Ibid., 109.

[7] Thomas A. Goudge, *The Thought of C. S. Peirce* (Toronto: University of Toronto Press, 1950) 84.

[8] Murray G. Murphey, *The Development of Peirce's Philosophy* (Indianapolis: Hackett, 1993) 23.

[9] Ibid., 36.

tions between the categories. I detected others; but these others, if they had any orderly relation to a system of conceptions, at all, *belonged to a larger system than that of Kant's list*" (*CP* 4.2).[12] Indeed, the reason for calling his first publication on the categories a *New List* is precisely his intentions to complete Kant's list,[13] and just like all fascination tends to involve ambivalence, so it does for Peirce. One must look to his later and more mature work in order to see how the promises contained in this early blend of fascination with and critique of Kant begin to be fulfilled.

According to Peirce's self-evaluation, the project of completing Kant's work on the categories is one he takes on only after unsuccessful attempts at employing "a direct speculative, a physical, a historical, and psychological manner" (*CP* 1.563). Pursuing this route for a while, Peirce finally concludes "that the only way was to attack it as Kant had done from the side of formal logic" (*CP* 1.563). In other words, he realizes what it is about Kant's philosophy that he must acknowledge and incorporate into his own philosophical system: "I was a passionate devotee of Kant, at least as regarded the Transcendental Analytic in the *Critic of the Pure Reason*. I believed more implicitly in the two tables of the Functions of Judgment and the Categories than if they had been brought down from Sinai" (*CP* 4.2). Evaluating the significance of Kant for Peirce's philosophy, it appears that Peirce is suggesting that the relatedness of the theory of the categories and the theory of knowledge must receive primary attention. Peirce's *New List* was, after all, released as the first in a paper series on cognition. Furthermore, "when Peirce set out to systemize his early thought, it was a system of metaphysics which he undertook to build,"[14] as Murphey argues. For the present project of suggesting a particular reading of Peirce's metaphysics, it is important to start where Peirce first starts, with Kant.

As for Peirce's critique of Kant, the main obstacle is his alleged nominalism. Just as it is Peirce's opinion that as "modern nominalists are mostly superficial men" (*EP* 1.53), the modern concept of knowledge in general must be critiqued on the same account. For Peirce, this means that virtually every philosopher since William of Ockham suffers an infection of nominalism. Very sensitive to this influence, Peirce detects the nominalist idea wherever he discerns that someone assumes the existence of the transcendental object, or the thing-in-itself, and also assumes that it is unknowable. Peirce is absolutely unsupportive of adherence to the belief that

---

[12] Italics mine.
[13] Peirce gives this ambivalent response to Kant more directly in *CP* 1.287, 8.279–80.
[14] Murphey, *Peirce's Philosophy*, 20.

universals can not possibly have objective reality in the individual things for which they are *nomina* (names)—independently of whether or not they are comprehended by any individual, or community of individuals. To understand what makes these classical critiques of nominalism uniquely Peircean, his definition of comprehension must now be our focus.

Nominalist belief is nonsense, Peirce holds, because it argues two contradictory things. On one hand it argues that the transcendental object, or the thing-in-itself, exists, and, on the other hand, it argues that it does not appear to the human mind in representation (i.e. by what he more properly calls *signs*). The fatal point here is that a nominalist makes something like an equation of cognition itself and the impressions the external world leaves upon the mind. Although Peirce does believe that a brute kind of encounter between the world and the human mind results in leaving sense impressions on the mind, he considers it highly problematic that cognition should happen when these impressions are absorbed as knowledge by way of what he refers to as introspection, or intuition. For Peirce, the mind can not simply be a container accumulating a manifold of sense impressions in order then for intuition to bring about knowledge of the external objects that originally left those sense impressions behind as a trail when they passed through the mind. It is nonsensical to claim that intuition should be a faculty enabling direct, causal transmission of cognition from the actual object to the subject. A synthetic judgment can not be explained by reference to something as magical as an intuitive fusion of object and predicate. To correct this misperception, Peirce argues that reliance on the illusory faculty of intuition conceals a refusal to acknowledge that sense impressions are part of a greater and complex realm of inter-related signs.

Hold this critique in mind and recall Kant's description of *a priori* synthetic judgment. Kant explains the possibility of synthetic judgment by assuming a *transcendental I* as its condition. By virtue of such a *hidden source in the human soul*, the human subject has active and determining influence on how it knows and understands the world. This is the autonomy and freedom of Kantian individuality. The bitter drop in Kant's description of autonomous freedom is the experience of a disturbing inner quality of *schizophrenia*, caused by a split between the freedom of rational, active reason and the bondage of empirical reason (i.e. the fact that the outside world exercises the same measure of determination on the human subject as the other way around). Kant argues that this *transcendental I* relates to rational reason and empirical reason the way a root relates to its two stems, which is how it accomplishes—by a *transcendental appercep-*

tion—the synthesis between a given object and its universal predicate. If one should insist on a full theoretical understanding of this mystery of synthetic judgment, Kant's simple advice is to stop further inquiry for, using a term from Friedrich Hölderlin, the *Kantian line of demarcation* has been reached. In other words, the event of *a priori* synthetic judgment is explained by assuming that unification of an object and its predicate is facilitated by a transcendental source of human subjectivity. One conclusion to draw from paralleling Peirce's critique of nominalism with Kant's description of *a priori* synthetic judgment is the following. Where Kant fences an explanation of *a priori* synthetic judgment off as a mystery, Peirce ventures on by envisioning a semiotic theory that initiates a break-down of the Kantian demarcation line. Or, in Corrington's words, "If Kant leaves us with an absolute abyss, Peirce puts us on the road toward true convergence in the infinite long run."[15] Again, this is not unlike Hegel's earlier and likewise critical response to Kant.

Making a transition into Peirce's semiotic, it is important to remember where it originates and where it is located within the greater scheme of Peirce's architectonic, namely in close proximity of his critique of Kant's *a priori* synthetic judgment. It is at the heart of Peirce's theory of knowledge that semiotic is introduced, and it must be remembered that many later and more elaborate semiotic theories can in some measure be traced back to Peirce's evaluation of Kant's critical philosophy.[16] Peirce's primary motivation for a semiotic theory of knowledge is a critical evaluation of Kant's epistemology: "Late in the last century, Immanuel Kant asked the question, 'How are synthetical judgments *a priori* possible?' . . . But before asking *that* question he ought to have asked the more general one, 'How are any synthetical judgments at all possible?'"[17] (*EP* 1.167). Hence, it is the virtue of a semiotic epistemology that it can explain how individual elements of a synthetic judgment interrelate to bring about knowledge. A Kantian reference to a *transcendental I* is unable to accomplish such an explanation.

---

[15] Robert S. Corrington, *An Introduction to C. S. Peirce: Philosopher, Semiotician, and Ecstatic Naturalist* (Boston: Rowman & Littlefield, 1993) 143.

[16] Peirce and Ferdinand de Saussure are widely accepted as the founding fathers of modern semiotic.

[17] Kant's question regards "the general problem of transcendental philosophy: *how are synthetic a priori judgments possible?*" (Kant, *Critique of Pure Reason*, B74).

Semiotic

If Peirce's critique of Kant is ambiguous, his critique of René Descartes certainly is not, for it is he who must be responsible for establishing the eighteenth and early nineteenth century idea of human freedom and self-consciousness on the notion of intuition. Descartes proposes a dualist separation of mind and matter—the former equals thought, the latter extension—along with an intuitionist method of determining whether or not some idea in the mind is true (i.e. whether or not it is a true representation of the external object). The intuitionist method is based on ascertaining the quality of that idea, for "whatever I perceive very clearly and distinctly is true,"[18] Descartes holds. The human subject evaluates the level of clarity and distinctness of its own ideas by an act of subjective introspection, ascertaining whether or not these ideas are true and in correspondence with the external reality of matter. This evaluation does not happen by way of inferential judgments, but by way of intuitive cognitions; an idea either appears clearly and distinctly, or it does not. This means that the Cartesian idea stands on its own, unrelated to other ideas. It simply appears to the mind. In Peirce's translation, a non-inferential cognition, i.e. a cognition unrelated to anything prior to itself, "not determined by a previous cognition of the same object, and therefore so determined by something out of the consciousness . . . is to be termed an *intuition*" (*EP* 1.11—12). It is important to note that this definition of intuition involves an entity "out of the consciousness," or what Peirce also refers to as "the transcendental object" (*EP* 1.12), which is the facilitator that makes intuition possible. In his critique of Cartesian intuition, Peirce's focus is not the transcendental object, however, but the alleged experience of clarity and distinctness, which can hardly be more than a potentially deceptive feeling of immediacy. Just as every "lawyer knows how difficult it is for witnesses to distinguish between what they have seen and what they have inferred" (*EP* 1.13), so it is nowhere near plausible "that we can always intuitively distinguish between an intuition and a cognition determined by another" (*EP* 1.12). Take the dream as an example, he recommends: "Not unfrequently a dream is so vivid that the memory of it is mistaken for the memory of an actual occurrence" (*EP* 1.14). Hence, to rely on something like a feeling of clarity and distinctness for infallible access to knowledge of reality is simply not a viable option; it is but an example of boastful

---

[18] René Descartes, *Meditations on First Philosophy*, trans. John Cottingham (New York: Cambridge University Press, 1986) 24.

self-confidence and illustrates how harmful the infection of nominalism is to logical thinking.

In contrast to Descartes' proposal, Peirce offers a kind of monism where mind and matter share a substantial identity because they are linked by signs. This idea is the heart of his semiotic realism. For Peirce, "A sign, or *representamen*, is something which stands to somebody for something in some respect or capacity" (*CP* 2.228), which means that an object functions as a sign merely by pointing to something other than itself.[19] In order to have something be a sign, then, the dyadic structure is sufficient because there need be nothing more happening than one thing pointing to another. That some object serves as a sign does not *complete* the relatedness of the two things involved, for even though the sign is a necessary part of the sign relation, it only *contributes* to the fulfilment. The fulfilled sign relation requires that the third element of purpose emerges also, which happens as the sign relation takes on meaning and a specific interpretation. A sign "is a First which stands in such a genuine triadic relation to a Second, called its *Object*, as to be capable of determining a Third, called its *Interpretant*" (*CP* 2.274). Hence, although Peirce agrees that a sign is a thought, it is one that (unlike the Cartesian idea) cannot possibly have any obvious meaning without a subsequent interpreting thought. It is the emergence of this subsequent thought that gives meaning to the sign relation and thereby makes it truly triadic. Peirce terms this subsequent thought an *interpretant*, "because it fulfils the office of an interpreter, who says that a foreigner says the same thing which he himself says" (*EP* 1.5). The interpretant is the carrier of cognitive meaning, and as cognitive meaning appears, the dyadic sign relation comes out as triadic because its purpose has found expression. In the process of developing cognition, there is a relatedness of the less developed and the more developed interpretation, of the representamen and the interpretant. A sign "addresses somebody, that is, creates in the mind of that person an equivalent sign, or perhaps a more developed sign. That sign which it creates I call the *interpretant* of the first sign" (*CP* 2.228).

Metaphysical Semiotic

One implication of the semiotic triad is that any interpretant (which is necessarily a more developed sign than its antecedent sign, the representamen) is, in turn, subject to interpretation by a yet more developed sign, and so forth. A sign can be both a representamen and an interpretant,

---

[19] Note that Peirce is not consistent in his use of the term *representamen* as synonymous of *sign*.

depending on the perspective (i.e. whether it is seen as the actual interpretant of the *present* sign relation or a possible representamen of the *next* sign relation). This is Peirce's principle of semiotic continuity where all individual sign relations take part in a larger and more complex, continuous semiotic relatedness. How this principle is supported by his metaphysical doctrine of synechism, contending that all matter is *effete mind*, shall be addressed in more detail later, but as a matter of sketching some potential perspectives of Peirce's metaphysics, a few comments are in place here. Raposa suggests that if universal "semiosis is the mechanics, the dynamics of objective mind . . . then everything is potentially a sign of God's presence."[20] In his judgment, this means that a Peircean semiotic is essentially supportive of a *theosemiotic*. He argues that interpreting Peirce's semiotic as a theosemiotic is a necessary consequence of Peirce's own vision and a suggestion of "the sort of text that Peirce might have written, given the table of contents that he provided."[21] A theosemiotic is just such a text in proposal of a Peircean philosophy of religion and an alternative to Peirce's own fragmented presentation of a philosophy of religion. Claiming continuous affinity of mind and matter, Peirce is out to establish metaphysical underpinnings for his semiotic and this gives it nothing less than cosmological and universal scope. In a word, Raposa's theosemiotic expands Peirce's semiotic to a cosmological level.

A theosemiotic is supported, for example, by Joseph Ransdell's observation that "a good ninety percent (if not more) of his [Peirce's] prodigious philosophical output is directly concerned with semiotic,"[22] and that therefore the systematic importance of the semiotic structure can not possibly be overestimated. Also, that Peirce's semiotic should have cosmological and universal scope is supported by his own inclusion of everything in this "most general science of semiotic . . . be it truth or fiction . . . whether it is interrogatory, imperative, or assertory" (*EP* 2:403), his appeal that "this general study must be done by somebody" (*EP* 2:461), and also his late life confession that he never studied anything except as a study of semiotic. Another supportive observation comes from Corrington who says that, "From first to last, Peirce was a metaphysician,"[23] in so far as Peirce envisioned a philosophical architectonic where the universal categories, the

---

[20] Michael L. Raposa, *Peirce's Philosophy of Religion*, Peirce Studies 5 (Bloomington: Indiana University Press, 1989) 146.

[21] Ibid., 3.

[22] Joseph Ransdell, "Some Leading Ideas of Peirce's Semiotic," *Semiotica* 19 (1977) 158.

[23] Murray G. Murphey, "On Peirce's Metaphysics," in *Trans.* 1 (1965) 12.

semiotic structure and the cosmological doctrine of continuity go hand in hand. Corrington keenly argues that Peirce's semiotic perspectives must be fully integrated into his metaphysics and that his philosophy "needs to be rethought from the standpoint of his pansemioticism."[24]

Clearly, Peirce's insistence on a metaphysical semiotic (although the purpose of his semiotic is initially epistemological and methodological) does give it much wider explanatory significance for his philosophical project at large. Still, I argue that appealing to the metaphysical significance of semiotic in support of an expanded semiotic, perhaps even a theosemiotic where everything is potentially a sign of God's presence, can be challenged by interpreting Peirce's semiotic from a different, less cosmological, perspective. This perspective emphasizes the role anticipation plays in Peirce's semiotic structure. The principle of anticipation is present in so far as it relies on something like an *inferential pattern*, or a pattern of cognitive expectation, in the semiotic process. This is to say that Peirce grants the future some measure of influential power over the present, even though the future still has not manifested the way it will at a later point in the process. In order to develop this thesis further, the following looks at Peirce's semiotic structure with an eye to the function of anticipation in it. Keeping in mind that Peirce is increasingly aware of the ability the semiotic structure has to support his categorial analyses, this happens by focusing on the triadic structure of the individual sign relation and the way it functions in argumentative support of his three ontological categories.

As already seen, Peirce's semiotic theory is a theory of thought as signification and emergence of meaning. As it unfolds, it also becomes a theory of language and communication, however. This only seemingly conflicts, Peirce argues, for "thinking always proceeds in the form of dialogue—a dialogue between different phases of the *ego*" (*CP* 4.6).[25] Arguing that the dialogical sign relation necessarily expresses the theory of the three irreducible categories, as does everything else, it is no surprise to find Peirce arguing that the semiotic structure of dialogue and communication is triadic, too. Furthermore, the sign relation is, in and of itself, his clearest

---

[24] Corrington, *Introduction to C. S. Peirce*, xii.

[25] Peirce argues that even the human self must be defined semiotically because its centre is the process of an inner dialogue, or the process of chaining inferential judgments, just as the larger community of inquirers is defined by the dialogue between its members and their shared pursuit of knowledge. Interestingly, the idea that all thought is dialogical in form is at least as ancient as Plato: "Thinking and discourse are the same thing, except that what we call thinking is, precisely, the inward dialogue carried on by the mind itself without spoken sounds" (Plato, *Sophist* 263e). See Ransdell, "Some Leading Ideas," 171.

example of the most complex of the three categories, Thirdness, which will always include the other two categories, Firstness and Secondness: "In its genuine form, Thirdness is the triadic relation existing between a sign, its object and the interpreting thought, itself a sign, considered as constituting the mode of being a sign. A sign mediates between the *interpretant* sign and its object" (*SS* 31).

Consider the verb "to give" as an example of the meditative function of a sign that constitutes Thirdness and thereby fulfils the triadic sign relation.[26] In a situation where two individuals exchange a gift, the verb "to give" construes a genuinely triadic relatedness of three elements: the giver, the recipient, and the gift. All three are involved simultaneously by virtue of the intentional and purposeful act of giving, in that a gift must be both given and received in order to be a gift. This is essentially the idea of *gift*. It is insufficient to say that a gift exchange occurs because A happens to leave B somewhere and then C coincidentally picks it up later. The simple transfer of an object between A and C can not constitute the act of giving. There must also be a transfer of *ownership* between the two subjects, and this, for Peirce, is a matter of law. That such transfer of ownership must be present for the gift exchange to be an instance of Thirdness is well illustrated by one of Peirce's own examples. A merchant throws away a date-stone that accidentally hits a boy on the breast. Tragically, this boy is in the wrong place at the wrong time and dies. Now, this event does *not* belong to the realm of Thirdness because the relation is merely causal, not intentional and purposeful. If the merchant had aimed the date-stone at the boy, "then there would have been a relation of aiming which would have connected together the aimer, the thing aimed, and the object aimed at, *in one fact*" (*CP* 1.366).[27] Consequently, the merchant can not be made responsible for the boy's death, even though his act was its direct cause; not primarily because that would be an immoral verdict, but because it would be illogical.[28] This example illustrates, for Peirce, the distinction between

---

[26] The tradition of anthropological structuralism makes particular use of the gift exchange as a principal semiotic figure. Generally, the tradition of contemporary semiotic has developed in two different directions, the Continental and the American. Saussure is one of the leading figures of Continental structuralism, the main focus of which is linguistics. For him (and anthropological structuralists with him) language is a system of signs that function sociologically as *cultural codes*. The American tradition draws mainly on Peirce's semiotic and, to varying degrees, his emphasis on the evolutionary and universal status of the sign relation.

[27] Italics mine.

[28] In line with Peirce's example, it is to be noted that, in the scheme of the normative sciences, Peirce refers to logic as a special case of ethics, and that, furthermore, it is Thirdness

a genuinely triadic relation which involves Thirdness, and a *degenerate* triadic relation which does not involve Thirdness.

Returning to the verb "to give," the process involved in Thirdness contributes the specific purposefulness that can not be removed without destroying the relatedness of giver and receiver because this would annul the gift itself. In epistemological terms, this means that cognitive knowledge, or meaning, establishes the triadic relation between an external object, its sign, and its interpretant, as genuine Thirdness. As the sign and the interpretant relate in the process of evolving cognition, the knowledge resulting from these two signs relating is the necessary third element in addition to the first two. This process is what Peirce calls *semiosis*, which is the same as rendering an object meaningful to consciousness. Intelligibility is therefore always an instance of Thirdness, as the continuous string of interpretants adds new knowledge to the world, and it is when we consider semiotic relatedness as a living and dynamic continuity that it reflects what Peirce means by semiosis.

The process of semiosis is governed by something like a futuristic necessity forced upon the triadic sign relation. Signs are not arbitrary, but nor are they strictly conventional and predictable. Rather, they are defined by a purposive relatedness to the future, and in that respect they supply the sign relation with a law of openness, or a kind of arbitrary conventionality. Strict conventionality would imply that a sign could be substituted by any other sign of random choice, but this is not possible as all signs have their own designated place in the chain of sign relations. Were signs completely arbitrary, on the other hand, it could not be said that the "sign stands for something, its *object*" (CP 2.228), and not just for anything. Functioning by a general law of conditional necessity in relation to the future, the *cognitive resultant*, as Peirce calls the triadic sign relation, follows what I term *a cognitive pattern of anticipation*.

This cognitive pattern of anticipation introduces the principle of anticipation and emphasizes that the intentionality and purposive nature of semiosis is not simply defined by an internal drive within the sign relation, pushing the sign into the future and thereby bringing about its interpretation. The future has determining influence upon the sign in the present. In a sense, "every given symbolic interpretation is, *qua* symbolic sign, hostage in its meaning to [the] interpretation subsequent to it."[29] The law of openness that the process of *semiosis* must be subject to is not an open-

---

that makes the ethical realm possible.
[29] Ransdell, "Some Leading Ideas," 175.

ness to any possible interpretation of a given sign but involves discovering the interpretation that is already the *destined* one: "A final cause may be conceived to operate without having been the purpose of any mind: that supposed phenomenon goes by the name of *fate*" (*CP* 1.204).

Illustrating this law of *open destiny*, Peirce uses the classical fairy tale of a king who has received the prophetic warning that his daughter will suffer a serious misfortune. The point is what all fairy tale readers know, namely that whatever strategy the king chooses in response (such as shutting his daughter up in a tower to protect her against misfortune, or disregarding the prophetic warning altogether) will prove the very means by which the prophecy is fulfilled. "Fate then is that necessity by which a certain result will surely be brought to pass according to the natural course of events however we may vary the particular circumstances which precede the event" (*CP* 7.334). This illustration is helpful for an understanding of the ideal form of semiosis, which is about the anti-nominalist task of unveiling what is true, regardless of whether or not any individuals have obtained knowledge of it. The purposive element of the sign relation makes it gravitate toward a certain *fated* interpretation, almost in the manner of automatic pilots.[30] Or to put it differently, Peirce says that when a sign functions as a symbol, it "depends upon a convention, a habit, or a natural disposition" (*CP* 8.335). It is important to note that this conventional habit of interpretation is a function of Thirdness, just as the symbolic function of a sign is a function of Thirdness. Therefore, an anticipation of a future interpretation establishes the symbolic function of signs and is dependent upon the influence that habits of interpretation exercise. In other words, introducing the notion of anticipation must pay focused attention to Peirce's understanding of the category of Thirdness as it plays out in the different areas of his philosophy. How Peirce's habits of interpretation reflect the principle of anticipation will be addressed in the discussion of Peirce's doctrine of tychism. This is his doctrine of absolute chance, designed to explain how reaching a predestined goal is always complicated by the fact that nothing is entirely predictable. How the symbolic function of signs reflects the principle of anticipation too will be addressed in the discussion of Peirce's speculative grammar. Thirdly, how Thirdness reflects the principle of anticipation will be addressed in the discussion of the three categories.

[30] Ransdell suggests this metaphor and also relates the tendency of a gravitational pull to what is often called the principle of *equifinality*: "even relatively simple cybernetic devices, such as thermostats and automatic pilots, continually tend toward a certain goal state in spite of the variations in the observational data which are fed into them" (ibid., 171).

At this point, my suggestion is merely this. The principle of anticipation is particularly well suited to explain the complex relatedness of continuity and chance (of synechism and tychism) in the semiotic structure. The role anticipation plays in Peirce's semiotic is perhaps better illustrated by reference to the verb "to promise" than to the verb "to give." By definition, a promise is exclusively about the future; it regards something that will happen at a later point in time. But, a promise still influences the *present* because its primary role is to give permission to anticipate the reality and fulfillment of what is promised. I argue that Peirce's semiotic structure is a function of such a permission to anticipate the future and that it thereby brings into the present what belongs to the future. The purposefulness, or intentionality, of Peirce's semiotic structure is precisely anticipatory because it does not rely solely on the emergence within the sign of an internal and forward push into the future. It strongly emphasizes that the reality of the future (i.e. what is promised) has influence upon the present *prior* to its own fulfilment and manifestation. The fulfilment of a promise is real before it is given. In the act of giving, the gift that is given does not originate in the present. In the act of promising, the promise (which is always a promise of a gift) does originate in the future and only has reality in the present because it is anticipated in the present. It is this principle of anticipation as constitutive of Peirce's semiotic structure that provides argumentative material for an interpretation of Peirce's metaphysics as a metaphysics of anticipation.

Granted, one of the most frequent criticisms leveled against Peirce's position is, as Sandra B. Rosenthal notes, that his "metaphysics is often accused of over-futurism,"[31] thereby causing an undue emphasis on the future. Rosenthal's view is in agreement with John Boler's diagnosis of this same criticism when he says that Peirce is tempted to "force into the future what is quite comfortable in the present."[32] In Rosenthal's analysis, however, Peirce places no undue emphasis on the past or the future but understands these to secure the "richness and thickness of the present."[33] In categorial terms, Rosenthal's point is to say that Peirce's Thirdness does not contract or concretize into Secondness, but that it emerges from Firstness and Secondness. There is, therefore, a logical (not temporal) movement

---

[31] Sandra B. Rosenthal, "The 'Would-be' Present of C. S. Peirce," *Trans.* 3–4 (1967) 155.

[32] John Boler, "Habits of Thought," in *Studies in the Philosophy of Charles Sanders Peirce*, Second Series, ed. Edward C. More and Richard S. Robin (Amherst: University of Massachusetts Press, 1964) 392. See also J. E. Smith, "Community and Reality," in *Perspectives on Peirce*, ed. Richard Bernstein (New Haven: Yale University Press, 1965) 118.

[33] Rosenthal, "The 'Would-be' Present," 155.

forward, where the past imparts quality to the present, and the future is in the present as potentiality, reflecting that Firstness is pure quality, that Secondness is blind and brute force, and that Thirdness is potentiality and rational law. Critiques of Peirce's over-futurism might relate to his belief that the process of inquiry is moving toward an objective goal *in the long run*. In this sense, these critiques would not address the significance of the future interpretation of a sign in the sign relation.

Speculative Grammar

Above, the sign was referred to as symbolic. But what is a symbol? Primarily, the symbol is a member of the icon-index-symbol triad. Interestingly, however, Peirce seems to ascribe more importance to the symbol than to both icon and index, and, as already suggested, Peirce's semiotic enumeration includes icons and indices merely "for the sake of completeness—Peirce's real interest is in symbols."[34] In Hookway's judgment, certain passages in Peirce's writing in fact suggest that "there are no *pure* icons or indicies; all the signs are, to some extent, symbolic."[35] This would imply that the icon-index-symbol triad is a subdivision of the symbolic sign. Recalling Peirce's most fundamental description of a sign—anything pointing to something other than itself—it is clear that all signs have some measure of symbolic quality. The situation is more complicated than this, however, for once Peirce has defined the fundamental nature of a sign, he develops a very intricate system of sign classifications. This results in a fascinatingly detailed *grammatica speculativa*, which is meant to "establish certain rules and standards that will enable us to determine how signs are related one to the other and how they function as signs,"[36] furnished by the three categories and spreading into further triadic subdivisions.[37] Keeping in mind that Peirce defines a sign in more than broad terms—a sign is anything that points to something else—it is only to be expected that he then turns to exploring the different ways signs can inter-relate, and what various roles they can play in the life of inter-relatedness. The discipline of speculative grammar serves the role of analyzing the various kinds of triadic relations,

---

[34] Murphey, *Peirce's Philosophy*, 92.

[35] Hookway, *Peirce*, 126.

[36] Christian J. W. Kloesel, "Speculative Grammar: From Duns Scotus to Charles Peirce," in *Studies in Peirce's Semiotic*, ed. Kenneth L. Ketner and J. Ransdell, Peirce Studies 1 (Bloomington: Indiana University Press, 1979) 128.

[37] For details on these subdivisions, several accounts of Peirce's speculative grammar can be consulted, for example, Murphey, *Peirce's Philosophy*, and Hookway, *Peirce*.

and speculating on their meanings. One might consider Peirce's "classification of signs as laying a groundwork for the long list of categories that he never attempted to articulate,"[38] and his speculative grammar certainly reflects the vision of his three ontological categories by repeatedly indicating that the categories converge with the different kinds of semiotic triads contained in his classifications.

The project of completing the speculative grammar happens gradually in the course of Peirce's life. His earlier efforts conclude that there must be three triads and, as combinations of these three, ten different kinds of signs. Eventually, however, Peirce comes to the conclusion that this classification must be expanded into a more complex and elaborate list that includes ten triads and sixty six different kinds of signs. For present purposes it is enough to bring some elements of the earlier classification to attention, as this is where Peirce's best known insights appear. The most prominent of these insights pertain to the triad of icon, index, and symbol.[39]

As already seen, the most basic semiotic triad consists of sign (representamen), object, and interpretant; it defines the fundamental relatedness of signs and the way signs evolve into the string of semiosis. As early as 1867, in *On a New List of Categories*, Peirce builds on this fundamental sign relation and makes his first attempt at a classification as he concludes that a sign can relate to its object in three ways:

> 1st. Those whose relation to their objects is a mere community in some quality, and these representations may be termed *Likenesses*.
>
> 2d. Those whose relation to their objects consists in a correspondence in fact, and these may be termed *Indicies* or *Signs*.
>
> 3d. Those the ground of whose relation to their objects is an imputed character, which are the same as *general signs*, and these may be termed *Symbols*. (*EP* 1.7)

A sign can relate to its object as icon, index, or symbol—all three of which correlate with the triad of his three ontological categories, Firstness, Secondness, and Thirdness. The icon is a reflection of the category of Firstness, the index reflects the category of Secondness, and the symbol reflects the category of Thirdness. Defining his terms, Peirce says an icon

---

[38] Douglas R. Anderson, *Strands of System: The Philosophy of Charles Peirce* (Indiana: Purdue University Press, 1995) 49.

[39] Peirce's correspondence with the British Lady Victoria Welby is a good source for details on this later classification. Compared to his manuscripts, the letters to Lady Welby make Peirce's mature thoughts on semiotic more accessible.

functions "merely by virtue of characters of its own" (*CP* 2.247). That is, the characters of an icon are analogue to, or *like*, those of the object it represents. Iconic relatedness is therefore established "where the dual relation between the sign and its object . . . consists in a mere resemblance between them" (*CP* 3.362), and, he continues, "I call a sign which stands for something merely because it resembles it, an *icon*" (*CP* 3.362). Examples of icons are mathematical formulas, geometrical projections (e.g. architectural sketches and floor plans), diagrams, pictures (e.g. photographs and portraits), imaginations, and dreams. Take the architectural sketch. Examining the sketch of a building complex provides the student of architecture with information about the actual buildings represented by the sketch. The iconic sketch has some character, property, or quality in common with the building complex, which does not depend on their relation, for both sketch and building would have the quality separately, regardless of whether or not the other had it too. It is shared only by analogue. In that an icon shares quality with the object it represents, it correlates directly with the category of Firstness.

Turning to the second kind of sign in the triad, "An *Index* is a sign which refers to the Object that it denotes by virtue of being really affected by that Object" (*CP* 2.248). It is clear that indexical relatedness is part of Peirce's critique of nominalism. It ensures that a sign is not detached from the realm of matter (like the Cartesian idea), but rather embodied in it by appearing in the form of what can be called a *bodily feeling*. Peirce uses the weathercock as an example. "A weathercock is a sign of the direction of the wind. It would not be so unless the wind made it turn round. There is to be such a physical connection between every sign and its object" (*PS* 141). The semiotic relatedness of a weathercock and the wind is constituted by the material quality of the indexical sign relation.[40] The indexical relation exploits dyadic relatedness of signs in that there must be a bodily and physical interaction between a sign and its object. In Douglas R. Anderson's formulation, indices find their utility "in drawing attention and providing directions to their objects, both physically and conceptually."[41] The indexical sign relation consists of both iconic and indexical

---

[40] This part of Peirce's argument works in support of the view that human thinking is a brain process and that thought evolves in so far as a material quality is processed by signs inter-relating. This view would, as James Hoopes comments, probably be "congenial even to many who do not otherwise agree with his [Peirce's] metaphysics"; James Hoopes, introduction to *Peirce on Signs: Writings on Semiotic by Charles Sanders Peirce*, ed. James Hoopes (Chapel Hill: University of North Carolina Press, 1991) 10.

[41] Anderson, *Strands of System*, 47.

elements, just as the category of Secondness also includes Firstness. The index correlates with Secondness.

Finally, there is the symbolic sign relation. Although a symbol has no existence, "it has a real being *consisting in* the fact that existents *will* conform to it" (*CP* 2.292), in the sense that it refers to a basic habit or belief-act, i.e. a general, law-like mode of interaction, on the basis of which some concrete action takes place. The symbol depends, in other words, on there being a law of interpretation that enables the activity of meaning and cognition to evolve. The symbolic sign relation is involved in what Peirce terms *habits of interpretation*, a notion to be addressed in detail in conjunction with the principle of rational self-control during the process of rational inquiry. The process of rational inquiry is guided by the fact that a symbolic sign "is related to its object only in consequence of a mental association, and depends upon a habit. Such signs are always abstract and general, because habits are general rules to which the organism has become subjected" (*CP* 3.360). Because they are under the influence of a habitual law of intentionality, symbols can be neither arbitrary nor conventional, but must work to supply meaning by some kind of conditional necessity. The symbolic sign correlates with Thirdness and involves both the iconic and the indexical sign relation, just as Thirdness also involves both Firstness and Secondness.

In summary, the triad of icon-index-symbol explicates how signs signify either an object's possibility (in which case they function as icons), its contingent necessity (by functioning as indices), or they signify the intentionality and purpose of an object (and function as symbols). Relating this back to where the discussion of semiotic started, namely the need Peirce sees to make substantial corrections to the modern theory of knowledge, a few things now fall into place. First, signs are the proper focus for any explanatory theory of knowledge because they function as *mediators* of knowledge through the formation of hypothetical inferences. Hypothetical inferences are reductions of sense impressions (*icons*) and their related interpretants (*indices*) to the unities that are propositions about the external world. A perceptual judgment unifies the manifold of given sense impressions; it deduces the manifold to unity by making a hypothetical inference. It is the hypothetical inference that is the product of sense impressions interpreted, and this hypothesis then transitions into the formation of the *next* hypothetical inference, and so forth. In that Peirce does not insist on "this or that logical solution . . . but merely that cognition arises by a *process* of beginning, as any other change comes to pass" (*EP* 1.27), knowledge of the world evolves as a process. Perceptual judgments are defined by the events of deduction that make up the process of semiosis, and therefore a perception is what it is by virtue of its function. It can not exist apart from the manifold sense impressions of our experience, but neither can we transfer our sense impressions to the realm of thought and comprehend their meaning without their assistance of signs as the mediators facilitating the transfer, and helping in the process of unifying sense impressions. It is only upon the event of a synthesis between a sense impression and its predicate that an inference can be made and a hypothetical statement about a given external object advanced. According to Peirce, only *this* properly defines the birth of cognition. Second, this gives epistemological status to Peirce's semiotic, for, as Hookway says, "a theory of meaning and signification is, at root, a theory of understanding: It must explain how we are able to understand or interpret the meanings of signs."[42] Clearly, a semiotic epistemology addresses the Cartesian misunderstanding of how cognition happens. Without change, Peirce holds, no cognition is possible, and no change will happen instantaneously, because of the developmental process that it requires. And so, intuitive knowledge, as Descartes understands it, is simply impossible. Third, cognition is absolutely dependent on being interwoven with matter. No hypothetical inference can emerge apart from observed facts.

It is very appropriate to conclude, with Karl-Otto Apel, that Peirce's suggested transformation of the modern concept of knowledge relies directly on his semiotic warrant of the three categories as an alternative to Kant's transcendental deduction: "This semiotic transformation of the modern concept of knowledge, based on the idea of hypothetical inference . . . makes possible Peirce's 'metaphysical' and 'transcendental' deduction of his fundamental categories."[43] Murphey echoes Apel's point and describes Peirce's metaphysical deduction of the three categories by first assuming that Peirce understands Kant's *I think*—the transcendent unity of apperception—to, in fact, mean *God thinks*. Consequently, everything we experience in representation springs from the original unity in God's mind of idea and sensory impression; idea and matter are in unity in God's mind. Keeping in mind that Peirce's phenomenology concerns all possible experience, he can establish a *semiotic phenomenalism* and maintain that whatever is true about the sign must be true for all possible experience because all representation has its origin within the unity of divine mind.

---

[42] Hookway, *Peirce*, 127.

[43] Karl-Otto Apel, *Charles S. Peirce: From Pragmatism to Pragmaticism*, trans. John Michael Krois (Amherst: University of Massachusetts Press, 1881) 22.

Peirce's next step then is, as Murphey continues, to initiate a comprehensive analysis of the sign relation, and this is the analysis that reveals the sign relation to be fundamentally triadic in its structure. In turn, this discovery then gives Peirce the proof he needs in order to establish an argument for the ontological status of his categories.

Understanding Peirce's semiotic epistemology as set in a Kantian frame of reference necessitates taking a look at an important added fourth element in relation to the triadic sign relation, namely Peirce's notion of *ground*. This will also conclude our discussion of the triad icon-index-symbol. In Peirce's own words, "The sign stands for something, its *object*. It stands for that object, not in all respects, but in reference to a sort of idea, which I have sometimes called the *ground* of the representamen. 'Idea' is here to be understood in a sort of Platonic sense, very familiar in everyday talk" (*CP* 2.228). This ground is, in other words, operative in the process of signification and leads the interpretation in a certain direction, which is to say that whether a sign functions as an icon, an index, or a symbol, is determined by the ground. As a kind of stabilizing idea, ground serves the purpose of establishing consistency and unity among the ideas one already possesses and those one is in the process of interpreting. Ground may therefore be best described as *recollection*, always working "backwards in relation to the past in that it grasps and generalizes . . . past facts, simultaneously leaving these regularities concerned with the future which one [therefore] anticipates will show the same tendentious characteristics."[44] As Anne Marie Dinesen explains, mere remembrance would concern the many particular facts of our past experiences, whereas recollection concerns the general ideas to which those particular memories are attached. This is why Peirce holds that the beliefs we have already established about the relations of signs and their objects are what determine how we should interpret signs later. "All our knowledge of the future is general, for we have no experience of it. My confidence that I know the sun will rise tomorrow consists in my thinking it *must* and under the circumstances (vaguely apprehended) always would" (*NEM* 813). Peirce's notion of ground means this: already established beliefs about how signs relate to their objects anticipate future sign interpretations, and they provide the unity of thought that is needed in order to guarantee that signs are not *misinterpreted*, but interpreted as they ought to be.

---

[44] Anne Marie Dinesen, *C. S. Peirce: Fænomenologi, Semiotik og Logik* [C. S. Peirce: phenomenology, semiotic and logic] (Århus: Tryk, 1992) 104; translation mine.

This takes us back to the question that originally necessitated a discussion of Peirce's semiotic, namely Peirce's question to Kant: How are any synthetical judgments at all possible? Peirce answers this question semiotically, explaining that the synthetic judgment is possible because of three irreducible elements that interrelate in order to bring about knowledge. This is the background for the semiotic sign relation where sense impressions and their predicates come together in a hypothetical statement about a given external object. Moreover, Peirce's semiotic is buttressed by a very detailed speculative grammar and secured by the three ontological categories. Next, it is important to pay more specific attention to Peirce's description of the categories of Firstness, Secondness, and Thirdness, and we now turn to this task.

The Indecomposable Elements of the Universe

An exposition of the three categories concerns the *real* phenomena of the world as well as the *possible*, as it will be recalled from the discussion of Peirce's linking of the non-normative with the normative sciences. It is with the discipline of applied mathematics that Peirce makes this link and it guarantees that the categories concern not only the phenomenologically real but also the *potentially* real. The three categories have, in other words, ontological status; they are indecomposable elements of everything that is—real or potential. As such, the categories First, Second, and Third must therefore be understood as "ideas so broad that they may be looked upon rather as moods or tones of thought, than as definite notions" (*EP* 1.247). Although Peirce insists that the categories are the abiding results of phenomenological investigations, he gives no reason to "deny that there are other categories. On the contrary, at every step of every analysis, conceptions are met with which presumably do not belong to this series of ideas" (*CP* 1.525). When, therefore, one takes to describing the content of the ontological categories, it is a challenging project where especially Firstness and Thirdness are difficult to portray accurately. This is due partly to their particularly complex nature and partly to the fact that the categories "are so intangible that they are rather tones or tints upon conceptions" (*CP* 1.353).

Firstness

Firstness is monadic. It is pure quality and "something *which is what it is without reference to anything else* within it or without it, regardless of all force and of all reason" (*CP* 2.85). The quality of Firstness is discernable apart from any sense of time, with no awareness of past and future. This means that Firstness can not involve any reflection or self-consciousness, for it "cannot be articulately thought: assert it, and it has already lost its characteristic innocence. . . . Stop to think of it, and it has flown!" (*CP* 1.357). Firstness is as innocent as immediate consciousness—it is a "*Quality* of Feeling" (*CP* 5.66)—and therefore it is, in fact, impossible to produce an adequate description of it. "It is so tender that you cannot touch it without spoiling it" (*CP* 1.358). To conceptualize an experience of Firstness would be like touching it. Compared to the categories of Secondness and Thirdness, Firstness is the most difficult to describe, and one must accept that the only available routes to an understanding of its nature are indirect.

It has been suggested that the experience of primitive, vegetating organisms could exemplify the kind of unspoiled reality of Firstness that Peirce attempts to distinguish by describing it as a quality of feeling.[45] An experience of Firstness would then be like a complete immersion in pure quality and make all awareness identical with that quality itself. An identity like this would be void of all time and self-consciousness, more like an isolated sense experience. Imagining a situation that might bring the human experience close to such a state of being leads us to consider how it would be "in a slumberous condition to have a vague, unobjectified, still less unsubjectified, sense of redness or of salt taste, or of an ache, or of grief or joy, or of a prolonged musical note. That would be, as nearly as possible, a purely monadic state of feeling" (*CP* 1.303). Pure colour, for example, without an object, but as an expression of its own is-ness (e.g. redness as such) is a monadic state of feeling. Unrelated to anything else, even its own past and future, redness in itself can only be found in the unadulterated present moment: "The present is just what it is regardless of the absent, regardless of past and future" (*CP* 5.44). Obviously, the difficulty here is to grasp Peirce's notion of a form of consciousness bereft of reflective self-consciousness: "Now a *quality* is a consciousness. I do not say a *waking* consciousness—but still, something of the nature of consciousness, a potential consciousness. A *sleeping* consciousness, perhaps" (*CP* 6.221).

With his account of the category of Firstness, Peirce reiterates his case against the position of nominalism, only now in the context of introducing his notion of Firstness. On the nominalist view, quality is always and necessarily related to an actual sense experience, and it is precisely this relatedness Peirce labours at great length to divide. He does so by isolating

---

[45] See ibid., 27.

pure quality from the actual. Describing Firstness as immediate, innocent, and unspoiled quality, Peirce emphasizes that it can know nothing of the laws of necessity that all actualizations imply. It is "absolutely undefined and unlimited possibility—boundless possibility. There is no compulsion and no law. It is boundless freedom" (*CP* 6.217). If pure quality is subjected to any measure of dependency upon the actual, he holds, it will no longer be unlimited possibility because its potentiality is reduced by the limitations of its objectified appearance. Speaking of the nominalist position, Peirce therefore explains that, "quality is a mere abstract potentiality; and the error of those schools lies in holding that the potential, or possible, is nothing but what the actual makes it to be" (*CP* 1.422). Using the example of colour, Peirce also criticizes nominalists for a more than obvious misperception. "That the quality of red depends on anybody actually seeing it, so that red things are no longer red in the dark, is a denial of common sense" (*CP* 1.422). Pure potentiality and possibility is absolutely independent of both actualization and someone in fact seeing it, for Firstness may or may not actualize, and it may or may not be seen. Either way, it remains what it is.

In his description of Firstness, Peirce takes the freedom to voice what he considers a stark disagreement with Hegel. Because Hegel defines abstraction as a result of rational processing, the Hegelian notion of abstraction can never be a true category; the rational process can always be reduced to that upon which reason initially began its reflection. The categories are absolutely irreducible. Hegel is committed, Peirce argues, to some kind of necessity by which reason unfolds over the span of historical development. What strikes him as a fallacy is that Hegel takes the universe to evolve by something like "the logic of events" (*CP* 6.218). This excludes, Peirce argues, a state of being where time is completely absent, for if the principle of a rationally evolving universe determines one's definition of reality, then there is no reality, and no state of being without time. "We have therefore to suppose a state of things before time was organized" (*CP* 6.214). In short, Peirce argues that Hegel subscribes to a permeating influence of reason as an intrinsic principle of reality, which excludes any talk about Firstness in its purity: "the absolutely First must be entirely separated from all conception of or reference to anything else . . . It precedes all synthesis and all differentiation: it has no unity and no parts" (*EP* 1.248). Two things influence Peirce's critique of Hegel and leave much to be desired in terms of sensitivity to the complexity of Hegel's work. First, Peirce is very quick to detect the enemy of nominalism in modern thinkers, and Hegel is no exception. He is a nominalist because he identifies abstraction as something irreducible when, in fact, it is only a product of human reflection. Second, Peirce joins those who criticise Hegel for giving absolute status to reason as the intrinsic and irreducible power of evolution. Logically, there must be a beginning state of affairs prior to the commencement of evolution where there is "absolutely undefined and unlimited possibility—boundless possibility.... So of *potential* being there was in that initial state no lack" (*CP* 6.217). This boundless freedom without rational processes and evolutionary movement is, for Peirce, true Firstness.

Secondness

"The idea of second must be reckoned as an easy one to comprehend" (*EP* 1.249). One reason is that "second is eminently hard and tangible. It is very familiar, too; it is forced upon us daily: it is the main lesson of life" (*EP* 1.249). So, what is this main lesson of life? It is found in all places where something *reacts* to something else. It always "meets us in such facts as Another, Relation, Compulsion, Effect, Dependence, Independence, Negation, Occurrence, Reality, Result" (*EP* 1.248). All of these necessarily involve something which is first in order for there to be a reaction, a differentiation, a splitting off, a disrupted unity, or any manner of encounter: "A thing cannot be other, negative, or independent, without a first to or of which it shall be other, negative or independent" (*EP* 1.248). Secondness is dyadic, in that it involves the monadic Firstness, for "Second is precisely that which cannot be without the first" (*EP* 1.248).

One of Peirce's examples of Secondness is the common experience of having to exercise muscular effort when trying to open a heavy door. The resistance of the door is what causes an increased effort to push it open. "I instance putting your shoulder against a door and trying to force it open against an unseen, silent, and unknown resistance. We have a two-sided consciousness of effort and resistance" (*CP* 1.24). As Peirce comments, this is "a two-sided sense, revealing at once a something within and another something without" (*CP* 2.84). Were there no resistance on the part of the door, there would be no reaction of pushing out against it on the part of the person opening it, which is to say, again, that the event itself is naturally and necessarily dyadic in nature. It is an instance of Secondness. And like this example, Secondness is everywhere a reality where there are some brute actions of one subject on another subject.

An important conception for Peirce's definition of Secondness is *experience*. "In youth, the world is fresh and we seem free; but limitation, conflict, constraint, and secondness generally, make up the teaching of experience" (*CP* 1.358). On a yet higher level, Peirce suggests that Secondness "blindly forces a place for itself in the universe, or willfully crowds its way in" (*CP* 1.459). In any case, all human beings feel the imposing nature of Secondness through whatever experiences involve an encounter with some external fact, or perhaps a foreign idea. On this account, all forms of experience are included, in that they all involve some level of effort and resistance, or cooperation with the surprising fact that happens to cause the experience: "We are continually bumping up against hard fact. We expected one thing, or passively took it for granted, and had the image of it in our minds, but experience forces that idea into the background, and compels us to think quite differently" (*CP* 1.324). It is the nature of Secondness to change the expected course of events. It is important to remember that Peirce's phenomenological backdrop ensures a definition of experience that includes both physical and mental encounters with the external and foreign. Secondness can be instanced by an encounter of actual, physical objects, but just as well by encounters of things like mental ideas.

Peirce also defines Secondness by the use of attributes like existence, actuality, and *haecceitas*. The phenomenological raw material of reality—the phaneron—is, in its actuality, "something *brute*. There is no reason in it" (*CP* 1.24). The example of putting one's shoulder against a heavy comes very close to this pure sense of actuality because it illustrates how one object defines another. In Peirce's argument, nothing—actual or mental—is anything in and of itself, but only truly exists when it is in a state of being second to something else, for "whatever it is, it is for what it is attracting and what it is repelling: its being is actual, consists in action, is dyadic. That is what I call *existence*" (*CP* 6.343). The mere fact that something exists establishes its actuality, which means that there is no generality to be found in actual existence. "Secondness, strictly speaking, is just when and where it takes place, and has no other being; and therefore, different Secondnesses, strictly speaking, have in themselves no quality in common" (*CP* 1.532). It is the *hic et nunc*, what happens right here and right now, that determines actual existence, without any relatedness whatsoever. As for the attribute of *haecceitas*, it too defines Secondness, although it does not appear in his writings until after 1890 which is more than twenty years after his first publication on the categories. For Peirce, Secondness "involves an unconditional necessity, that is, force without law or reason, *brute* force" (*CP* 1.427). So, even though an event as a whole (a piece of rock breaking away from a cliff and rolling into the valley, for example), is explainable by law and reason, its mere *this-ness*, the naked reality of its *happening*, its matter-of-fact and individual reality, still has something accidental and unpredictable about it. It is in this technical sense of reality's unintentional and almost irrational quality that Peirce applies the term *haecceitas*.

Peirce does not attempt to emphasize the temporal and spatial conditions of existence by employing the "here and now" terminology. Rather, referring to one of his favorite philosophers, he points to the simple actuality of a thing's appearance: "*Hic et nunc* is the phrase perpetually in the mouth of Duns Scotus, who first elucidated individual existence. It is a forcible phrase if understood as Duns did understand it, not as describing individual existence, but as suggesting it by an example of the attributes found in this world to accompany it" (*CP* 1.458). Contrary to Firstness, then, Secondness relates to time, although not time in a historical sense, but time as "already closed," as it were. What has obtained existence will have no later opportunity to live a life of change, without moving from a state of being second to a state of being third. In other words, time can only play a *mediating* role in the *hic et nunc* actualization of some possibility; it can not establish temporality. This notion of mediating, non-temporal time may be clarified by situating Secondness in the context of all three categories. It is impossible to have pure Firstness if there is any trace of something second going along with it, and "likewise to think the Second in its perfection we must banish every third" (*EP* 1.248). Secondness can not be without Firstness, and would most certainly dissolve with any touch of Thirdness involved. Also, if Firstness is restricted to the absolutely present, then Secondness is an event of the past. In fact, because there is no trace of Thirdness in Secondness, "Second is therefore the absolute last" (*EP* 1.248).

Other examples of Secondness could be a sudden sound breaking into silence, or the discovery of an impressive idea. In both cases some external reality imposes itself with some measure of forceful effort, followed by an immediate reaction of astonishment. Effort meets with resistance. Another example is human will. We employ our will to bring about some desired change, but what effect our efforts have depends on the state of affairs beyond the control and influence of our will, perhaps someone else's will. For instances of Secondness, such as these three examples, the pure potentiality and absolute freedom found in Firstness is limited by the actual, for whenever some possibilities are actualized, others are ruled out. When a sudden sound breaks the silence, it is no longer possible that some other sound could take its place. When I encounter and contemplate an impressive idea, there are a vast number of ideas I exclude from my experience. Just as when I make a certain choice, many other choices are no longer possible for me to make. The definite always limits the indefinite.

Defining Secondness, Peirce once again hits Hegel with a serious point of critique. In his review of Josiah Royce's *Religious Aspect of Philosophy*, Peirce includes the comment that the "capital error of Hegel which permeates his whole system in every part of it is that he almost altogether ignores the Outward Clash" (*EP* 1.233). This has the serious consequence, he continues, that Hegel neglects the "direct consciousness of hitting and of getting hit [which] enters into all cognition and serves to make it mean something real" (*EP* 1.233). Although at this point Peirce may not have seen, as Max H. Fisch remarks, that he "is on his way to a three-category realism in which ultimate reality is ascribed to seconds rather than to thirds or firsts,"[46] in retrospect this comment is clearly concerned with the category of Secondness, upon which all actual reality hinges.

Thirdness

"First and Second, Agent and Patient, Yes and No, are categories which enable us roughly to describe the facts of experience, and they satisfy the mind for a very long time. But at last they are found inadequate, and the Third is the conception which is then called for" (*EP* 249). With this appeal, we now turn to the category of Thirdness, which completes Peirce's triad of irreducible categories.

There will be no genuine triad without the involvement of Thirdness, but nor "will it be possible to find any Secondness or Firstness in the phenomenon that is not accompanied by Thirdness" (*CP* 5.90). A genuine triad is, in other words, impossible without the involvement of the first and the second ingredients of the triadic synthesis established by Thirdness, which is triadic, therefore, by virtue of including both Firstness and Secondness. This is another way of saying that all phenomena—physical as well as mental—involve the three categories, and that if the phaneron should reveal instances of more categories than three, then "analysis will show that every relation which is *tetradic, pentadic*, or of any greater number of correlates is nothing but a compound of triadic relations" (*CP* 1.347). The three categories always involve each other, and also always remain irreducible. In categorial terms, this means that nowhere is there anything else to be found except Firstness, Secondness, and Thirdness.

---

[46] Max H. Fisch, *Peirce, Semeiotic, and Pragmatism: Essays by Max Fisch*, ed. Kenneth Ketner and Christian Kloesel (Bloomington: Indiana University Press, 1986) 190.

Keeping in mind that Peirce understands the relatedness of icon, index and symbol as the most fundamental triad of all, it is no surprise to see him contend that "in this genuine Thirdness we see the operation of a sign" (*CP* 1.537), when we remember that, in this case, Peirce refers to sign in the general sense of semiotic process. For Peirce, genuine Thirdness is representation, "*composition*" (*CP* 1.297), predication, or intention, all of which point to a repetition of Peirce's semiotic doctrine that in order for a sign to take on meaning (i.e. to be interpreted in one specific way as opposed to other ways) it must find itself in a triadic relatedness of representamen, object and interpretant. For meaning to occur, that is, Thirdness emerges in the form of "a permanent conditional force, or *law*" (*CP* 3.435) that functions as the mediator between two elements. Anchored in Peirce's semiotic, the category of Thirdness becomes the forward drive of mental intentionality, or the piercing power of mind, whose mediating laws of judgment establish syntheses between estranged elements. Thirdness is the tendency of mind to *synthesize* Firstness and Secondness by bringing them together in an intentional composition of meaning, and to express "the peculiar flavor or color of mediation, we have no really good word. *Mentality* is, perhaps, as good as any, poor and inadequate as it is" (*CP* 1.533).

For the sake of illustration, Peirce uses the example of a recipe, the nature of which is to provide something like a general formula of guidance, but unrelated to the actual ingredients going into the dish or cake in question. Just as Thirdness involves the idea of composition, so does the recipe—with a very specific intention—provide a detailed description of the right combination of ingredients needed in order to arrive at the result promised in the recipe. If the recipe is one for making apple pies, then some form of apple must be involved in the actual process of making it. The recipe provides the force of law that ensures the right kind of apple and the right kind of supplemental ingredients that are needed for the making of an apple pie. One emphasis Peirce wants to make is that "we seldom, probably never, desire a single individual thing" (*CP* 1.341)—a single individual apple pie, for example. Rather, "What we want is something which shall produce a certain pleasure of a certain kind" (*CP* 1.341), in this case the pleasurable taste of apple pie, and any pie made on the basis of the recipe for apple pie can satisfy this desire. Hence, the fact that Thirdness always gravitates toward an *undetermined* objective gives every genuine triad an aspect of generality, as Peirce will say, for "no triad which does not involve generality, that is, the assertion of which does not imply something concerning *every possible* object of some description can be a genuine triad" (*CP* 1.476). Just like a recipe for apple pie is the basis for an indefinite number of actual future apple pies, so genuine Thirdness always involves generality; it is the conditional law that makes circumstances gravitate toward a certain kind of result.

Because Peirce applies his categories to physical as well as mental reality, some consideration must be given to the fact that he understands the law of mind to be part of physical nature also. In some way nature thinks too, and shows characteristics similar to that of rational thinking. Evidently, the thinking that nature does can not be of a reflective and perceptive kind, like human reflection, because it can not release analytical and synthetic judgments, but Peirce argues fervently that nature follows the same rational laws that only mind can manufacture. Natural phenomena have the characteristics of living mind, which is to say that both human reflection and the realm of nature are involved in the categorial scheme and abide by the triadic semiotic structure. Consciousness is therefore not restricted to human existence, where it is governed by active reflection; it may just as well be the consciousness of organic, and even inanimate, existence. Arguing this, Peirce maintains that "what we call matter is not completely dead, but is merely mind hidebound with habits. It still retains the element of diversification; and in that diversification there is life" (*CP* 6.158). Thus, the law of mind reigns everywhere, regardless of the environment in which it is actually realized, be it that of mental activity or that of physical phenomena. This is also the reasoning behind Peirce's belief that "our thinking only apprehends and does not create thought, and that . . . thought may and does as much govern outward things as it does our thinking" (*CP* 1.27). All human reflection can do is to form hypotheses about the external world—the *real* home for the laws of mind—in that what the external world already possesses simply is that which the human mind will echo in its reflection upon it. Is that not exactly what reflection means, after all, to reflect upon a reality already there? Along these lines, Peirce inverts the traditional view that sees mind as something akin to human possession, to say that *we* belong to mind, rather than vice versa. Mind is not within us; we exist within mind. Again, Descartes must take a hard blow when Peirce contends that "modern philosophy has never been able quite to shake off the Cartesian idea of the mind, as something that 'resides' . . . in the pineal gland. Everybody laughs at this nowadays, and yet everybody continues to think of mind . . . as something within this person or that" (*CP* 5.128). In the mental realm, then, conceptualization constitutes Thirdness by virtue of establishing mental habits of interpretation, and this corresponds to the laws of nature. It must never be forgotten that these convictions rest on Peirce's theory of the categories in the sense that it is *categorically* that there is no difference between mental habits and natural laws. Arguing for a likeness of mind and matter, Peirce's point is that the difference between the rational mind and physical nature is of absolutely no categorial significance.

Recalling that Firstness is exclusively embodied in the present, and completely separated from both future and past, and also that Secondness is exclusively an event of the past, a *fait-accompli*, or *esse in praeterito*, Thirdness is always an event of the future. Thirdness is *esse in futuro*. Even though it is impossible to predict the future with certainty, Thirdness relates to the future by virtue of its general aspect (i.e. in the form of conditional law). Using the example from before, a recipe for apple pie justifies the expectation that an actual apple pie is likely to appear at some point in the future. Likewise, there is reason to expect certain things about the future, based on experiences of the past and based on knowledge of the laws that govern certain behavior. "Being *in futuro* appears in mental forms, intentions and expectations. Memory supplies us a knowledge of the past by a sort of brute force, a quite binary action without any reasoning. But all our knowledge of the future is obtained through the medium of something else" (*CP* 2.86). This is to say that we continually observe causal laws on the basis of past experiences and then subsequently apply these laws to the future. "Five minutes of our waking life will hardly pass without our making some kind of prediction. . . . To say that a prediction has a decided tendency to be fulfilled, is to say that the future events are in a measure really governed by a law" (*CP* 1.26).

With this short description of Thirdness, Peirce's triad of irreducible categories is complete. It is the third category, however, that indicates the next natural step for a project of besieging Peirce's metaphysics. "Continuity represents Thirdness almost to perfection" (*CP* 1.337), as he says, and an exposition of the category of Thirdness therefore introduces a doctrine that plays a significant role for Peirce's metaphysics and adds to it a distinctively cosmological character. This is the doctrine of synechism.

Cosmology

It is a small wonder to realize that even though the doctrine of synechism is our next object of attention, what we find is another *world of three* opening up. Peirce's systematic project almost explodes into ever increasing outgrowths of triadic structures and sub-structures. In his evolving philosophical system, it is hard to know which direction to follow as it keeps expanding into added new branches. In any case, the doctrine of synechism is involved in another triadic set of categorial doctrines, this time appearing in the form of three absolute, cosmological categories, which Peirce identifies as the three universes of tychism, agapism, and synechism.

First, there is the universe of absolute chance, expanded upon in the doctrine of *tychism*. This universe reflects the category of quality, or feeling, and is therefore an expression of Firstness. Then there is the universe of evolution, explicated in the doctrine of *agapism*, which is the principle of growth and development of habits (i.e. a manifestation of Secondness). Finally, there is the universe of continuity, addressed by the doctrine of *synechism*, also found in the principle of generality and regularity (i.e. the category of Thirdness). For Peirce, these three categorial forms establish nothing less than a "perfect cosmology of the three universes" (*CP* 6.490). These universes are the three categories played out at a cosmological level. Moreover, by giving the ontological categories cosmological significance, Peirce instigates an entirely new and separate area of study, namely cosmology. For our discussion, it is important to approach Peirce's cosmology as an independent area of study because of its strong ties to his metaphysics. But, in effect, it is by an acquaintance with Peirce's metaphysical methodology that one understands why Peirce is forced to develop a cosmology as a separate field of study. We shall next turn to this connection of metaphysics and cosmology in Peirce.

Metaphysics must, as Peirce has explained, provide some objective criteria for the assessment of rational claims, and as the discipline describing the most general character of reality, it is fundamentally dependent upon the phenomenological method. "Metaphysics, even bad metaphysics, really rests on observations, whether consciously or not; and the only reason that this is not universally recognized is that it rests upon kinds of phenomena with which every man's experience is so saturated that he usually pays no particular attention to them" (*CP* 6.2). Placing metaphysics on the shoulders of phenomenology, it is from Peirce's phenomenological investigations that the three irreducible categories of Firstness, Secondness, and Thirdness appear. This should already be clear.

Peirce is ambiguous about the order of appearance, however, for do the categories precede the phenomenological investigations, or is it the other way around? He argues that the cosmos consists of the complete phaneron and everything subject to phenomenological investigation. He is also convinced that a study of the complete phaneron should consider "not everything in the phaneron, but only its indecomposable elements, that is, those that are logically indecomposable, or indecomposable to direct inspection" (*CP* 1.288). Peirce now seems to launch investigations of the complete phaneron, purposely looking for the categories, expecting their appearance before they have actually appeared. It is a reversal of the previous argument when he says, "So prolific is the triad in forms that one may easily conceive that all the variety and multiplicity of the universe springs from it" (*CP* 4.310).[47] Considering the discrepancy of the two arguments, Peirce is clearly ambiguous on the issue of whether the categories are findings based on phenomenological investigations, or whether the phaneron is a manifestation of the three pre-established ontological categories. Do the categories determine the results of Peirce's phenomenological results, or do his phenomenological investigations yield the categories? This is what Murphey wonders when he comments that "the universality and necessity of the categories can be proven only in a relative sense."[48] Even if a thorough phenomenological investigation reveals nothing but the three categories, it does not mean that all *possible* experience of the phaneron will reveal nothing but the three categories.

Peirce is, of course, aware of this problem and in order for him to support his theory of the irreducible categories, he is therefore under pressure to retain metaphysical affinity of mind and matter, which is another way of saying that he is in a systematic bind that causes him to introduce the now necessary doctrine of continuity, or synechism. This move ensures that no phenomenological encounter can possibly fall outside the categories that reflect the logic of mind. But even though affinity of mind and matter should truly represent Thirdness in its perfection, as Peirce maintains, and therefore be evidence of the doctrine of continuity, what is the guarantee that any of the categories, including Thirdness, is reliable at all? The challenge Peirce faces is the serious critique that the categories may very well be the most fundamental components of reality, but without some epistemological qualification, this observation is fundamentally unreliable, and can be nothing but a claim. If it should turn out to be nothing but a claim, then the doctrine of continuity is of no argumentative value either. Peirce is forced to argue for a metaphysics based on affinity of mind and matter, for only thus can the categories rest on phenomenology, and phenomenology in turn be a trustworthy discipline. But *additionally*, this must be a metaphysics with solid cosmological underpinnings, for it must be anchored in an ontological realism that accepts the existential uni-

---

[47] Within a Kantian frame of reference, it is worth mentioning that first supporting Kant's definition of the categories, Peirce soon discovers that they must be *relational* (he defines the three individual categories as triads) rather than *conceptual*. For details on this shift, see Murphey, "On Peirce's Metaphysics," 12–17.

[48] Ibid., 17.

verse with unshakable confidence. Peirce needs more than a cosmological *doctrine* of continuity. He needs a cosmological *realism*, which demands, for him, an entire science of cosmology.

Commenting on the fact that Peirce bases his cosmology on ontological realism, James Feibleman comments that for "both idealism and materialism . . . there is no need for a special science of cosmology. But in realism, neither the subject nor that which he knows is identical with the existential universe."[49] Cosmology is irrelevant for the idealist because he or she is committed to the idea that reality is what it is by virtue of passing through some manner of subjective comprehension. For the idealist, reality is defined by the comprehending subject. In contrast, the materialist relies solely on the objective character of reality and would therefore never require a cosmology. Left is the realist who, as Feibleman continues, "accepts ontology at its face value, and clears away from the discussion those . . . topics concerning the nature of knowledge and of reality, and the refutation of subjectivism or objectivism."[50] For Peirce, cosmology is the science that concerns the entirety of the universe and it is impossible to sustain what Fisch calls his "three-category realism,"[51] apart from an ontological cosmology.

In conclusion, Peirce's metaphysics necessitates that he retain affinity of mind and matter, which in turn calls for an ontological realism and finally an independent study of cosmology. Hence, the following attempts to address the triadic cosmological doctrines of synechism, tychism, and agapism. It is difficult to keep the three absolutely separate, especially because the doctrines of synechism and agapism seem to be variations on the same theme, if not two terms for the same thing, namely the opposite of tychism. Perhaps Peirce's desire to construct a cosmology based on the categorial triad is more ambitious than realistic, and a result of his commitment to the triadic structure. It appears to me that the triadic structure is forced upon his cosmology and that the juxtaposition of synechism and tychism is more true to the actual state of the matter. Is there really a triadic structure to Peirce's cosmology? In my judgment, the heart of Peirce's issue here is that he is forced to develop a cosmology at all because he faces the difficult challenge of dealing with the tension between synechism and tychism. It is exactly the seriousness of this challenge that necessitates a

---

[49] James Feibleman, *An Introduction to Peirce's Philosophy: Interpreted as a System* (New York: Harper & Brothers, 1946) 400.

[50] Ibid., 399.

[51] Fisch, *Peirce, Semeiotic, and Pragmatism*, 190.

constructive reassessment of Peirce's metaphysical project and which is the incentive for my proposal of a metaphysics of anticipation. By comparing Peirce's cosmology to Schelling's speculative metaphysics, I intend to demonstrate that the tension between synechism and tychism in Peirce's philosophy concerns the reality of a metaphysical voluntarism more than it concerns a cosmology of a triadic structure, and that it is the principle of volition that makes it possible and viable to propose a metaphysics of anticipation. Therefore, the following begins with an account of the universe of synechism, dealing with agapism conjointly. Looking at these two (the third and second universes) then leads naturally to a discussion of the first universe, that of tychism.

Synechism and Agapism

It is Peirce's doctrine of synechism that claims all of reality continuous. Strongly dependent on his mathematical reflections and writings on continuity, the doctrine of synechism holds up Peirce's confidence that all matter is *effete mind* and explains his belief that there "is a reason, an interpretation, a logic, in the course of scientific advance . . . that man's mind must have been attuned to the truth of things in order to discover what he has discovered" (*CP* 6.476). As a result of being attuned to the truth of things, synechism not only argues all of reality to be a continuum; it also provides the parameter for which hypotheses our succeeding scientific and empirical tests are most likely to confirm as true. In Peirce's formulation, synechism is "that tendency of philosophical thought which insists upon the idea of continuity as of prime importance in philosophy and, in particular, upon *the necessity of hypotheses involving true continuity*" (*CP* 6.169).[52] In other words, synechism is meant to assist in the decision of which hypotheses to privilege above others, or which regulative hopes to invoke as worthy of trust, among the multitude of possible hypotheses, most of which are wrong. Moreover, this particular function of the cosmological doctrine of synechism is, as Hookway comments, one example of the way adequate metaphysical doctrines are meant to serve as the grounding of regulative hopes.[53] We must, Peirce therefore says, "be guided by the rule of hope, and consequently we must reject every philosophy or general conception of the universe, which could ever lead to the conclusion that any given general fact is an ultimate one" (*CP* 1.405). This indicates how one of synechism's functions is to be "a regulative principle of logic, prescribing

---

[52] Italics mine.
[53] See Hookway, *Peirce*, 264.

what sort of hypothesis is fit to be entertained and examined" (*CP* 6.173). This is exactly what occurs in the process of abductive reasoning when the faculty of choice and volition is engaged in the pursuit of the right hypotheses among the many possible ones. For now, the thing to note is that the favored hypotheses are always those involving true continuity because we must avoid the conclusion that any particular, general law is the ultimate one. Peirce simply will not know anything of reliance upon *inexplicable ultimates* or metaphysical absolutism. "It is . . . no explanation at all of a fact to pronounce it *inexplicable*" (*CP* 1.139), he claims. In fact, "Once you have embraced the principle of continuity, no kind of explanation of things will satisfy you except that they *grew*" (*CP* 1.175).

Peirce's doctrine of synechism is based on his contention that the cosmos evolves purposively according to the principles of life and growth in the manner of an extraordinarily complex general idea, which is Absolute Mind. A general idea is one that brings out many more ideas, thereby telling us that ideas live on their own and do not need the human mind to develop. An idea is not limited to any one location or point in time, for ideas become continuous as they spread throughout the universe and across time. Like the quality of feelings, ideas are universally interrelated. "We can hardly but suppose that those sense-qualities that we now experience, colors, odors, sounds, feelings of every description, loves, griefs, surprise, are but the relics of an ancient ruined continuum of qualities, like a few columns standing here and there in testimony that here some old-world forum with its basilica and temples had once made a magnificent *ensemble*" (*CP* 6.197). The underlying principle of synechism is the inter-related flow of ideas, for "an idea can only be affected by an idea in continuous connection with it" (*CP* 6.158), and so the relatedness created between a limited number of ideas will gradually cause larger systems of ideas to emerge and the great whole to appear as a truly continuous, synechist reality.

This continuously evolving system of ideas is at the core of Peirce's claim that all matter is mind, for matter is simply "mind whose habits have become fixed so as to lose the powers of forming them and losing them."[54] The doctrine of synechism is another term for Peirce's doctrine of identity between mind and matter, and so he contends that the cosmos is mind because it is governed by the laws of mind, and matter is mind because it consists of the laws of mind, only in a fixed, or muted, form.

---

[54] Peirce, "Uniformity," in *The Dictionary of Philosophy and Psychology*, vol. 2, ed. James Mark Baldwin (New York: Macmillan, 1901–1905) 726.

So, the synechist continuum is determined by the general laws, according to which all facts are grouped and systematically related. The relatedness ensuing from the connectedness of all facts defines the continuum, which is held together by the perfect generality of a law of relationship. Facts and matter are regarded as unrelated atomic units; they define the cosmos as essentially continuous. Still, Peirce holds that synechism is no ultimate and absolute metaphysical doctrine, but rather a regulative principle of logic. This is another way of introducing his doctrine of tychism, or the doctrine of absolute chance.

Before transitioning to a discussion of tychism, we must dwell on Peirce's doctrine of agapism. Although Peirce treats agapism separately, I consider it a slightly varied form of his doctrine of synechism, as already indicated. Nevertheless, it is because Peirce is not convinced that the influence of chance accounts adequately for the evolutionary process of growth that he introduces agapism and identifies it as the expression of evolution in its truest form. In a sense, Peirce tries to connect agapism to chance, or tychism, but it is, in effect, closer to his doctrine of synechism, as the following shows.

Agapism "means nothing but *growth* in the widest sense of the word" (*CP* 1.174), and is, more specifically, a direct reference to the influential and purposeful love of God. Agapism is evolution by love; it is the principle of evolutionary love, and in this sense evolutionary growth happens according to a divine cosmological "law of love" (*CP* 6.302). It is this law that adds the gravitational pull to the evolutionary process and sets it on the course toward a definite end goal. The law of love draws growth out of nothing and reveals love to be synonymous with evolution, and therefore Peirce logically enough chooses to use a form of the Greek word αγαπη. It is unimaginable for Peirce to think of the universe as having no ultimate meaning. So, to explore the doctrine of agapism is to explore this meaning, i.e. the purest meaning of evolution.

Understanding synechism conjointly with agapism does not answer the question of what it is that determines the appearance of regulative hopes when Peirce strictly enforces that the continuum is "continuous and unbroken, [and] contains no definite parts" (*CP* 6.168). Because regulative hopes spring forward in the form of surprising hypotheses, they can not be accounted for as inherent parts of the cosmic continuum. If a hypothesis is inconsistent with reality, it must be disruptive of the continuum, and since some are consistent and others are not (otherwise the guiding help of synechism would not be needed for the process of choosing some hypotheses as plausible and leaving others as implausible), they must, at least partially, originate apart from the continuum. Addressing this issue is another way of asking what happened to the category of Secondness in Peirce's cosmology. If indeed "*all things* so swim in continua" (*CP* 1.171) that "we may suppose that one portion of matter acts upon another because it is in a measure in the same place" (*CP* 1.170), then where is the brute encounter, or clash, between two foreign elements? Where are the parts of the universe that will act up and surprise us with disruptive events of unpredictable ideas? The indecomposable reality of Secondness makes such clashes sure events of the existent universe, but synechism and agapism are unable to account for them. Responding to this challenge, another of Peirce's cosmological doctrines, tychism, is a helpful lead.

Tychism

Tychism is evolution by chance, and therefore not truly evolutionary. This makes Peirce exclaim that "as for explaining evolution by chance, there has not been time enough" (*CP* 5.172). Giving up explaining what tychism is not, Peirce then describes it positively as the doctrine of absolute chance (*CP* 6.47, 6.102). Tychism is what allows for variety and new possibilities to appear and for changing the course of evolutionary processes, just as it supposedly explains miracles. Although tychism means it is impossible to predict evolutionary outcomes of the future because impulses of spontaneity recurrently cause deviations, Peirce maintains that this does not compromise the rule of synechism and can not possibly introduce any principle that originates independently of the evolutionary process itself. The evolving universe is all there is. But how so? Are synechism and tychism two conflicting doctrines? Only seemingly, for it is Peirce's contention that, exactly because all matter is mind, all changes leave impressions behind that eventually establish themselves as habitual patterns, in turn forcing the developmental process onto a certain route, thereby excluding other possible routes. This way, the actuality of possibilities (that some appear in reality and others do not) is a matter of will, of choice and of action, and a process by which the original range of possibilities is gradually reduced.[55] The appearance of these habitual patterns translates into *habits of interpretation* and means that everything is no longer possible as it was in the beginning of the evolutionary process, for the emergence of a specific directedness into the future has exercised shaping influence on reality

---

[55] The doctrine of tychism is the main force behind Peirce's critiques of mechanical necessitarianism, which, in his opinion, pervades the modern sciences of his time as trails of Newtonian physics.

and diminished its potentiality. Hence, included in Peirce's universal continuum, which he also calls Absolute Mind, or God, is *volition*. This is to say that his cosmology involves a metaphysical voluntarism that provides him with the justification for arguing the actual shape and characteristics of the cosmos. By account of an origin within itself, the cosmos is what it is. This argument is not unlike that of establishing the origin of God's existence as an eternally internal part of God's own being.

An interesting issue now is whether Peirce's habits of interpretation can be fully accounted for as birthed from within the cosmos itself (i.e. as part of a spontaneously emerging wave of volition). If not, then the extent to which the reality of the future is merely an *emergent* from within would define the extent to which it is *independent* of the process that leads to its appearance. In other words, Peirce's ambiguous account of the doctrine of tychism raises some questions. Is it possible to comprehend the act of volition and choice without a directedness toward something that has reality *apart* from the cosmological mass, out of which volition appears? Can choice be defined apart from something to choose? Relating these questions to Peirce's notion of rational inquiry, and the question of where hypotheses and regulative hopes originate, indicates the difficulty of understanding what we shall call Peirce's metaphysical voluntarism. That hypotheses emerge by virtue of volitional force may suggest that they come from within the cosmos itself, but it does not automatically necessitate that their appearance should be accounted for cosmologically. At least it is clear that the question of why "in general we have more reason to trust our instinctive judgements of rationality than we do the products of distinctively philosophical reasoning,"[56] is directed toward the active dynamics of will and choice. At this point, the most promising escape from Peirce's onto-cosmological impasse seems to be the systematic significance of volition as it relates to tychism and subsequently also to his theory of abduction. The theory of abduction is infiltrated by the mystery of choice (the power not only to choose, but also to choose correctly), thereby suggesting some kind of objective reality that does not necessarily comply with onto-cosmological principles, and that therefore relates back to Peirce's doctrine of tychism.

Suggesting a broader perspective, I propose that Peirce's general approach to metaphysics is not unlike that of Pannenberg's metaphysics of anticipation. Peirce says, "The first to go must be the proposition that

---

[56] Christopher Hookway, *Truth, Rationality, and Pragmatism: Themes from Peirce* (Oxford: Clarendon, 2000) 249.

every event in the universe is precisely determined by causes according to inviolable law" (*EP* 1.273). The laws of nature are subject to some measure of unpredictability in the natural processes because some phenomena and surprising appearances in the universe can only be accounted for by a principle of spontaneity. Peirce therefore contends that our aspiration must be for "a wonderful degree of approximation, and that is all" (*EP* 1.273). Now, in so far as this is a repetition of Pannenberg's thesis that metaphysical reflection about the absolute must "take on the form of *conjectural reconstruction* in relation to its object,"[57] Peirce and Pannenberg argue the same point about the necessary form of the metaphysics each of them wishes to propose. And in so far as this conclusion is accurate, Peirce and Pannenberg propose the same *kind* of metaphysics, namely one that is *able to meet the requirements established by Kant's critical philosophy*. Although Peirce does not make it a primary argument to say that the metaphysical project as such should meet Kantian requirements, my argument is that it does exactly this, which is evidenced by the anticipatory structure of Peirce's metaphysics. Supporting this argument, there is even more reason to engage in a comparison of Peirce and Schelling than Peirce's own references to Schelling suggest. Schelling takes, as we are soon to see Walter Schulz argue, credit for the collapse of German idealism, because he is able to assume a unique philosophical position between Kant and Hegel. That is, in his later philosophy, Schelling demonstrates an equal measure of commitment to the conditions given by Kant's critical philosophy and Hegel's vision of remedying the split created by Kant's critical philosophy. As we are soon to see also, it is via the argument for metaphysical voluntarism that Schelling places himself between Kant and Hegel and, considering this an accurate assessment of Schelling's later philosophy, I suggest the following. Not only does Peirce's commitment to the anticipatory structure of metaphysical reflection line his metaphysics up with Pannenberg's. In so far as his application of volition reflects the later Schelling's argument for a metaphysical voluntarism, he also places himself, with Schelling, between Kant and Hegel. In other words, Peirce's metaphysics meets the requirements given by Kant's critical philosophy, but does so without subscribing to the kind of cosmological absolutism that the later Schelling criticized in Hegel. In order, therefore, to support this argument, we now turn to a more detailed discussion of Peirce's appropriation of the philosophy of the later Schelling.

---

[57] Wolfhart Pannenberg, *Metaphysics and the Idea of God*, trans. Philip Clayton (Grand Rapids: Eerdmans, 1990) 94.

Peirce and the Later Schelling

As part of developing his cosmology, Peirce's article *The Law of Mind* announces that he has "begun by showing that *tychism* must give birth to an evolutionary cosmology, in which all the regularities of nature and of mind are regarded as products of growth, and to a Schelling-fashioned idealism which holds matter to be mere specialised and partially deadened mind" (*EP* 1.312). Following this sentence, Peirce takes immediate measures to appease potentially concerned readers and insists that he has contracted none of the virus that spread when acquaintances of his youth "were disseminating the ideas that they had caught from Schelling, and Schelling from Plotinus, from Boehm, or from God knows what minds stricken with the monstrous mysticism of the East" (*EP* 1.313). Also, it is important for Peirce to make clear that any cultured bacilli that he still may have contracted are now harmless, because they have been "modified by mathematical conceptions and by training in physical investigations" (*EP* 1.313). Clearly, these comments give voice to some fairly strong and critical opinions about Schelling's philosophy. In my judgment, however, they are scarcely more than paper thin and, if challenged, quickly turn ambiguous, if not affirmative of Schelling's position. Consider, for example, the article *The Seven Systems of Metaphysics*, where Peirce inserts (and later removes) a comment that would shine an unmistakably positive light on Schelling: "The doctrine of Aristotle is distinguished from substantially all modern philosophy [except perhaps Schelling's and mine] by its recognition of at least two grades of being. That is, besides *actual reactive existence*, Aristotle recognizes a germinal being, an *esse in potential* or I like to call it an *esse in futuro*" (*EP* 2.180).[58] Although one should not give such a passing comment more weight than it can carry, it is still interesting to notice that Peirce does flirt with the idea of identifying himself with Schelling. Hence, I venture to argue that even if Peirce's remarks about Schelling are little more than casual, Peirce will, upon closer systematic examination, appear in much closer proximity to Schelling than he leads us to believe.

Historically, post-Kantian idealism is introduced in America through the New England Transcendentalists and is no unexpected source of inspiration among intellectuals of the nineteenth century. It is therefore only natural that the German idealists catch Peirce's attention too, and that

---

[58] The comment in brackets is Peirce's insertion, as the editors of *The Essential Peirce* explain: "Peirce originally inserted 'except perhaps Schelling's & mine' after 'modern philosophy'; he then apparently changed his mind, crossed out the insertion, and added instead the word 'substantially' earlier in the sentence" (*EP* 522, n. 4).

especially Hegel's thought turns out to be as formative for Peirce's thought as it does. For anyone attracted to the tradition of German idealism, Hegel must be of primary interest, and Peirce makes no exception of this. Also, it is characteristic of Peirce, as it is of many, that his fascination with Hegel is tempered by a great deal of caution; he continues to be ambivalent about Hegel, just as Schelling is, and with both of them also Søren Kierkegaard. Interestingly, Peirce is not as clear as Hegel and Kierkegaard about how he might have appropriated Schelling's philosophy, and the references he does make never appear in the context of thoroughly analytical assessments of Schelling's work. On a critical note concerning the relatedness of Hegel and Schelling, Peirce insinuates, in *A Guess at the Riddle*, that Schelling's significance is limited to that of being in league with Hegel. With an unusually Kierkegaardian metaphor, he contributes to the choir of those who struggle to come to terms with the magnitude of Hegel's philosophical influence when he comments about "the new Schelling-Hegel mansion, lately run up in the German taste, but with such oversights in its construction that, although brand new, it is already pronounced uninhabitable" (*EP* 1.247). Reading a remark like this, one is reminded that Kierkegaard too refers to Hegel's system as an impressive mansion—impressive because it is utterly uninhabitable. The point being that Hegel has asked himself to reside in his own dog-house.

Now, is it not the case that many a philosophy attempts to buttress its thinking by some manner of adapting Hegel's three notions, thesis, antithesis and synthesis? Without determining here whether or not all such adaptations are true to Hegel's own intentions, it is important to notice that both Schelling and Peirce admit to some level of reliance on this Hegelian triad. After all, Peirce gives clear credit to Hegel when he talks about his own development of the theory of the triadic categories, and Schelling develops the theory of God's triadic potencies (explored in detail later). Provided one agrees with this generalizing observation: are similarities between Schelling and Peirce necessarily evidence of more than the broad influence of idealist thought (Hegel's in particular) which characterizes the nineteenth century? In my opinion, there is reason to maintain that this is in fact the case. Even though Peirce's remarks about Schelling are casual, Peirce is closer to Schelling than one might at first think. Apparently, Peirce does not pay much attention to the complexity and systematic details of Schelling's philosophy, and openly overlooks the significant divergences there are between Schelling's early and later philosophies. Having encountered, in Peirce, the same lack of sensitivity to the complexity of Hegel's thinking, we have reason to suspect that the same is true in relation to Schelling. Nevertheless, there is clearly something about Schelling's philosophical approach that appeals to Peirce, and this may prove more significant than his casual reading of Hegel and Schelling would allow us to believe. So, what is this appeal?

The following discussion focuses on two specific points that contribute to answering this question. The first is that there are manifest similarities between Peirce's theory of the categories and Schelling's theory of God's potencies when it comes to the way they both appropriate the Hegelian triad—*and do so in a manner that implies a critique of it*. My thesis is that the shared uniqueness of their individual critiques is the fact that they are furnished by a *metaphysical voluntarism*, which distinguishes them quite significantly from Hegel. Surprisingly, Peirce does not realize that he and Schelling share a fascination with Hegel that they both struggle to shake off, and which they both manage to do, precisely by arguments implying the metaphysical significance of volition. On Schelling's part, this move is the very thing that gives him the legacy of having caused the collapse of German idealism, as we shall see in the discussion of his epistemological justification of speculative metaphysics. On Peirce's part, volition is the particular component of his philosophy which remains, in my opinion, one of the most important challenges for contemporary Peirce scholarship because Peirce himself lets it play a systematically very important role, but one he does not explain in a sufficiently comprehensive manner. This relates to his ambiguous account of the doctrine of tychism in relation to the doctrine of synechism. Had Peirce recognized Schelling's commitment to the metaphysical importance of volition, then he could have drawn directly from Schelling's insights and perhaps achieved a more complete formulation of his own understanding of it. As it is, the issue of volition is left for interpreters of Peirce to understand, especially the role it plays in the process of abductive reasoning and therefore also its significance for his attempts to integrate the two doctrines of synechism and tychism. Just as Peirce struggles to account for the role of volition in the process of abductive reasoning, as we shall see later, so he struggles to give an account of the reality of absolute chance and spontaneity (tychism) in an architectonically coherent universe whose stability is secured by the doctrine that everything is continuous (synechist). For a project pursuing clarification of the relatedness of these issues, I argue that it is necessary to consult Schelling's argument for the metaphysical significance of volition.

Consider, on this proposal, the review of Royce's *Religious Aspect of Philosophy* where Peirce starts out grouping Schelling with Hegel (and Royce!) and then sharply criticizes their shared ignorance of the philosophical importance of volition: "ordinary people make, at once, the very same criticism that the profoundest students of philosophy have made, namely, that the Hegelian school overlooks *the importance of the will as an element of thought*" (*EP* 1.230).[59] Turning to a detailed study of Schelling's theory of the potencies of God, it shall become clear why it is reasonable to conclude that Peirce fails to notice the strong argument Schelling makes for a metaphysical voluntarism. Their shared commitment to the principle of volition can bring Schelling out of league with Hegel and explain how Peirce can be more than momentarily identified with Schelling.

Tied to this first point about the appeal Schelling's philosophy has on Peirce is my second point, which concerns the epistemological justification that both Schelling and Peirce provide for their reliance on the speculative discourse. I argue that Peirce's science of cosmology is a systematic parallel to the speculative metaphysics of Schelling's later work, and that both thinkers offer epistemological justification for the speculative form and content of these two undertakings, in anticipation of the criticism they might—and do—elicit. Both Schelling's speculative metaphysics and Peirce's cosmology have received much critique. I argue, however, that there is reason to show precaution with one's criticism, for both are well

---

[59] Italics mine. Historically, *will* has been applied philosophically in various contexts of responding to the question of human freedom and deliberate action: What does it mean to act deliberately and freely? There are two main responses to this question. One builds on the principles of rationalism, the other on the principles of voluntarism. First, it has been argued that the will is subject to the faculty of reason. The will is released into action because a person has first gone through a process of rational deliberation and concluded that a certain action is preferable. Kant's distinct treatment of practical reason belongs here, as it defines the ability to act according to rational principles. Second, it has been argued that rational deliberation is subject to the will, which is rather a spontaneous and unrestrained, even irrational, impulse in the human being. Although the technical details of these two responses shall not be explored further here, Friedrich Nietzsche takes an interesting middle-position worth mentioning. Nietzsche argues that the will (as a fundamental drive in all creatures, a *will to live*, or, ultimately, a *will to power*) is not a restrained impulse, but nor is it determined by reason, for that would make it more like conscious decision than actual will. Rather, in the words of Nietzsche's Zarathustra, the will is described by the language of creative activity: "All 'it was' is a fragment, a riddle, a dreadful accident—until the creative will says to it, 'But thus I willed it; thus shall I will it'" (Friedrich Nietzsche, *Thus Spoke Zarathustra*, in *The Portable Nietzsche*, ed. and trans. Walter Kaufmann [New York: Viking, 1954] 253). As this quote also indicates, the will is more than just creative in the traditional sense of giving artistic expression to some insight or novel idea, whatever that might look like. The most significant virtue of the will is the power it has over the past (not the future) and so it is reckoned not only creative but also *redemptive*. Thus, Zarathustra: "As creator, guesser of riddles, and redeemer of accidents, I taught them to work on the future and to redeem with their creation all that *has been*" (ibid., 310).

aware of the deep waters they are getting themselves into by unleashing the faculty of speculation. As a way of countering unnecessary critique, they both provide something like an epistemological justification of the speculative freedom they grant themselves in the areas of metaphysics and cosmology respectively. Peirce justifies his cosmology by the systematic necessity that forces him to institute the science of cosmology, as we have already seen. For Schelling, speculative metaphysics is justified by drawing the logical consequence of the Hegelian notion of rational absolutism. This enables him to dismantle reason, announce its powerlessness and thereafter reinstate it in the office of speculative metaphysics. Turning to a more detailed discussion of these two points, we will start with the first.

Schelling's Theory of God's Three Potencies

The relational dynamics of Peirce's three categories is already discussed in sufficient detail to let us turn directly to an account of the most central role of the triadic structure in Schelling's philosophy. For Schelling, it is a challenging thing to describe God, although he is sure of one thing, namely that God contains the two opposites of necessity and freedom: "The concept of God is of wide, yes of widest, scope and cannot be articulated in a single word. In God there is necessity and freedom."[60] Now, it is within the divine pole of necessity that the opposing powers of good and evil (light and dark, *Ideal und Real* (ideal and real), rational and irrational), are located.[61] Even though evil originates from within God, it is, according to Schelling, held in check by virtue of the structure of God's inner nature because evil's battle with good is ongoing and always takes place in submission to God's other pole, divine freedom. This is to say that within God's necessity there is first of all the antithetical tension between

---

[60] F. W. J. Schelling, *Friedrich Wilhelm Joseph von Schellings sämtliche Werke*, vols. 1–14, ed. K. F. A. Schelling (Stuttgart: Cotta, 1856–61) 1.209; translation mine. Hereafter referred to as *SchW*, followed by volume and page number. (In the original, "Der Begriff Gottes ist von grossem, ja vom allergrössesten Umfang, und nicht so mit Einem Wort auszusprechen. Es ist in Gott Nothwendigkeit und Freiheit.")

[61] Schelling's teaching on God's potencies relies heavily on Jakob Böhme's response to the problem of evil, the most important part of which is the argument that evil is rooted within God and therefore not a power opposed to an only good God, as orthodox Christianity teaches. It is worth noticing that Böhme's teaching is broadly influential during this time. At first it is the poet Ludwig Tieck who introduces Böhme's thought to the intellectual group around K. W. F. Schlegel and the Jena Romantics. When, in 1806, Schelling moves to Munich, he finds the interest in Böhme no less significant there than it was in Jena. Here, Böhme's thoughts are appropriated by thinkers like F. H. Jacobi and the theosophists F. von Baader and F. C. Oetinger.

good and evil, ideal and real; these two opposed impulses are God's first and second potencies. But there is also a third and unifying power in this pole, which brings about the unity of the first two potencies. Moreover, this unifying power is God's third potency and functions, in Robert F. Brown's words, as "another principle alongside the other two, possessing an equal, but not a greater, claim to be."[62] The three potencies are of equal status and none of them is superior to the others. For Schelling, this is how he perceives the necessity of God as a triadic, dynamic power-field of God's three potencies, and a power-field with a life of its own, evolving in the following way.

The three potencies arrange themselves naturally in relation to each other, for only by spontaneous submission to a natural order can they escape a competitive mode of relatedness. Which is to be first, second, and third is of no importance; it just happens. God's first potency is the destructive, and, left to itself, "the 'real' is at once the power of grimness and strength, the principle of egoity, . . . power that pushes being into the dark."[63] Egoity, or egoism, is essentially contractive; it bends in upon itself more and more, and eventually disappears altogether, taking with it all light and leaving only darkness behind. In contrast, God's second potency is essentially expansive and comes as a counter-active response to the first potency of contraction. It is the ideal, appearing through the first potency by changing contraction to expansion, which is the same as reversing the essentially negative nature of the first potency. This way, the first potency is transformed through and into the second, demonstrating that the second potency can not exist without the first because the first potency is its only possible place of origin. This means that, in so far as the first potency functions at the service of the second potency, it becomes a positive and expanding principle, and Schelling can now claim that "the real . . . is motion par excellence. . . . From it, all being has its motion and its drive, its vitality, which means: the energy of the living, its 'will to live,' the urge to growth and light, strength of evolvement and self-assertion."[64] It is the mutuality and the inter-dependent relatedness of the

---

[62] Robert F. Brown, *The Later Philosophy of Schelling: The Influence of Boehme on the Works of 1809–1815* (Cranbury: Associated University Presses, 1977) 204.

[63] Horst Fuhrmanns, "Einleitung und Anmerkungen," in F. W. J. Schelling, *Über das Wesen der menschlichen Freiheit* [Philosophical inquiries into the nature of human freedom] (Stuttgart: Reclam, 1995) 23; translation mine. Hereafter referred to as *Freiheitsschrift*. In the original: "das 'Reale' zugleich Macht der Grimmigkeit und der Strenge, Prinzip der Egoität, . . . Macht, die das Dasein ins Dunkle drängt."

[64] Ibid., 25–26; translation mine. In the original: "Das 'Reale' . . . ist Bewegtheit schlec-

first and second potencies that establish, for Schelling, life and relatedness in itself—the very thing that therefore can not exist apart from the reactive encounter of good and evil.

With the emergence of life through the encounter of the first two potencies, something more than a mere encounter has happened. We have the appearance of yet another element alongside the first two. This is God's third potency and "the eternal end of the process of alternation, the goal that is always present."[65] With this formulation, Brown calls attention to the fact that, involving the first two potencies, God's third potency is dependent upon the first and second potencies for its existence. It is not only the second potency that depends on the first, in other words, and one is reminded here of a similar principle in Peirce's theory of the three categories, namely that the second category involves the first while the third involves both the second and the first. In a certain sense, Schelling's third potency crowns the encounter between the first and second by facilitating the result of this encounter, namely their unity, and hence it could not exist without them. This should clarify how it is by virtue of the logic of their interaction that God's three potencies live in a movement of self-prioritizing positions, naturally organizing themselves as the first, second, and third potency. Because the potencies still have and can not escape their individual existence, however, this inter-active movement inevitably returns to its starting point where the first potency will contract, the second expand, their unity come about, and this same unity fall apart again. There is a double movement of gravitation toward unity and gravitation toward individuality. As soon as unity happens, separation is bound to follow, which only means that the process of unification can start all over again. It is a cyclical movement and it is permanent. For Schelling, this eternally circular process of transformation constitutes God's necessity and is parallel to a worm incessantly eating its own tail, gaining neither death nor life because its tail keeps growing back. His conclusion is that God's necessity, or *the inner life of God*, needs emancipation.

Schelling now continues his teaching on God's three potencies by explaining how the emancipation of God's living personality can only happen through the interaction of God's necessity (where the three potencies reside) and God's other pole, God's freedom. God's freedom is not a potency but is the highest principle beyond and above the potencies (i.e.

---

thin. . . . Aus ihm hat alles Sein seine Bewegtheit, seinen Schwung, seine Vita-lität, will sagen: die Energie des Lebendigen, seine 'Lebenswillen', den Drang zu Wachstum und Licht, Kraft der Entfaltung und des Sichbehauptens."

[65] Brown, *Later Philosophy of Schelling*, 208.

beyond God's necessity). God's freedom is unconditional eternity and pure will; it is without a will to anything specific because it is free and indifferent in relation to everything. It does not have consciousness because it does not hold any discrepancies within itself. It is *purus actus*.[66] By its sheer presence, Schelling argues, God's freedom calls out an intense *Sehnsucht* (longing) from within the potencies for independence from each other, or for lasting emancipation, which is the same as freedom from their cyclical process of endless, circular movement. His argument is that a full and complete realization of God's personality will only happen when it, "associates itself eternally and inseparably with the Highest as its immediate subject, by the strength of *an eternal will or determination*."[67] That is, divine being is only realized when the triadic power-field of God's three potencies is dynamically fixed *under* the highest principle beyond everything else, including the part of God that struggles with itself, and this highest principle is *eternal volition or decision*—another term for God's freedom. When this happens, the three potencies can finally appear in a form of organic unity, "not [as] something that 'happens' to or in God but . . . [as] an aspect of his eternal reality."[68] When God's will appears, emancipation has occurred.

In conclusion, Schelling's theory of God's three potencies is based on a metaphysical voluntarism. The unconditional and absolute background for God's reality and actual existence as a personal God is the principle of pure volition, of will in and of itself, completely stripped of all reaction-

---

[66] In Scholastic philosophy the term *purus actus*, or *actus purus*, expresses God's absolute perfection.

[67] *SchW* 1.241; italics mine, translation mine. In the original: "kraft *eines ewigen Willens oder Entschlusses*, sich ewig und untrennbar jenem Höchsten als sein unmittelbares Subjekt verbündet."

[68] Brown, *Later Philosophy of Schelling*, 214. For Schelling then, God does not suffer self-estrangement and does not need to integrate *God's own opposite* in order to become God-self, as Hegel would argue. Even though Hegel claims that God's self-integration is independent of temporality and therefore is a process that unfolds at the very core of being itself, rather than going through different states of being over a span of time, Schelling's position differs significantly from Hegel's. Within God's self, Schelling claims, evil is transformed into good by virtue of God's *in sich bleibende Potentialität* (self-abiding potentiality) and *this* preserves God's pure goodness and independence of the developmental process. It is a permanent indissoluble potentiality within God that gives God an eternal beginning anchored in the movement of the three potencies within God's self. God's own reality is therefore dependent upon the negative presence of evil within God's first potency. Again, it is only by virtue of the darkness within God's self (i.e. within God's pole of necessity) that the reality of God's personality can come forward. The evil within God is the condition for God's freedom and will to be expressed.

ary and inter-active impulses. Appropriating the Hegelian triad, Schelling unveils about it what he considers a need for emancipation and thereby moves beyond a description of how its three components interrelate. He demonstrates the need for a metaphysical principle of volition to facilitate freedom from the restrictive and repetitive conditions established by triadic relatedness.

Justifying Speculative Metaphysics

The difference one finds in the ways Peirce and Schelling offer epistemological justification of the science of cosmology and speculative metaphysics respectively is hardly more than one of degree. As already seen, Peirce is under logic and systematic pressure to support his metaphysics by the science of cosmology. Conversely, Schelling earns permission to launch the speculative philosophy by first reinstating reason in the service of positive and speculative philosophy. When Schelling argues, for example, that the history of the world is a direct expression of God's inner nature, it is simply nothing more than a claim, unless he can assure his audience that the knowledge of God's divine nature, which he finds by analyzing world history, is epistemologically justified. Just like Peirce, Schelling needs to demonstrate that reason can be trusted with confidence and that the speculative theories it delivers are reliable. The following shows how Schelling supplies such justification.

First of all, if one agrees there is a distinction between the early and the later Schelling, the demarcation line is the publication of his peculiar little book, *Freiheitsschrift*. In it, Schelling leaves his earlier *Natur-und Identitätsphilosophie* (Philosophy of nature and identity) and conveys a lessened interest in the pantheism of Baruch Spinoza who had previously been a significant source of inspiration for him. Because pantheism leaves little, if not no, room for human freedom, it is, on Schelling's account, fatalism. In the process of breaking away from Spinoza's pantheist fatalism, Schelling makes the surprising move of turning his deepest concern about pantheism against his own tradition, German idealism, and especially its reliance on the capabilities of the faculty of reason: "All philosophy that is only rational is or will be Spinozism!"[69] This move is primarily directed toward Hegel and what Schelling criticizes as a conceited kind of rational absolutism. It is important to understand that it is *not* Schelling's errand to repeal the most fundamental category of idealist thought: the

---

[69] Schelling, *Freiheitsschrift*, 59; translation mine. In the original; "Philosophie, schlechthin alle, die nur rein vernunftsmässig ist, ist oder wird Spinozismus!"

notion that all of reality is determined by a self-determining subjectivity, or that reality is what it is because the process of passing though human consciousness has defined it so. For Hegel, reality can not be defined on the basis of keeping human rationality and the world separate; it finds existence within the human subject by and through its rational thought movement. This definition of reality is a product of Hegel's philosophy and the prime category of idealist thinking which Schelling wholeheartedly affirms. Schelling's errand is exactly to pursue the utmost capacity of this category, but he manages to do it in such a way that it reveals its own limitation and powerlessness at the pinnacle of its ability. He forces the idealist category of the power it claims to have and thereby lures it into revealing its own powerlessness.

In accordance with Hegel, Schelling insists that all true philosophy is idealist philosophy. He agrees that reality is fundamentally rational and only comprehensible by means of rational reflection. But, he is still provoked by the pretension that reason should derive from itself and he therefore charges Hegel with leaving reason to itself in an eternally restless circle of meaninglessness—like a worm incessantly eating its own tail, achieving neither life nor death. Astounded by the meaningless nature of rational activity, Schelling can not but ask, "why is there anything at all? why is there not nothing?"[70] He realizes that "knowledge only reproduces the absolute act of cognition,"[71] and that it justifies why "knowledge must affirm itself as *its own beginning, behind which it cannot reach*."[72] Reason can not account for its own power and therefore has to concede that it is defined by its own powerlessness. Schelling's description of rational activity outbids Hegel's in his claim that rational reflection is a self-circulating but also an unavoidably self-transcending movement that will proceed beyond its self-relatedness to a point of making a final and ecstatic move where it encounters its own facticity and limitation. Reason is *Erstarrt* (paralyzed) and confronted by its own *dasshafte Wesenlosigkeit* (factual insubstantiality); it stands not opposite itself, but opposite the fact that it is there at

---

[70] *SchW* 13.7; translation mine. In the original, "warum ist überhaupt etwas? warum ist nicht nichts?"

[71] Manfred Frank, *Der unendliche Mangel an Sein: Schellings Hegelkritik und die Anfänge der Marxschen Dialektik* [The endless absence of being: Schelling's critique of Hegel and the beginning of the Marxist dialectic] (Munich: Fink, 1992) 215; translation mine. In the original: "das Wissen den absoluten Erkenntnisakt nur reproduziert."

[72] Ibid., 215; italics mine, translation mine. In the original: "das Wissen sich selbst als unhintergehbaren Anfang behaupten muss."

all.⁷³ In this, the ultimate rational initiative is revealed to belong not to reason itself but to *Seyende selbst* (being itself), or pure *Seinkönnen* (ability of being), to the permanent and constitutive potentiality, which is real before materialized reason is real. It is, however, the privilege of reason to find itself face to face with its own naked powerlessness because thereby it suddenly becomes more than negated rational power. At this point of no return, reason realizes the fact that even before exercising its own power (which leads to its self-negation), it necessarily is negated reason. At the pinnacle of its capacity, reason flips into materiality, so to speak, and is *thereby* authorized to be the thing it always was. Through an uncovering of the powerlessness of reason, reason is reinstated as reason.

In conclusion, Schelling manages to revoke the idealist vision of defining human subjectivity in terms of pure rationality alone: "the movement in which self-transcending subjectivity starts to circle within itself occurs, for the first time, in Schelling."⁷⁴ Or, redefining subjectivity in more structural terms, the following paradigm for the collapse of German idealism identifies the most important accomplishment of Schelling's philosophy: human subjectivity is a pre-established and self-affirming twofold movement of *Aus-sich-herausgehens* (going out of itself) and *In-sich-zurückkehrens* (returning to itself). The human subject has, with Schelling, claimed the pre-rational nature of its own existence and implicitly also brought closure to any further progress of idealist thought, since the future of its central category, human subjectivity, has come to a halt. The notion of human subjectivity can reach no next developmental level.

For Schelling, a reinstatement of reason as reason is the same as a revelation of God's reality; his God is the God of the philosophical system, the source and pure initiation of being, compared to which reason is realized to be what it always has been, namely derived and negated being. This also entails, for Schelling, that a philosophical system is possible only as a per se religious system, and that the discipline of speculative religious philosophy, or speculative metaphysics, is sanctioned because reason is now a reliable means of acquiring insight into the divine truths about God's eternal being. Hence, rational philosophy has acknowledged the necessity of conceding that human subjectivity can no longer be defined apart from intimate knowledge of divine reality and a new urgency is given to the

---

⁷³ Walter Schulz, *Die Vollendung des Deutschen Idealismus in der Spätphilosophie Schellings* [The completion of German idealism in Schelling's later philosophy] (Pfullingen: Neske, 1975) 295–96.

⁷⁴ Ibid., 272; translation mine. In the original: "In Schelling vollzieht sich erstmalig die Bewegung, in der die sich übersteigende Subjektivität in sich selbst zu kreisen beginnt."

task of exploring God's inner nature and divine reality in rational detail. Now that reason is reinstated as reason, Schelling's speculative metaphysics can begin because he has obtained the confidence in reason that was required in order for metaphysics to be a reliable science. Turning to his later philosophy—first *Die Weltalter* (The ages of the world) and later his *Philosophie der Mythologie und der Offenbarung* (Philosophy of mythology and revelation)—one should remember that Schelling rises from the ruins of Hegel's rational absolutism, a ruin Schelling himself first brought about. His chief vision is that the history of the world is a literal reflection of the metaphysical reality of God and that, therefore, human reason can gain empirically verified insight into the truths about God's inner being, through studies of history.

Metaphysical Voluntarism: A Trajectory of Schelling's Speculative Metaphysics and Peirce's Science of Cosmology

The trajectories of Schelling's speculative metaphysics are not altogether beautiful, for with reason's newfound freedom to speculate, Schelling's later work unfortunately also exhibits an inopportune gravitation toward excessive speculation and exaggeration. Even though he is fundamentally committed to keeping speculative freedom in check by the critical voice of reason, and also intends a balanced view of reason's competence, many of Schelling's later speculations are somewhat questionable and toward the end oftentimes of limited persuasion. Schelling must have felt this too, considering the fact that he gives up the project of finishing *Die Weltalter*, which he intended as a definitive account of his cosmological vision. It turns into a project of such overwhelming proportions that he is unable to bring it to completion. At the same time, Schelling must also have felt that he could not possibly relinquish his underlying vision, for he resurrects his vision in his following writing project, the *Philosophie der Mythologie und der Offenbarung* not long after leaving the project of *Die Weltalter*. To complicate matters even more, this new project too takes on overwhelming proportions and the speculative web of his thinking eventually gets so thick that it causes him to lose sight of the philosophical vision that first motivated it. Schelling works on *Philosophie der Mythologie und der Offenbarung* for the remaining forty years of his life. Unfortunately, he never sees it to publication. All of Schelling's later philosophy was published posthumously by his son.

In anecdotal style, Kierkegaard's reaction to Schelling's speculative metaphysics may give as accurate a description of Schelling's developing intellectual problems as one will ever find. Kierkegaard was one of the guests attending Schelling's famous Berlin lectures during the winter of 1841–42.[75] He was concerned about Schelling's teaching and commented on his performance in the lecture hall, "Schelling babbles quite unbearably . . . Furthermore he has now gotten the idea that he will read longer than usual . . . I am too old to listen to lectures, just like Schelling is too old to give them. His entire teaching about potencies reveals the highest impotence."[76] Reading through Schelling's later writings, one is apt to agree with this evaluation.

Turning to the trajectories of Peirce's cosmology, many scholars have commented that even though synechism (the doctrine of affinity of mind and matter) is the backbone of Peirce's scientific logic, it is also "one of the darkest areas of his philosophy"[77] as well as the teaching that leads into cosmological speculations of an excessive character. Again, this situation is not unlike that of the later Schelling who eventually finds himself entangled by increasingly obscure explanations of how, in very exact comparisons, the progressing history of the world is a direct expression of God's own living nature. Bryce W. Gallie's remark about Peirce's cosmology that it is "the white elephant"[78] of his system expresses concerns not unlike those uttered by Kierkegaard about the later Schelling's increasingly obscure thoughts. With their cosmological speculations, both Peirce and Schelling do, in other words, occasion critical responses of similar kinds. Why the tendency to speculative exaggerations?

---

[75] Kierkegaard travels to Berlin, partly because it was the cultural center of Europe at the time, but also "because of his will to verify the vicissitudes of Hegelian idealism and speculative theology in light of the development of Schelling's philosophy" (Salvatora Spera, "La Philosophie de la Religion de Schelling dans son développement et son rejet par Kierkegaard" [Schelling's philosophy of religion in his development and his rejection by Kierkegaard] in *Kierkegaard and Dialectics*, ed. Jørgen K. Bukdahl [Aarhus: University of Aarhus Press, 1979] 147; translation mine). In the original: "par sa volonté de verifier les vicissitudes de l'idéalisme hegelien et de la théologie spéculative, à la lumiere de l'évolution de la philosophie de Schelling." Kierkegaard saw in Schelling a critique of Hegel's idealism that he was already exploring in his own philosophical reflections, and Schelling's work stirred in Kierkegaard the first existentialist impulses. The influence Schelling has on the emergence of existentialism from the ruins of Hegelian absolutism is another important aspect of Schelling's critical response to his own tradition of German idealism.

[76] Søren Kierkegaard, "Breve," in *Breve og Aktstykker vedrørende Søren Kierkegaard I* [Letters and documents concerning Søren Kierkegaard I] (Copenhagen: Munksgaard, 1953) 109–10; translation mine.

[77] Hookway, *Peirce*, 174.

[78] Bryce W. Gallie, *Peirce and Pragmatism* (Harmondsworth, UK: Penguin, 1952) 215.

Concluding this brief discussion of the motivations behind Schelling's speculative metaphysics, some evaluating remarks are in place. Peirce and Schelling exhibit a shared commitment to the principle of metaphysical voluntarism and they both expound this commitment in the course of developing complex theories of the triadic structure. They give the triadic structure a clearly paradigmatic role in their philosophy as a whole, and especially in their cosmo-metaphysical reflections. Also, their thoughts on the triadic structure are quite similar in this way: the First provokes a reaction of the Second, and the Second includes the First as its own point of origination; the Third mediates between the First and the Second, and requires the reality of both for its own existence.

Even if one decides to support Gallie's evaluating remark (that Peirce's cosmology is the white elephant of his system) one must remember that Peirce's philosophical vision is unable even to get off the ground without it. Therefore, if Peirce's cosmology can not be annulled, it must be reconstructed, and I suggest that this can happen successfully by an evaluation of that which originally necessitated its appearance, namely the systematic tension between the doctrines of synechism and tychism. My contention is the following. The problem Peirce faces with the tension between synechism and tychism is evident at both the cosmological and the epistemological levels of his philosophy. When he launches the cosmological doctrine of tychism, and when he deals with the epistemological question of rational self-control in the process of abductive reasoning, he is in fact responding to a systematic need to acknowledge the principle of volition. In order, therefore, to reconstruct Peirce's cosmology, or to propose a constructive interpretation of it, it is a systematic necessity to also include a constructive interpretation of his theory of abduction. In my reading, this suggests that the reason why Peirce does indeed have a difficult time integrating the philosophical and the religious lines of argumentation in his own philosophy relates to the systematic role of the principle of volition—and the fact that Peirce does not address this issue exhaustively. In other words, a focus on the principle of volition, with the purpose of identifying its systematic centrality in Peirce's system, offers a constructive opportunity to reassess Peirce's systematic thought in a way that makes its religious parts less ostracized from its philosophical parts. Moreover, a constructive outcome and the one I propose is to argue that the principle of volition is a significant element of the metaphysical realism that Peirce seeks to define but does not complete.

Relating this proposal back to the beginning of the present chapter, the principle of volition is identified as the systematic heart beat of the metaphysical realism that Peirce needs, and seeks, in order to provide "a specification of how reality must be if the various regulative hopes that are introduced at different stages of the investigations are all to be fulfilled."[79] In Peirce's philosophy, volition is a metaphysical principle. If related to the definition of anticipatory hope, further contours of such a constructive interpretation of Peirce begin to appear. Defining anticipatory hope as a willingness to bring into the present what still rightfully belongs to the future, one of its innermost components is the motivational force of volition. As Peirce lets regulative hopes define his own metaphysics, their regulative function adds to his metaphysics exactly what anticipation adds to hope: one of its innermost components is the motivational force of volition. All of this is to say that we now have enough theoretical background to make the constructive suggestion that Peirce's metaphysical realism is best described as, structurally, a metaphysics of anticipation. With Peirce's philosophy as frame of mind, I argue that at a cosmological as well as an epistemological level, volition is an integral part of anticipatory hope and, as such, one way to account for the fact that hope is willed activity, preceded by a reliable promise and infused by the effects of this promise, namely the emergence of the motivational force of volition. Peirce's metaphysics is a metaphysics of anticipation.

---

[79] Hookway, *Peirce*, 79.

3

Peirce's Theory of Abduction

Discussing Peirce's theory of abduction in relation to the systematic need for him to formulate a cosmology, but considering the fact that the actual form and content of this cosmology are problematic, it is helpful to revisit his semiotic. The previous chapter followed a line of argumentation from Peirce's semiotic to his theory of the categories, culminating in a discussion of his cosmology and the doctrines of synechism and tychism, all with the purpose of addressing his espousal of a metaphysical voluntarism not unlike that of the later Schelling. This chapter revisits Peirce's semiotic, especially the speculative grammar which is part of his semiotic. It then follows a slightly different trajectory from there, through Peirce's logic, its divisions and sub-divisions where it finds, as one such subdivision of logic, the theory of abduction. Discussing the theory of abduction then leads to reflections on how Peirce tries to determine the importance of volition in the process of abductive reasoning and how this suggests, again, that volition has metaphysical significance in Peirce's system.

First of all we notice that Peirce's *speculative grammar* (his elaborate study of the different ways signs can inter-relate) is identical with the first division of his logic. The speculative grammar is one division out of three, again reflecting the categorial structure of the universe. It is the first division. The second division of logic is the *critical logic*, the third division is *methodeutic*, and, looking further, we discover that it is among the subdivisions of his critical logic (the second division of logic) that the epistemological methods of induction, deduction, and abduction are situated.

Peirce's logic is not only interesting in the present context because abduction is one of its subdivisions. It is of more specific importance because of his logic of relatives, which is part of his speculative grammar. In fact, it is widely agreed that Peirce's main contribution to the field of logic is precisely his logic of relatives. Two connections are explored here, as Peirce makes clear references in his writing to the pioneering work that Augustus De Morgan (1806–1871) had already initiated in the field of the logic of relatives, and to Francis Ellingwood Abbot, especially his book, *Scientific Theism*, which is also among the early contributions to the logic of relatives. De Morgan, British mathematician and logician, is of the opinion that the discipline of logic is in a seriously miserable state of affairs because it has made no advancements since Aristotle. The study of logic is unprogressive and stuck, he says. Abbot echoes this claim, as does Peirce. Later, Peirce was able to erect some hope for the future of logic and also takes credit for having helped reverse the unfortunate situation it was in: "I am as confident as I am of death, that Logic will hereafter be infinitely superior to what it is as I leave it; but my labors will have done good work toward its improvement" (*CP* 2.198). Perhaps this is even an understatement, for his work with the logic of relatives turns into a very influential accomplishment and establishes him as an academic pioneer in the area of logic. Interestingly, the starting point for Peirce's logic of relatives is his argument that there is identity between logic and semiotic, which is what makes him distinct in that area too, and which produces self-evaluating remarks like this: "I am, as far as I know, a pioneer, or rather a backwoodsman, in the work of clearing and opening up what I call *semiotic*, that is, the doctrine of the essential nature and fundamental varieties of possible semiosis; and I find the field too vast, the labor too great, for a first-comer" (*CP* 5.488).

With a specific interest in the theory of abduction, we note that the logic of relatives (the logic of how the individual elements of the universe inter-relate, or logic "treated by means of a special system of symbols" (*CP* 4.372)) is the broader background against which Peirce's theory of abduction is understood. The logic of relatives builds directly on his doctrine of synechism and the contention that all of reality is a continuum of inter-related entities, and it is precisely the role of abductive reasoning (the faculty of guessing) to conjecture the laws that govern these relationships of the cosmic continuum. So, to explore the relational intricacies of the continuum and the logic that governs it, the method of abductive reasoning is indispensable. Along these lines, Peirce thinks there is more than a superficial connection between logic and the onto-metaphysical truths about reality. He contends, "Metaphysics is the science of being, not merely as given in physical experience, but of being in general, its laws and types" (*EP* 2.36). In this sense, metaphysics concerns the reality of being itself and its results do not merely have regulative validity in the realm of the physical sciences. Rather, metaphysics has the functional role of unifying the variety of results that the physical sciences provide and, as such, demonstrates that the universe has meaning. In this context of deciphering the meaning of the universe, the role of abductive reasoning is indispensably linked to the metaphysical logic of the way everything interrelates. Abductive reasoning can uncover metaphysical truths.

In summary, there are two reasons to address Peirce's logic separately as a way of setting a frame for exploring his theory of abduction. First, abduction appears as a systematic sub-division of logic, and in order to approach abduction within its proper context, it is only natural to explore Peirce's logic first. Second, the logic of relatives explains why the method of abductive reasoning is a necessary addendum to the doctrine of synechism, and since an important focus of my argument is the problematic relatedness of synechism and tychism, it is natural, again, to start with Peirce's logic. The following explores these two reasons for the study of Peirce's logic.

Logic

Peirce says a logician was the first thing he wanted to be. This was already clear, he tells us, at the age of twelve when he happened upon Archbishop Whateley's book, *Logic*. Peirce was immediately taken in by it and spent no more than a few days to manage and absorb its content. Also, as Peirce arrived at the "demonstrative certitude that there was something wrong about Kant's formal logic" (*CP* 4.2), his early paper, *Memorandum Concerning the Aristotelian Syllogism* (circulating through the Lowell Institute in 1866), accused Kant of an inability to understand the logic of syllogisms. It was also at this point, in his early twenties, that Peirce read De Morgan's work on logic and, having read his memoir on the logic of relatives, he thought it was "a brilliant and astonishing illumination of every corner and every vista of logic" (*CP* 1.562). Clearly, Peirce experienced this early fascination with logic and it stayed with him throughout his career, continually playing a fundamental role in his work. That logic remained so important for Peirce as he moved through the different stages of his philosophical development relates to his confidence in its methodological importance for the creation of optimal conditions for the growth of knowledge. "In logic, it will be observed that knowledge is reasonableness; and the ideal of reasoning will be to follow such methods as must develope knowledge the most speedily" (*CP* 1.615). As we shall see, it is in Peirce's third division of logic that he reveals more specifically what he means by "such methods," and how he applies these in the struggle to escape doubt and pursue knowledge. Appropriately, he entitles this third field *methodeutic*.

In his most elementary definition of logic, Peirce makes a direct identification of logic and semiotic by claiming that logic is "only another name for semiotic σημειωτικη" (*CP* 2.227). This is an elementary and broad definition of logic because it identifies semiotic as its most general aspect. Logic is "the science of the necessary laws of thought, or, still better (thought always taking place by means of signs), it is general semeiotic, treating not merely of truth, but also of the general conditions of signs being signs" (*CP* 1.444).[1] In other words, the focus of Peirce's logic is not the semiotic structure per se, but rather the necessary laws that signs follow in their various ways of inter-relating. Already here, the structural elements for a new emphasis on the logic of relatives are beginning to emerge and, against traditional Aristotelian logic, Peirce argues that logic must concern *logical* language (the laws of thought), not everyday language. Everyday language is merely an expression of thought and therefore derived from logical language. In the same way that Aristotle should concentrate on common thought, rather than common language (as De Morgan argues), so Peirce argues that the logician should make a commitment "to embrace all the necessary principles of semeiotic" (*CP* 4.9), for "the woof and warp of all thought and all research is symbols, and the life of thought and science is the life inherent in symbols" (*CP* 2.220).

It is in Peirce's work with the semiotic relatedness of signs, and the laws of thought governing them, that he finds these laws to be of three kinds. The laws are grouped in two areas, pure logic and applied logic. Belonging to pure logic we find the first two divisions of logic (speculative grammar and critical logic), while the third, methodeutic, represents the area of applied logic.[2] These three divisions of logic each relies on the preceding one for its results, much like Thirdness involves Secondness and

---

[1] Goudge points out that there is some confusion about whether Peirce is referring here to *all* signs or only signs that function as symbols. He suggests that this confusion is due to Peirce's interchangeable use of the words *symbol* and *sign* (examples are *CP* 1.191, 2.93), and at the same time explicitly says that the three sub-divisions (*speculative grammar, critical logic*, and *methodeutic*) concern the logic of symbols, *not* the logic of icons or indices. (See *CP* 4.9.)

[2] Peirce lets all three divisions bear classical and old names but, as is his signature custom, he also redefines them. From a contemporary point of view, Feibleman comments that Peirce's pure logic (i.e. the first and second divisions) "includes what is now called symbolic or mathematical logic" (Feibleman, *Interpreted as a System*, 88), and that it examines syllogisms in the context of the validity of reasoning (as does traditional Aristotelian logic). Peirce's applied logic (i.e. the third division) "includes modern semantics, pragmatics, and scientific method, or the logic of discovery" (ibid., 88), which Peirce gives a classical name also, namely *speculative rhetoric*.

Firstness, and Secondness involves Firstness. Methodeutic relies on speculative grammar and critical logic, and critical logic relies on speculative grammar.

We have already looked at Peirce's general theory of signs in the earlier discussion of semiotic, along with its more complex outcropping, the speculative grammar. The speculative grammar now reappears as the first division of his logic, and therefore we need not repeat the details of it in this new context. The only thing to note is that Peirce's identification of speculative grammar as logic's first and most fundamental division happens because of his basic contention that all logic deals with "the formal conditions of symbols having meaning" (*CP* 4.116, 2.93); that is, with the conditions for understanding the "reference of symbols in general to their objects" (*CP* 1.559).[3] This is to say that the most fundamental laws that dictate the behavior of signs, or the process of signification, set the conditions for symbolic referencing, and logic is precisely a study of the most basic form of symbolic signification. Recalling that speculative grammar concerns the very complex but still general functions of signs and simply organizes the various types of signs, so does the first and most fundamental division of logic concern the bare conditions for the way symbols take on meaning and how they behave as signs.

In propositional language, Peirce explains that the meaning of a symbol is determined by the way it functions and becomes a building block for terms and propositions. He distinguishes between terms and propositions by saying that "a 'term' or class-name, is for me nothing but a proposition with its indices or subjects left blank, or indefinite" (*CP* 3.440). As such, a term may appear in the form of a building block for a proposition and thereby "be a direct constituent of a proposition" (*CP* 2.328). Propositions are "symbols which . . . independently determine their *objects* by means of other term or terms, and thus, expressing their own objective validity, become capable of truth or falsehood" (*CP* 1.559). Compared to the proposition, a term is the simpler function of a symbol but one that can merge into the more complex function of propositions. Terms and propositions

---

[3] Keeping in mind that this first sub-division of logic helps define the initial stage of exploring the most fundamental patterns and functions of signs, this is the one of the three divisions closest to phenomenology. As such, it assists in the discovery of the three irreducible categories, Firstness, Secondness, and Thirdness. It is not necessary to pursue this theme further, since it has already been shown how signs behave in accordance with the dynamics of the categorial triad.

concern meaning only, and therefore can not be more than fragments of arguments.[4]

Critical Logic

Peirce terms the second division of logic *critical logic*, and argues that it "classifies arguments and determines the *validity* of each kind" (*CP* 1.191).[5] Where speculative grammar concerns the meaning of symbols, critical logic concerns the validity of arguments consisting of the symbols already analyzed in the context of speculative grammar. Moving beyond the first division of logic (i. e. speculative grammar, which deals with the meaning of symbols as it appears in terms and propositions), the critical logic now analyzes and estimates the validity of complete arguments, or syllogisms. That is, a syllogism consists of terms and propositions but does more than just communicate meaning. By also making a claim to truth, the second part of pure logic (critical logic) does not limit itself to meaning; it also concerns "the formal conditions of the truth of symbols" (*CP* 1.559). Compared to the *grammatica speculativa*, the speculative grammar, a truth standard is now involved and the task of critical logic is to ask about the relevance of the complete argument in relation to truth. In Peirce's formulation, a syllogism "represents its object as being an ulterior sign through a law, namely, the law that the passage from all such premisses to such conclusions tends to the truth" (*CP* 2.263), so that the new focus is to determine the manner in which conclusions gravitate toward truth. The syllogism asserts something that goes beyond mere communication of meaning; it aspires to be truth. Or, in the reverse sense, terms and propositions can only be derived from an argument as its parts; they do not qualify for a position at the level of argumentation. It is important to note that a syllogism does not have to declare the actual truth in order to still principally be about truth, for even if its declaration should be untrue, it "can in some conceivable case lead to absurdity . . . [and] as soon as we admit the idea of absurdity, we are bound to class the rejection of an argumentation among argumentations" (*CP* 2.356). Whether or not a syllogism is actually true does not annul the fact that it aspires for the truth,

---

[4] For the sake of systematic clarity, the three sub-divisions of logic are speculative grammar, critical logic and methodeutic. The first two belong to pure logic and the third belongs to applied logic. The logic of relatives is a division of speculative grammar. The critical logic consists of induction, deduction, and abduction. The principle of pragmatism is part of the methodeutic.

[5] Italics mine.

so it is not that the syllogism is an impeccable deliverer of truth, but rather that it always gravitates toward the truth.

All of this is to say that the syllogism must "be a Symbol, or Sign whose Object is a General Law or Type. It must involve a Dicent Symbol, or Proposition, which is termed its *Premiss*: for the Argument can only urge the law by urging it in an instance" (*CP* 2.253). There is "a peculiar force, or relation to the Interpretant" (*CP* 2.253) within the symbol that causes it to assert itself by way of urging its interpretant (who or which is its interpreter) to declare a certain interpretation of it. In the argument there is an urge toward a specific conclusion, and an urge for a specific passage to occur from certain premises to certain conclusions. Therefore, the interpretation of a symbol will, at best, be the inevitable truth about it, or the one that, at the least, tends toward it. The peculiar force within the symbol is the assertiveness that makes an argumentation. Peirce also says that the proposition is "but an argumentation divested of the assertoriness of its premiss and conclusion" (*CP* 3.440).

With the definition of a syllogism in hand, Peirce now claims that there are three different classes of syllogisms: "An Argument is always understood by its Interpretant to belong to a general class of analogous arguments, which class, as a whole, tends toward the truth. This may happen in three ways, giving rise to a trichotomy of all simple arguments into Deductions, Inductions and Abductions" (*CP* 2.266), or hypotheses.[6] So, here we finally encounter Peirce's notion of abduction; it defines the third class of arguments in addition to the two traditional ones, induction and deduction. We complete this brief exposition of the three divisions of Peirce's logic by first visiting his methodeutic, and then continue through his logic of relatives to a more focused study of his three classes of syllogisms, especially abduction.

Methodeutic

The third division of logic is termed methodeutic and "studies the methods that ought to be pursued in the investigation, in the exposition, and in the application of truth" (*CP* 1.191). Concerning the application of the truth tended to by critical logic, methodeutic (also called *speculative rhetoric*) builds on both the second and the first divisions of logic. Peirce thinks

---

[6] Remember that deduction, induction, and abduction are not limited to concrete forms of human reasoning. They are argumentative forms that the rational process exemplifies. This relates to Peirce's understanding of reasoning, which is not limited to the form it takes in the human mind. Reasoning and the human mind live within the Absolute Mind, not vice versa.

of methodeutic as "the logical study of the theory of inquiry" (*CP* 2.106); it is the practical method of how to pursue truth and, in effect, the very thing that reasoning does. Although—or perhaps because—this is "the highest and most living branch of logic" (*CP* 2.333), Peirce never brings his methodeutic to completion. Taking the study of symbols to this third and highest level, he does reveal that methodeutic "would treat of the formal conditions of the *force* of symbols" (*CP* 1.559, 4.116).[7] In Feibleman's formulation this means that it deals "with the *communication* of reasoning and the discovery of truth,"[8] or quite simply the process of rational inquiry. As such, the methodeutic is *applied* logic and investigates "the laws by which . . . one sign gives birth to another" (*CP* 2.229), and therefore how argumentative reasoning grows. For present purposes, the most important aspect of Peirce's methodeutic is its focus on the compelling force within symbols and how it moves them not only toward a certain truth interpretation, but also toward actual realization.[9] With the third division of logic, it is Peirce's interest to explore whether "there be also a greater life-history that every symbol furnished with a vehicle of life goes through, and what is the nature of it" (*CP* 2.111). He also identifies this "vehicle of life" as the activity of a symbol, or the *effect* symbols have in the greater picture of symbolic representation. That is, effect is something that characterizes a symbol in addition to what can be known about its meaning (determined by speculative grammar) and what can be known about the way it tends toward truth (determined by critical logic).

Essentially, this activity of symbols becomes the logical background for Peirce's epistemology. As already discussed, the semiotic sign relation of icon, index, and symbol expresses truth, and in so far as truth happens in the human mind, it becomes the means for obtaining knowledge. Epistemology is more concerned with the actual emergence of knowledge than it is with the semiotic technicalities preceding the appearance of knowledge and it therefore focuses on the experience of the force by which the process of semiosis (the emergence of knowledge) imposes itself upon the mind. "The assertion [syllogism] represents a compulsion which experience, meaning the course of life, brings upon the deliverer to attach the predicate to the subjects as a sign of them taken in a particular way" (*CP* 3.435). The knower's experience is characterized by the compulsory effect

---

[7] Italics mine.

[8] Ibid., 88.

[9] This focus on realization relates Peirce's third division of logic to modern semantics, pragmatics, the logic of discovery, and scientific methodology.

of the semiotic process overruling the semiotic process itself. Semiosis is not experienced as a process, but rather as one singular force that presses in upon the mind in the form of propositions that make claims to truth. This experience of being imposed upon is the experience of knowledge, or "that determination of belief and cognition generally which the course of life has forced upon a man" (*CP* 2.138). Not until propositions have appeared in the human mind can exchange of knowledge begin to happen in the form of communication of reasoning and the discovery of truth. Exploring the methods of rational inquiry presupposes that knowledge already exists, as it were, and *this* is where epistemology has its home. Epistemology operates in the realm of communication about already asserted truth. Peirce's methodeutic turns out to be very important in our study of abduction as guarantor for religious instinct because it defines the methodological possibilities and limits of knowledge of God.

Logic of relatives

In a text from 1877, Peirce distinguishes between ordinary metaphysics and his own metaphysics. "According to the former, there are ultimate sensations without any general relations between them; according to the latter, although the differences between different sensations can never be completely covered by a general description, yet we may make an indefinite progress toward such a result" (*EP* 1.107). We have already heard from Peirce that metaphysics can only hope to make wonderful approximations toward the truth about all reality. Now he repeats this point by letting us know that the metaphysical discourse must focus on the general relations between ultimate sensations, which he has already treated in his cosmological doctrine of synechism. With his logic of relatives, it is precisely this focus that Peirce wishes to pursue. Although he is historically the rightful author of the logic of relatives, it was under way for quite a while and, in effect, already took its beginning with De Morgan and Abbot whose thoughts were indispensably important for Peirce's theory.

Augustus De Morgan and Francis Ellingwood Abbot

In 1849, De Morgan publishes quite an innovative statement that redefines algebra as *a system of symbols*. The symbols of the algebraic system, he says, are all without definite meaning, simply and merely identified by their formal inter-relatedness. In his statement, he first makes the move of reducing the number of algebraic rules to five and then argues, "Any system of symbols which obeys these laws and no others, except they be formed by combination of these laws, and which uses the preceding symbols and no others, except they be new symbols invented in abbreviation of combinations of these symbols, is symbolic algebra."[10] Based on De Morgan's approach and new focus on how symbols relate, rather than focusing on the symbols themselves, it is possible, as Murphey explains, "to apply algebra to nonquantitative subjects. Among the first such applications to be made was the development of the algebra of logic—the forerunner of modern symbolic logic."[11]

Related to this shift in focus, from quantitative classification to formal relatedness, is also De Morgan's criticism of Aristotelian logic. De Morgan argues that logic must concern the *necessary laws of thought*, not the laws of everyday language, which are merely expressions of thought. His argument against common logicians addresses their inability to distinguish between a judgment and a relation. As for the principles of logic, he says, there is in fact only one formal principle: "*there is the probability a that x is in the relation l to y.*"[12] In other words, logic should analyze nothing but the possible and actual relatedness of subjects and the laws that determine how these relations are structured. De Morgan even goes as far as suggesting that thought be conceived as a branch of algebra, and we see why, considering his definition of symbolic algebra. If the analytical focus is the relatedness of symbols, then thought and algebra are subject to the same analytical process. In fact, De Morgan's work with the logic of relations initiates a tendency of making mathematics essential in the emerging transformation of the discipline of logic. His thoughts have a particular influence on Peirce's pursuit of "an indisputable theory of reasoning by the aid of mathematics" (*CP* 3.618) and help him on the way toward his own logic of relatives. Although it is De Morgan who initiates the relation theory of logic, its actual development is to Peirce's credit.

Peirce is quickly fascinated with De Morgan's thought. Having received a copy of his paper on the logic of relations, Peirce comments that he "at once fell to upon it; and before many weeks had come to see in it, as De Morgan had already seen, a brilliant and astonishing illumination of every corner and every vista of logic" (*CP* 1.562). About four years later, Peirce then has the opportunity to visit De Morgan, and has by this time appropriated his thoughts about the logic of relations. So, Peirce seizes

---

[10] Alexander Macfarlane, *Lectures on Ten British Mathematicians of the Nineteenth Century* (New York: Wiley, 1916) 26–27.

[11] Murphey, *Peirce's Philosophy*, 185.

[12] Quoted in Dinesen, *C. S. Peirce*, 72.

the opportunity to present to him his own first major publication on the subject.[13] Much later, Daniel D. Merrill describes this publication as "the first attempt to expand Boole's algebra of logic to include the logic of relations,"[14] and it clearly marks Peirce's pioneer work in the field of logic; it marks the first beginnings of a full mathematical treatment of abstract relations. In evaluation of Peirce's work on the calculus of relatives, Murphey even makes the comment, "Not until the *Principia* appeared was Peirce's work superseded and then only by a theory based in large part upon his own."[15] It is commonly agreed that modern symbolic logic originates in Peirce's logic of relatives, which builds on De Morgan's work on the intersection of algebra and logic and the insight that logic concerns the formal relational system of things rather than their quantitative classifications. In spite of Peirce's many other contributions in the field of logic, his logic of relatives remains very significant.[16]

Similar to the way Peirce appropriates De Morgan's thesis on the logic of relations, he also finds inspiration in Abbot's reflections on the notion of *relationism*, or *scientific realism*, as he also calls it. Like De Morgan, Abbot criticizes Aristotelian logic and argues that the challenge is this: "Translating the Moderate Realism of Aristotle into the more accurate language of Relationism."[17] One important thing to remember about both De Morgan and Abbot's (and in turn Peirce's) critiques of Aristotle is that they seek to expand his logic rather than replace it. They affirm Aristotle's work and appropriate its basic elements although they are still disturbed by its inadequacies. Peirce is fundamentally affirmative of Aristotle's realism but also sympathetic to Abbot's critique of it. Contemplating the emerging ideas about the calculus of relations, he finds it wanting. Aristotle does not understand the full scope of realism and is blind to the fact that it can not continue to limit itself to the monadic level of reality. It strikes Peirce as particularly significant that the "great difference between the logic of rela-

---

[13] This publication is entitled *Description of a Notation for the Logic of Relatives, Resulting from an Amplification of the Conceptions of Boole's Calculus of Logic (DNLR)* (*CP* 3.45–149). The visit with De Morgan is possible because Peirce participates in a group visit to Europe (1870) with the purpose of studying a solar eclipse.

[14] Daniel D. Merrill, "The 1870 Logic of Relatives Memoir," introduction to *Writings of Charles S. Peirce: A Chronological Edition*, ed. Max Fisch et al. (Bloomington: Indiana University Press, 1982–) xlii.

[15] Murphey, *Peirce's Philosophy*, 152.

[16] Note that Peirce changes De Morgan's term *logic of relations* to *logic of relatives*. Later, around 1903, when Peirce regrets this change, he finds it too late to revert it because his own term is now in general use (*CP* 3.574 n2; 3.574).

[17] Francis Ellingwood Abbot, *Scientific Theism* (London: Macmillan, 1885) 41.

tives and ordinary logic is that the former regards the form of relation in all its generality and in its different possible species while the latter is tied down to the matter of the single special relation of similarity" (*CP* 4.5). Aristotelian logic is the prime example of just such an ordinary logic that is restricted to the monadic relation of similarity between two members of the same class, rather than being open to a consideration of relatedness per se, as it might happen between any and all entities. So, when Abbot already evaluated Aristotle's realism and emphasized not "forgetting to correct its capital error of making the universal inhere in each individual as an individual (*in re*) rather than in all the individuals as a group (*inter res*),"[18] he also foretold the story of Peirce's more elaborate treatment of symbolic relatedness.

As it should be clear, Peirce's response to Aristotelian logic centers on the contention that "where ordinary logic talks of classes the logic of relatives talks of *systems*" (*CP* 4.5). But what is a system? For Peirce, a system concerns more than individual things relating to other individual things on the monadic level; it includes interactive relations of dyadic and triadic relatedness in addition to those of monadic relatedness. Using Abbot's language of relationism, the relational system deals "with general laws rather than with the peculiarities or accidents of individual objects."[19] So, when Peirce argues that ordinary logic has a great deal to say about genera and species, or about classes, he recognizes the incompletion it suffers by restricting itself to an interest in the monadic level of reality. Reality can not possibly be reduced to the various classes and their members, but should include levels of far deeper complexity, of which monadic classifications are only parts. Peirce's critique of ordinary logic addresses the inability it causes to ever exceed the boundaries of determining similarity of objects and reflecting on the traits that members of a given class might share. For Peirce, logic is about the governing *laws* of reality, not simply the individual objects that make up reality. The rationale behind Peirce's self-pronounced title of *extreme realist* is precisely this expansion of the meaning of reality to also include the laws that govern it.

Peirce's relational definition of reality also implies that we can not approach reality by the simple criteria of true and false, for (as De Morgan would agree, too) there are different types of truth, not just the kinds determined by the classical theory of proposition, and we must be able to distinguish one kind from the other. Considering the fact that it is Kant's

---

[18] Ibid., 42.
[19] Ibid.

logic and his own work with syllogisms that first inspire Peirce's interest in logic, his logic of relatives is not unrelated to the work he does with the propositional and syllogistic form.[20] The simple principle of identity between subject and predicate in the copula is too narrow and needs revision, Peirce argues, for the copula is the distributor of relatedness, not of identity.

What is the difference between monadic, dyadic and triadic reality, and how does this difference relate to the need to distinguish between different kinds of propositional truth? For the sake of illustration, Peirce uses the classification of verbs. The verb "to be" is monadic and, as an example, makes the copula of soft and cotton ("cotton is soft") a monadic proposition of the traditional kind. In contrast, Peirce considers "to love" or "to kill" examples of dyadic verbs because they imply a relationship between two separate entities. Someone loves, or kills, someone else. He then considers "to give" as an example of a triadic verb because it involves a giver, a receiver, and an object to be received, thereby establishing the triadic expression "____ gives ____ to ____." It is important to be aware that the triadic verb applies to more than simply material gifts. To say, for example, that "*quantity* gives *form* to *quality* completes the expression also,"[21] and shows how the primary matter of Peirce's classification of verbs is to establish a logical principle by which phenomena can be classified according to their structural complexity rather than the class to which they belong. Also, since it is the logical task of the copula to distribute a relation, and not truth, it therefore has no logical consequences to negate the verb "to kill" and replace it with "not to kill." Logically, the dyadic relation remains unchanged, for whether a person does or does not kill, the relationship is there between either an actual or a potential killer on one side, and either an actual or a potential victim on the other.

In the context of my argument, it is particularly interesting to also consider the triadic structure of the verb "to promise" because the reality of promise is crucial to the definition of anticipation and anticipatory hope. In Dinesen's observation, the verb "to promise" is structurally similar to the verb "to give" and must be identified in terms of hope because it includes the *absence* of what is actually promised. She makes this observation in relation to Peirce's notion of belief: "And this [our belief] consists of the non-realization of a promise given, seen as an expectation."[22] Compared

---

[20] See *Critical Logic*, 79–80.
[21] Feibleman, *Interpreted as a System*, 108.
[22] Anne Marie Dinesen, "Tout signe est une promesse: Note sur l'habitude du croire selon

to a gift, then, a promise is only different because of the added aspect of temporality; it still requires a simultaneous involvement of both giver, recipient, and gift. As in the case of the triadic verb, which remains logically unchanged in spite of being negated, the verbs "to promise" and "to give" are structurally the same, regardless of whether the gift is actually or potentially real. A promise is a gift. Furthermore, Dinesen opts for an understanding of the sign relation per se as a type of promise. A sign is given as an indication, or a promise, of a possible future interpretation.[23] In a theological context—where the divine promise is the ultimate gift of all gifts—Dinesen's suggestion is significant. In order not to disrupt the proper order of things and anticipate a later discussion, however, Peirce's logic of relatives still needs further clarification.

The prime interest of Peirce's logic of relatives is the relation, but how does he define a relation? First of all, the relation is the glue that holds the system together. Considering what may be called an "empty sentence," for example, is to consider a relation in and of itself (i.e. the structure which allows for the emergence of an actual sentence once its blanks have been filled). In Peirce's words, a relation consists in "the possibility of a fact which could be precisely asserted by filling the blanks of a corresponding relative rheme with proper names" (*CP* 4.354).[24] A relation, stripped of its actual content, Peirce also calls a fact. "A *relationship*, or *fundamentum relationis*, is a fact relative to a number of objects, considered apart from those objects, as if, after the statement of the fact, the designations of those objects had been erased" (*CP* 3.466). The atom is another example that illustrates the nature of relation. The "unsaturated bonds" (*CP* 3.469) of an atom function in a similar way to the blanks of a sentence that need to be filled, and in both cases, the relation is understood as a universal. "Every relative . . . is general; its definition describes a system in general terms" (*CP* 3.220). Its generality also describes something of an incomplete nature, because it is "without attachments to experience, without 'a local habitation and a name' [yet with] indications of the need of such attachments" (*CP* 3.459). The relation is essentially incomplete, although

---

C. S. Peirce" [Every sign is a promise: note on the habit of belief according to C. S. Peirce], in *Qu'est-ce qu'une promesse?* [What is a promise?], ed. Per Aage Brandt and Annie Prassoloff, Peotica et Analytica, Supplément 1 (Århus: Aarhus University Press, 1991) 135; italics mine, translation mine. In the original: "Et celui-ci [nos *belief*] consiste dans la *non-réalisation d'une promesse donnée, vue comme une espérance*." *Espérance* can also mean *hope*.

[23] See Dinesen, *C. S. Peirce*, 74.

[24] The *relative rhema* is Peirce's elaborate name for the shorter term *relation* (*CP* 3.636). In the following, relation and relative may therefore be used synonymously.

thereby it also embodies a longing for completion, which is how Peirce can say that the relation "is, therefore, an *ens rationis* and mere logical possibility; but its subsistence is of the nature of a fact" (*CP* 3.571).

Some interpretive points are now relevant again. For Peirce, the relation is an embodiment of the tension between actuality and possibility—much in the sense that a promised gift is simultaneously actual and possible. In my judgment, this makes the very nature of the relation anticipatory. It holds together two separate objects and sustains a permanent encounter between them, in the present. The two separate objects are protected from collapsing into one and also from falling completely away from each other; they are held in perfect and permanent tension. What makes the relation anticipatory, then, is that the relation's inherent longing for completion, or the need of its *unsaturated bonds* to be attached to experience, is its essential nature. The relation subsists because it has reason to long for completion. Its completion is a promise and can therefore be rightfully anticipated. That the completion of the relation is permanently a reality of the future does not diminish its effect in the present, for this completion is just as much a present reality.

Metaphysical and Religious Implications of Peirce's Logic of Relatives

In a broader perspective, defining the relation as an incomplete sentence, an *ens rationis*,[25] or a logical tension of actuality and possibility, refers back to Peirce's extreme realism and its focus on the laws that govern monadic, dyadic, and triadic reality. It suggests that the relation is equivalent to the intelligibility and rational principles that govern the symbolic system Peirce considers reality to be. In other words, with the logic of relatives, Peirce ties the study of logic back to his metaphysics and perhaps most especially to his doctrine of synechism. To support this statement, it is clarifying to revisit Peirce's claim that logic exceeds the ordinary logic of monadic similarity and direct comparison.

The way Peirce's logic of relatives expands monadic reality with dyadic and triadic reality involves more than just adding two levels of reality; it is essentially a *redefinition* of monadic reality. Peirce makes this move with the contention that monadic existence is itself nothing but a degenerate form of relatedness. In Peirce's observation, the monadic can not possibly exist in separation from the dyadic and the triadic, which means that if the monadic is brought into isolation, it becomes a degenerate of

---

[25] *Ens rationis* refers to a *rational being* as opposed to a real being, *ens reale*.

what it was supposed to be. Recalling Peirce's argument that no individual category appears in isolation from the other two categories, we see how he brings the theory of the categories to bear on the things that disturb him about Aristotelian realism: mere Firstness, or isolated monadic existence, is an impossibility, it is always accompanied by Secondness and Thirdness, or dyadic and triadic existence. Since it is the responsibility of Thirdness to provide meaning, purpose, and intelligibility, for Peirce then to claim, as Raposa suggests, "that 'X is hard' is to do more than simply ascribe a particular quality to X; rather, it is to affirm that under certain specifiable conditions X will tend to behave in a certain specifiable manner."[26] In other words, qualitative possibility (Firstness) always appears as a matter of an infused tendency (Thirdness) to pursue a certain form of its own realization. So, at the back of all monadic reality is a governing law that keeps individual things tending toward certain behavioral patterns, for example the tendency to be hard, and this is the law of Thirdness that completes monadic reality and rescues it from being a merely degenerate relational form. The complete, relational form embodies the intelligibility of reality. Keeping in mind that the relation is essentially open ended and longs for completion, this law of Thirdness (infusing mere possibility with a tendency to actualize in a particular manner) is ultimately the focus of Peirce's logic of relatives. The relational encompasses the structure, or intelligibility, of reality.

At this point, Peirce's doctrine of synechism comes into view again. To argue that all monadic reality involves intelligibility, or that there is intelligibility at the back of everything, is another way of saying that even if "one is confronted with nothing more than the case of an individual object enduring through time, real *continuity* is involved and the properties that inhere in such an object are themselves 'general.'"[27] Individual things are incomplete elements of the continuum although the continuum still accounts for the generality displayed in each individual object in the behavioral tendencies that move it toward actualization and make it available for interpretation in merely monadic (and degenerate) predicates. In other words, the incompletion of monadic reality is an illusion, for individual things simply would not exist were it not for the intelligibility involved in their existence. Furthermore, the fact that generality originates in the reality of cosmic continuity enables individual objects to inter-relate in an infinite number of ways, precisely because they are first and primarily

---

[26] Raposa, *Peirce's Philosophy of Religion*, 18.
[27] Ibid., 18.

placed against the background of the infinite continuum. "In short, the idea of a general involves the idea of possible variations which no multitude of existent things could exhaust, but would leave between any two not merely *many* possibilities, but possibilities absolutely beyond all multitude" (*CP* 5.103).

These reflections leave us no more than a few steps short of Peirce's metaphysical contention that all matter is effete mind, and that all of reality is an expression of Absolute Mind. For Peirce, Absolute Mind is a synonym for the reality of God and the instinctive need for human reasoning to become and be sensitive to divine reality. Peirce develops a distinct metaphysics when he employs a form of extreme or objective idealism that comprises logic, evolutionary cosmology and now also the theory of abduction. As we shall see later, this metaphysics also involves his principle of pragmatism. For now, we see that Peirce's logic of relatives necessitates a narrow consideration of his theory of abduction. Why? Because Peirce reckons it the task of abductive reasoning to ascertain the relational laws of intelligibility that govern all of reality and which the logic of relatives identifies. But not only that, for it is also by virtue of abductive, hypothetical ideas that Peirce renders interaction with God possible. These ideas are able instinctively to comprehend not only the logical laws at the back of all of reality but also the divine mind with which they correlate. Indeed, Peirce's logic of relatives has metaphysical as well as religious implications.

Approaching Peirce's theory of abduction, we now turn to a discussion of the epistemological triad where it is situated.

Tending toward Truth: Deduction, Induction, and Abduction

Even though Peirce's epistemological notions of abduction, deduction and induction appear as subdivisions of his critical logic, Peirce's epistemology is also intimately related to his methodeutic. In the methodeutic, his observation is that knowledge comes in the manner of mental experiences of intrusive and imposing propositions that make specific claims to truth. Knowledge is an experience of the "forcible modification of our ways of thinking . . . [by] the brutal inroads of ideas from without" (*CP* 1.321). Propositions, or syllogisms, appear as "resultant ideas that have been forced upon us" (*CP* 4.318), and Peirce groups them in three kinds: abductive, deductive, and inductive. The triadic structure of Peirce's epistemology is again a manifestation of his theory of the three categories. Cognition too is a triadic set of logical operations.[28] Although Peirce uses logical operations synonymously with syllogisms, they are not logical conclusions, but only truth claims that function as fundamental building blocks for the cognitive process of arriving at logical conclusions. Syllogisms are the results of the preparatory process of semiosis and enter the epistemological field in the form of propositional arguments. They simply appear in the human mind and demand to be considered true. Peirce's epistemology pays very focused attention to the logical operations of human cognition that is defined as the movement, or tending, toward truth. Taken together, it is the role of abduction, deduction and induction to explain how this movement happens; they encompass the mental activity of cognitive gravitation toward truth.

Peirce's epistemological triad is spearheaded by abduction because it is only abductive propositions that have the ability to break new ground of knowledge. "Abduction is the process of forming an explanatory hypothesis. It is the only logical operation which introduces any new idea; for induction does nothing but determine a value, and deduction merely evolves the necessary consequences of a pure hypothesis" (*CP* 5.171). In other words, abduction suggests that something *may be*, deduction that something *must necessarily be*, and induction that something *actually is*. This means that both deduction and induction depend on abduction in such a way that induction depends on both deduction and abduction, and deduction depends only on abduction. What *may be* influences what *must necessarily be*, as well as what *actually is*, for the necessary and the actual should always be able to account for even the merely potentially possible. The possible can never exceed the sum total of the necessary and the actual. In contrast, that which *must necessarily be* is independent of what *actually is*, because it is determined by logical necessity only, apart from any realization of it.

Another way to compare abduction, deduction and induction is to say that deduction moves—backward—from a major premise (all men are mortal) through a minor premise (Socrates is a man) to a conclusion (Socrates is mortal). Induction moves—forward—from a minor premise (Socrates is a man) through a conclusion (Socrates is mortal) to a major premise (all men are mortal). Finally, abduction moves sideways, so to speak, in so far as it relates premise and conclusion the way two icons relate (i.e. not necessarily via a mediating element, but as a deliberately

---

[28] Technically, Peirce operates with one kind of abduction, two kinds of deduction, and three kinds of induction. Here the subdivisions of deduction and induction are only discussed in so far as they are important for the context.

established connection). In this sense, abduction is nothing but instinctive guessing that happens according to no modal truth value but rather according to the simple claim that guessing correctly is a reliable method. After all, "instinct seldom errs, while reason goes wrong nearly half the time, if not more frequently" (*EP* 2.349). Adding to the two classic examples of how Socrates' mortality can be employed either deductively or inductively, it might be employed abductively by reference to Socrates' actual death.[29] Reflecting on the death sentence he has received, Socrates expresses great certainty of the "good hope that death is a blessing,"[30] and that his soul will not be harmed by the so-called penalty of death that he is soon to receive. Socrates' fearless acceptance of death is, in other words, an expression of the instinctive manner in which he connects the two icons of life and death. He conceives abductively of death as harmless to the life of the soul and is therefore able to consume the hemlock drink with neither stoic indifference, nor presumptuous optimism, but confident peace. As we will see later, Peirce contends that the logic of abduction is at work in the doctrine of pragmatism, and, in turn, that the doctrine of pragmatism is the method of right thinking in the sense that conceiving the truth of an idea is impossible without also conceiving of its practical bearings. Hence, Socrates' death exemplifies the logic of abductive reasoning in that he conceives of death by also conceiving of its practical bearings, just as the doctrine of pragmatism states.

Even though abduction takes the epistemological lead, it still borrows characteristics from the two logical operations of classical epistemology, induction and deduction. What Peirce emphasizes with this hierarchical order is the urgent need that he sees for introducing a new kind of proposition because previous philosophy has been unable to provide an adequate logical description of the growth of knowledge. With this, he argues that epistemology must seek the help of scientific methodology, giving deduction and induction only secondary importance: "Now, that the matter of no new truth can come from induction or deduction, we have seen. It can only come from abduction; and abduction is, after all, nothing but guessing" (*CP* 7.219). Science has always progressed by the plain discipline of guessing, Peirce argues, and the scientists have a very important lesson to teach philosophers because they, too, facilitate the progress of knowledge by the discipline of mere guessing.

---

[29] I owe the suggestion of this example to Dr. Vítor Westhelle.

[30] Plato, "Apology," in *Complete Works*, ed. John M. Cooper and D. S. Hutchinton (Indianapolis: Hackett, 1997) 41.

Contemplating Peirce's triadic epistemology, there is, in my judgment, reason to pause at the tendency for him to reinforce a hierarchy of abduction first, followed by deduction and induction. Why does abduction stand out so significantly? And what importance does it have that he distinguishes abduction from deduction and induction by virtue of its ability to break new ground of knowledge? I suggest that a viable response to these questions comes as, principally, a repetition of the point made earlier, namely that the doctrines of synechism and agapism are two words for the same thing, and that they are contrasted by the doctrine of tychism in such a way that there is, in fact, more of a contrast between two opposing doctrines than a triad of three. It seems to me that placing abduction in contrast to deductive and inductive propositions taken together is a systematic reflection of the problematic tension there is between synechism and tychism. Just as tychism, which expresses the principle of absolute chance, breaks into the undisturbed synechist whole, so abduction expresses a cognitive power of initiation that introduces the principle of disruption into the yet undisturbed. New knowledge breaks the solid ground of already established knowledge. Systematically, my point is that at both the cosmological and the epistemological levels, Peirce tries to come to terms with one and the same issue, namely a very strong tension—or perhaps even an unsolvable conflict—between the stable and the unstable, the rational and the irrational, the synechist and the tychist, the immediate and the volitional. Again, we face the principle of volition and a need to understand its systematic importance for Peirce's thinking. First, we now turn to a brief, descriptive account of deduction and induction, followed by a lengthier discussion of abduction,[31] and then eventually we discuss the role of volition in Peirce's theory of abduction. We pursue this latter point by trying to understand what role Peirce ascribes to rational control in the process of abductive reasoning.

Deduction

Deduction relates two different elements by unconditional necessity. It is necessary reasoning and, in contrast to abduction, does not introduce any new thought elements that were not there before. Deduction reasons on the basis of hypothetically established general rules, and then concludes all possible consequences that have to be true in so far as the rule is true.

---

[31] On occasion, Peirce employs the term *retroduction* synonymously with abduction, perhaps in order to indicate the spontaneous non-mediated way abduction relates conclusions back to hypothetical premises. Abduction is the preferred term here.

Deduction is deeply influenced by the logic of mathematics and deals with what would be the case if the considered set of premises is, in fact, true. This means that deduction does not necessarily have any relatedness to a real phenomenon. A deduction is an analytical conclusion, or proof, and, as such, only true in an imaginary universe because the rule it employs can not be both true and applicable in a universe where nothing is absolutely true or absolutely false, which is the case in the world as we know it. Deductive reasoning has no interest in what actually is the case; it is only interested in the necessary connectedness of premise and conclusion. Where abduction suggests an explanatory hypothesis, deduction explicates the hypothesis itself and determines what consequences it will necessarily have if the hypothesis is accepted.[32] If we consider a proof in the form of a sequence of sentences, each of which follows, by a rule of inference, from preceding sentences, a deduction is such a proof.

Induction

Induction relates two different elements by *conditional* necessity. It tests the inferences drawn from a given hypothesis by deduction.[33] For inductive reasoning, the relation between premise and conclusion is symbolic because it is governed by conditional necessity. The "validity of an inductive argument consists . . . in the fact that it pursues a method which, if duly persisted in, must, in the very nature of things, lead to a result indefinitely approximating to the truth in the long run" (*CP* 2.781). Induction

---

[32] Peirce works with two subdivisions of deductive reasoning: *necessary deductions* and *probable deductions*. Necessary deductions "have nothing to do with any ratio of frequency, but profess . . . that from true premises they must invariably produce true conclusions" (*CP* 2.267). He then sub-divides necessary deductions into *corollarial deductions* (observing the premises leads to the conclusion directly) and *theorematic deductions* (a conclusion is only obtained as result of a mental experiment conducted on the premises). Probable deductions "are Deductions whose Interpretants represent them to be concerned with ratios of frequency" (*CP* 2.268). These probable deductions Peirce sub-divides in two also. He does not decide on final terms for them but suggests that they be called *probable deductions* and *statistical deductions*.

[33] Peirce sub-divides inductions in three: *crude inductions, quantitative inductions*, and *qualitative inductions*. Crude induction judges the truth of universal claims by asking whether there be any known counterexample to it. Quantitative induction observes a relative frequency in a sample and makes hypothetical conclusions about relative frequencies in the population from which it was randomly drawn. Qualitative induction consists "of those inductions which are neither founded upon experience in one mass, as Crude Induction is, nor upon a collection of numerable instances of equal evidential values, but upon a stream of experience in which the relative evidential values of different parts of it have to be estimated according to our sense of the impressions they make upon us" (*CP* 2.759).

depends on both deduction and abduction. It makes synthetic conclusions based on several observed instances by observing the manifold and making general conclusions based on those observations. In contrast to deduction, induction operates in a historically evolutive universe where nothing is absolutely true or absolutely false, and the results will therefore always be only probable, even if at a high level of probability. Induction either verifies or falsifies results of deduction by experimental testing. In a narrow sense, induction is inference to a generalization from its instances. It is induction when the premises support the conclusions without logically necessitating those conclusions. In a broad sense it is any inference where the claim made by the conclusion goes beyond the claim jointly made by the premises.

Abduction

Peirce gives no exhaustive description of abduction. Still, it is safe to say that the sparse and tentative descriptions he does give appear in roughly two different ways. His early descriptions gravitate toward a definition that makes use of the experience of encountering something unexpected, a surprising fact that has the startling effect of immediately producing in a person's mind some plausible explanation for the appearance of that fact in answer to why it happened. This explanatory suggestion is an embodiment of the logical operation of abduction and one that happens in accordance with iconic likeness, rather than in accordance with a modal truth standard. Peirce's later definition includes and expands the earlier by stating that abduction refers to a choice of the *qualified* guess among the many possible ones. This is to say that all the candidates of explanatory hypotheses are limited by abductive reasoning to those that are likely to be approved by the processes of inductive testing. On a broad view, then, Peirce intends for abduction to cover the productive activity of bringing forth hypotheses as well as the selective activity of choosing among those hypotheses once they have come forward.

Beginning with Peirce's early definition of abduction, the argument is that abduction embodies the process of suggesting provisional conclusions, or of supplying explanatory hypotheses for observed facts. In other words, an abductive conjecture opens the process of inquiry with an immediate and yet unqualified response to a given problem that simply presented itself. The process of conjecturing an abductive proposition excludes the overruling presence of logical conventionality because it is engendered by pure spontaneity. Nevertheless, Peirce makes an argument out of ascribing logical form to the spontaneous hypothesis, for even though abductive reasoning asserts conjectural conclusions, these conclusions still reflect a definite logical form. Peirce identifies three steps in this logical form of abduction:

> The surprising fact, C, is observed;
> But if A were true, C would be a matter of course,
> Hence, there is reason to suspect that A is true. (*CP* 5.189)

Even though abduction is an irreducible part of the process of inquiry, it is still stained by obvious weaknesses. In fact, Peirce considers abduction the weakest propositional form, and therefore it should never be considered in and of itself but always accompanied by the corrective influence of its two companions, induction and deduction. To make a point of this is to say that the strength of the abductive proposition is established as its conjectured hypothesis is proved *possible* by way of deduction, and shown to be *actual* by way of induction. Abduction's weakness is complemented by the strengths of deductive and inductive reasoning, so to speak, because they offer the possibility for an abductive proposition to have its validity established. Abduction is only complete in so far as it entails experiential consequences and is inductively testable. Any perception begins by a brute and unmediated encounter with "some surprising phenomenon, some experience which either disappoints an expectation, or breaks in upon some habit of expectation of the *inquisiturus*" (*CP* 6.469).

As we shall see later, there is an attitude of playful Musement involved in abductive reasoning, for in response to a given unexpected experience, the inquirer ponders, if only for a split second, the experienced phenomena in something like a free play with explanatory ideas and then simply announces the most plausible hypothesis. This, of course, involves both the productive and the selective activities of abduction, which are representative of Peirce's earlier and later definitions respectively.

Peirce's later definition of abduction relates to his doctrine of synechism and the contention that the reliability of abductive reasoning is guaranteed because the cosmos itself resembles rational mind and because the human mind therefore is instinctively attuned to the truth about all of reality. When abductive reasoning establishes hypotheses, we have warranted hope that among those hypotheses there will be those that are true representations of reality. Considered against the fact that Peirce does not provide an exhaustive and final description of the theory of abduction, the way he connects abduction and the doctrine of synechism recommends, as Raposa suggests, that "the depth and significance of his contribution . . . have yet to be fully assessed."[34] Raposa's thesis is, of course, particularly interesting when integrated with the project of reassessing Peirce's religious thinking. Pursuing it, Raposa argues that Peirce relies more heavily on Duns Scotus' work than immediately visible in his writings. Raposa makes a case for Duns Scotus as the primary source of inspiration for Peirce's notion of abductive propositions. Early in his career, Peirce formulated a theory of *unconscious ideas* that survived in his later work as a theory of *instinctive beliefs*, exemplified by abductive, hypothetical propositions. Raposa argues that a "major impetus in the development of Peirce's thinking about this topic was supplied by his encounter with the Scotist notion that ideas can exist in the mind *habitualiter*."[35] Raposa's point of connection is Peirce's comment that a

> notion is in the mind *actualiter* when it is actually conceived; it is in the mind *habitualiter* when it can directly produce a conception. . . . Just as sense affords sensible images of things, so the intellect affords intelligible images of them. It is such a *species intelligibilis* that Scotus supposes that a conception exists which is in the mind *habitualiter* . . . independent of *consciousness*. (*CP* 8.18)

What Peirce seems to learn from Duns Scotus is that the human mind can, in a sense, be acted upon *sensually* and thereby conceive actual notions that lay dormant until they come present to the mind *habitualiter* (without the influence of consciousness) as full-fledged conceptions. Transplanting this insight to Peirce's notion of abductive propositions, Raposa argues, it might be "by virtue of the operation of a habitual 'rule' of thought"[36] that the abductive, hypothetical proposition decides to state what it states. That Peirce might be more than superficially dependent upon Duns Scotus' theory still does not explain completely what it is that qualifies a hypothetical idea, however, and as illustrated in Peirce's own account of how he first happened upon the faculty of abductive reasoning, it is, again, the notion of volition that is central.

First, we notice that Peirce initially classifies abduction and induction as identical because they both have the ability to add something new to thought. In the beginning, he simply does not operate with two different terms for the one rational activity of *conceiving new ideas*, and he manages only slowly to separate these *Siamese twins* into two separate and

---

[34] Raposa, *Peirce's Philosophy of Religion*, 135.
[35] Ibid., 23.
[36] Ibid., 24.

individually named forms of reasoning. The mystery detective, however, earns a living by never allowing the two to melt into one. In the words of the fictional detective Peter Wimsey, the distinction of abduction and induction comes to very clear expression: "Go on with your theory—only do remember that to guess how a job *might* have been done isn't the same thing as proving that it *was* done that way."[37] Nor does Peirce hesitate to compare abductive reasoning to the method of the detective, as we well know already. In fact, it was his personal experience with the theft of his expensive Tiffany watch—on that infamous Friday, June 20, 1879—that initiated him into the logic of abduction. Reading his own account of the incident one quickly gets the sense that his first experience with the logic of abduction was a true detective's experience where cognitive instincts lead him to the very location of the stolen watch. He describes these cognitive instincts by simply claiming that, "abduction is, after all, nothing but guessing" (*CP* 7.219).

Seen in the context of scientific imagination, abduction refers to the creative process of hypothesis-formation and the astonishing fact that the skilled, scientific inquirer is very successful at hitting upon that one correct hypothesis among all the possible "trillions of trillions of hypotheses. . . . By chance he would not have been likely to do so in the whole time that has elapsed since the earth was solidified" (*CP* 5.172). As opposed to Karl R. Popper's purely tychist *conjecture-refutation* account of scientific discovery, Peirce is relentlessly committed to solving the riddle of how we happen upon hypotheses that prove true, and so he must ask the question of how hypotheses come into being in the first place. Popper's contention that "there is no such thing as a logical method of having new ideas, or a logical reconstruction of this process,"[38] is one that Peirce simply can not

---

[37] Dorothy L. Sayers, *Busman's Honeymoon* (New York: Harper, 1937) 232.

[38] Karl Raimund Popper, *The Logic of Scientific Discovery* (London: Routledge, 1959) 32. Popper greatly appreciated Peirce's work and, in his lecture, *Of Clouds and Clocks*, considers him "one of the greatest philosophers of all time"; Karl Raimund Popper, *Of Clouds and Clocks: An Approach to the Problem of Rationality and the Freedom of Man*, the Arthur Holly Compton Memorial Lecture (St. Louis: Washington University, 1966) 5. Popper, like Peirce, argues that the novel and good idea (i.e. what we had not thought about before) is something we happen upon inadvertently. Popper's method is different from Peirce's, however, in that it does not rely on "some external permanency . . . upon which our thinking has no effect" (*EP* 1.120). For Peirce, "the new conception here involved is that of reality" (*EP* 1.120) (i.e. something real beyond and apart from our knowledge of it). For Popper, however, there can be no impartation through our instincts, of anything objectively real to which our minds are already attuned. Rather, "every discovery contains 'an irrational element', or 'a creative intuition,' in Bergson's sense"; Popper, *Logic of Scientific Discovery*, 32.

accept, for why should instinct and logic be mutually exclusive? In his assessment, there is no such thing as the golden apple of insight dumping into the inquirer's turban unless one also accepts surrendering to Cartesian intuitionism, which is the same as a sad defeat at the hands of nominalism. It is the main force behind Peirce's critique of nominalism that pure intuition involves the existence of the transcendental object, and this, he holds, can only be an illusion.[39] In compliance with Peirce's metaphysical categories of triads, even the appearance of the novel is defined by relatedness, so although the insightful element of abduction is the seat of spontaneous and creative imagination, it never comes about unmediated: "The order of the march of suggestion in retroduction is from experience to hypothesis" (*CP* 2.755).[40] This means that abduction depends on both the will to risk reliance on what is no more than a hypothetical explanation *and* the fact that there is no other option: "our mind will be able in some finite number of guesses, to guess the sole true explanation . . . *That* we are bound to assume, independently of any evidence that it is true. Animated by that hope, we are to proceed to the construction of a hypothesis" (*CP* 7.219). The paradox that rational inquirers are bound by their own readiness to hope, but also thusly animated to produce deliberate constructions of hypotheses, introduces the problematic issue of how the inquirer exercises rational control in the process of abductive reasoning. Ultimately, it is with this issue that we can address and respond more fully to the question of abductive reasoning; that is, how qualification of an abductive hypothesis is established, and what the role is, in this process, of rational self-control. At this point, however, we need to discuss Peirce's pragmatism, since this provides another important doctrinal frame of mind for his theory of abduction and the significance he ascribes to it.

Pragmatism: A Method of Right Thinking

Together with aesthetics and ethics, logic is, on Peirce's account, a normative science.[41] But although a normative science "studies what ought to be"

---

[39] Most evidently, this includes Kant's transcendentalism but also British empiricism, particularly that of John Locke, which argues that all knowledge stems from the immediate perceptions produced by experience.

[40] Here, retroduction is used synonymously with abduction.

[41] In Peirce's system, normative science has three separated divisions: esthetics, ethics, and logic. The term *normative* emerged with the teachings of the Schleiermacher school although here it included logic and ethics only, and Peirce appears somewhat hesitant about the addition of esthetics when he says that "a thing is beautiful or ugly quite irrespective of any purpose to be so. It would seem, therefore, that esthetics is no more essentially norma-

(*CP* 1.281), it is not the role of logic to pass judgments on particular statements or situations by the standards of true or false. Rather, its aim is to study what ought to be the proper *method* of inquiry into truth, which is to say that "logic is not concerned with any specific state of affairs but with how to proceed in order to attain the truth."[42] Upon closer inspection, it is in Peirce's methodeutic, as its name indicates, that we find the one particular division of logic that gives clearest expression to logic's normative status, because this is where he gives most explicit attention to "the logical study of the theory of inquiry" (*CP* 2.106). In short, logic functions normatively when it gives us directions as to how we pursue truth and steer clear of doubt and confusion—and this is what methodeutic does.

Peirce's methodeutic is already described as applied logic (i.e. the rational inquiry of discovering truth through communication). But, in Apel's formulation, Peirce's proposal now is that methodeutic reaches even further into his philosophical system because it is "a theory of interpretation and the community of interpretation which finally also *includes the pragmatic theory of meaning*."[43] This is to say that methodeutic relates to the semiotic process as an epistemological vehicle for producing and obtaining meaning. In light of the historically most common understanding of pragmatism, it may surprise that Peirce would establish such a direct correlation between pragmatism and the method of rational inquiry. In his view, however, the pragmatic principle is exactly that, a methodological principle for rational inquiry. Defending this position, Peirce introduces the term *pragmaticism* in replacement of what he judges to be the seriously misguiding term *pragmatism* which has been "abused in the

---

tive than any nomological science" (*CP* 1.575). It may be, as Goudge suggests, that "the doctrine of the categories provides a strong reason for grouping the three disciplines under one heading. Logic is clearly concerned with Thirdness and ethics with Secondness. Esthetics, then, must be concerned with Firstness" (Goudge, *The Thought of C. S. Peirce*, 301–2). Whether or not Peirce is motivated by his theory of the three categories, his final conclusion is that esthetics indeed is a normative science: "Esthetics is the science of ideals, or of that which is objectively admirable without any ulterior reason. I am not well acquainted with this science; but it ought to repose on phenomenology. Ethics, or the science of right and wrong, must appeal to Esthetics for aid in determining the *summum bonum*. It is the theory of self-controlled, or deliberate, conduct. Logic is the theory of self-controlled, or deliberate, thought; and as such, must appeal to ethics for its principles. It also depends upon phenomenology and upon mathematics" (*CP* 1.191).

[42] Beverly E. Kent, *Charles S. Peirce: Logic and the Classification of Science* (Montreal: McGill-Queen's University Press, 1987) 170.

[43] Apel, *From Pragmatism to Pragmaticism*, 21; italics mine.

merciless way that words have to expect when they fall into literary clutches" (*CP* 5.414).⁴⁴

Peirce designs the term pragmaticism to capture a very old philosophical insight, one even as old as Socrates. In fact, it "appears to have been virtually the philosophy of Socrates" (*CP* 6.490) who bathed in the waters of pragmatism. Peirce also detects pragmaticism and the method of pragmatism in thinkers as diverse as Duns Scotus, Spinoza, George Berkeley, David Hume, and even Kant who appears to him "nothing but a somewhat confused pragmatist" (*CP* 5.525) because he ignores the foundational value of logic. In his own definition of pragmatism, Peirce synthesizes what all these thinkers teach about it, although both its ancient origin and its historical reappearance have left Peirce unaware "of its having been definitely formulated, whether as a maxim of logical analysis or otherwise, by anybody before my publication of it in 1878" (*CP* 6.490).

Peirce thinks that his original doctrine of pragmatism has been subject to abuse. His original idea that thinking should "*apply* to . . . *conceived* action" (*CP* 5.402 n.) has been distorted and popularized by some of his contemporary philosopher friends to convey instead that thought *consists* in acts. To argue for identity of thought and action, as the new and popular movement of pragmatism would have it, and to argue for the applicability of concepts to the world of actions, are clearly two different things.⁴⁵ What Peirce means by his original definition is clarified by this explanatory statement: "*In order to ascertain the meaning of an intellectual conception one should consider what practical consequences might conceivably result by necessity from the truth of that conception; and the sum of these consequences will constitute the entire meaning of the conception*" (*CP* 5.9).⁴⁶ For example, "The parallelogram of forces is introduced as a mathematical rule which enables us to resolve forces into their components, and to calculate the results of compounding a number of different forces."⁴⁷

In any case, by virtue of its obvious ugliness, Peirce says, the new term pragmaticism seems sufficiently "safe from kidnappers" (*CP* 5.414) and other future misrepresentations. Although the history of philosophy

---

⁴⁴ Explaining his choice of terms, Peirce also thinks that "the name of a doctrine would naturally end in *–ism*, while *–icism* might mark a more strictly defined acception of that doctrine" (*CP* 5.413). In what follows, the two terms will be used interchangeably.

⁴⁵ For illustrations of this difference, see Hookway, *Peirce*, 236–37. The illustrations of Peirce's pragmatism that concern the applicability of mathematical concepts to the experiential world of physics are especially helpful.

⁴⁶ Italics mine.

⁴⁷ Ibid., 237.

gives such figures as William James, John Dewey, and F. C. S. Schiller credit for the philosophical movement of pragmatism, Peirce considers this a very sad event. Peirce simply claims that they stole his idea and popularized it at the expense of its essential meaning and that this is a complete misunderstanding of his original vision for the notion of pragmatism. "Pragmaticism is not a system of philosophy. It is only a method of thinking" (*CP* 8.206). Pragmaticism is, he argues, very important for the discipline of logic because it describes the method by which knowledge develops. Peirce revolts against the prospect of identification with popular philosophies of pragmatism. He provided their conceptual foundation but no longer recognizes it.

But why the need for a methodeutic at all? One of the most fundamental problems is the fallibility of our reasoning faculty and the fact that it is in constant danger of pursuing lines of thought that dead-end, or perhaps falsify our hypotheses. It is necessary to anticipate the traps of fallible reasoning and this is what Peirce does by acknowledging "a practical need of methodeutic: an economy of research,"[48] as Anderson formulates it. Considering Peirce's claim that abductive reasoning produces all kinds of possible hypotheses means that abduction must be a place where reasoning is particularly vulnerable to fallibility. Peirce affirms this concern: "If you carefully consider the question of pragmatism you will see that it is nothing else than the question of the logic of abduction" (*CP* 5.196). That is, we must acknowledge that abductive reasoning has a particular need for a *built-in economy of research*, because it suggests hypotheses that are wrong, as well as hypotheses that are right.

There must be some economic principle to guide the abductive process, if we desire not to waste the hopes we invest in the explanatory propositions that we contemplate. To make efficient use of them, we must adhere to the methodological principle of pragmatism. Ideally, Peirce conjectures, in a situation where the pragmatic principle is carried to perfection, a proposition has the property that anyone who inquires into it would, over the course of some finite time, come to accept this proposition as valid. This is how Peirce envisions the community of inquirers so committed to the method of pragmatism that, in the long run of finite time, it gravitates naturally toward the formation of agreement on what is true.

It is noteworthy that what has been said here about the nature of abduction implies that abductive reasoning is more than just hypothesis *production*. It is also hypothesis *selection*. The selective function of abduc-

---

[48] Anderson, *Strands of System*, 54.

tion is an addition Peirce makes in his later definitions of abductive reasoning, as also the complication emerges of how to determine the role of volition and choice in the process of abductive reasoning. Peirce brings the methodological principle of pragmatism to bear on abductive reasoning, emphasizing that the pragmatic method relates to the selective function of abduction, more than it relates to the productive: "pragmatism proposes a certain maxim which, if sound, must render needless any further rule as to the admissibility of hypotheses to rank as hypotheses, that is to say, as explanations of phenomena held as hopeful suggestions" (*CP* 5.196). The pragmatic methodology is directly dependent upon the faculty of choice and volition in what must be a self-controlled rational activity of sifting and weighing all available hypotheses. Only those hypotheses should be admitted that give reason to expect that our hopes in their viability and truth bearing qualities will not be disappointed.

Again, we realize that one of Peirce's central doctrines, this time the doctrine of pragmaticism, introduces the systematic importance of volition. As we try to understand what manner of metaphysical significance Peirce gives to the principle of volition, it is interesting to discover that his pragmaticism relates very closely to his metaphysics. To this matter we now turn.

Metaphysical and Religious Implications of Peirce's Pragmatism

Peirce understands logic to be "the science of the necessary conditions of the attainment of truth" (*CP* 1.444), as we know. We also know that the principle of pragmatism, which is part of the third and highest division of logic, is particularly important for his scientific inquiry into truth because its purpose is to define the best logical methodology. Peirce argues, "Metaphysics consists in the results of the absolute acceptance of logical principles not merely as regulatively valid, but as truths of being" (*CP* 1.487), which is to say that the logical principle of pragmatism assists in his constructive project of establishing a metaphysics. In other words, logic does more than just regulate our metaphysical reflections methodologically; it frees us to establish a speculative metaphysics. Indeed, "Peirce thought that pragmatism could only be plausible if a form of metaphysical realism was adopted,"[49] and if therefore the inquirer can speculate confidently about metaphysics because it is founded on the principles of logic. "Peirce was serious in his endeavor to follow Aristotle and Kant in mak-

---

[49] Hookway, *Peirce*, 239.

ing metaphysics directly dependent on logic,"[50] as Anderson points out. So, referring his definition of the *real* to the term's invention and use in the thirteenth century, Peirce's notion of realism concerns reality as it is independently of any human knowledge of it. "That is *real* which has such and such characters, whether anybody thinks it to have those characters or not. At any rate, that is the sense in which the pragmaticist uses the word" (*EP* 2.342). In the context of Peirce's pragmatism, there is such a thing as an ultimate opinion, or an indisputable, ultimate reality, and so he continues to say that, "according to the adopted definition of 'real,' the state of things which will be believed in that ultimate opinion is real" (*EP* 2.342–343). To illustrate this ultimate opinion, Peirce uses the classical example of colour. "*Red* is relative to sight, but the fact that this or that is in that relation to vision that we call being red is not *itself* relative to sight; it is a real fact" (*EP* 2.343).

As we now inquire into the nature of Peirce's metaphysical realism, my thesis is the following. Peirce offers argumentative material for a rationally coherent argument for the reality of God in a way that makes his later, religious writing a natural, theological consequence of a metaphysics based on pragmatic methodology and its logically established truths of being. In other words, we can address the metaphysical implications of Peirce's pragmatism in relation to theism for, as he says, he makes considerable use of material from the Christian tradition in his reflections on religion, especially the gospel of John.

Before actually advancing to his proposal of a rational argument for the reality of God, it is interesting to notice that Peirce critiques those who have been traditional authorities on metaphysical issues, namely theologians and nominalist scientists. Neither group makes use of the proper methods in their metaphysical reflections, he claims. Theologians' attitude is often one of uncritical and blind acceptance of metaphysical statements and this results in dogmatic, unreflective—and ultimately useless—metaphysics. Nominalists' attitude is simply one of stubborn resistance to any form of metaphysical realism whatsoever. Peirce is not out to declare the discipline of metaphysics redundant, but with his attempts to prove pragmatism correct, he does strike out against people like "Messrs. Bradley, Taylor, and other high metaphysicians, on the one hand, and of the entire nominalistic nation on the other" (*CP* 5.468). All of these have, together with the theologians, left current metaphysics in a "deplorably backward condition" (*CP* 6.2). In order to remedy this situation, Peirce

---

[50] Anderson, *Strands of System*, 56.

argues that metaphysics must "be reconstructed in light of methodeutic and, in particular, of pragmaticism."[51] This will liberate the discipline of metaphysics from the dominance of blinded theologians and "high metaphysicians," as well as ignorant nominalists. For Peirce, metaphysics simply must be established on the logical principles of pragmatic methodology.

Considering Peirce's strong emphasis on methodology, it is tempting to conclude that "pragmatism . . . [is] nothing more than the method that complements the correspondence theory of truth"[52]—only reformulated by the help of Peirce's ever innovative vocabulary. The correspondence theory claims that truth is what corresponds to the way things really are (i.e. to the actual facts of reality) so that a proposed statement of truth can be tested directly against the objective facts of reality. The truth of a proposition is akin to the faithfulness of a portrait where "we effect a confrontation of the purported facts with the objective situation and carry out a comparison to determine whether the two are in agreement."[53] Applying, then, a *pragmatic correspondence theory of truth* to Peirce's need for a metaphysical realism is another way of saying that his pragmatic methodology leads to a true and actual portrait of a metaphysical reality at the back of all things, guaranteeing the validity of our knowledge. This conclusion would not convey the full scope of Peirce's position, however. For how could a pragmatic correspondence theory of truth avoid the problem classical correspondence theories of truth encounter too? Namely the inability to give precise descriptions of the *kinds* of correspondence required between reality and proposition. What are the proofs of correspondence? How do we determine whether or not there actually is correspondence? "Maps are very different from terrains, musical performances from music-scores,"[54] as Nicholas Rescher says, and so is true knowledge of an object very different from the actual object, be it a physical object, or an objective, metaphysical reality.

That Peirce's pragmatism is aware of this problem is clear when we consider Peirce's need to connect abductive reasoning with the religious experience of God's reality. First of all, Peirce frequently talks about religious experiences and, without much critical reflection on the nature of these experiences, connects them with the Christian tradition. Recall the three most important examples where he makes such connections. First,

---

[51] Ibid., 57.
[52] Feibleman, *Interpreted as a System*, 294.
[53] Nicholas Rescher, *The Coherence Theory of Truth* (Oxford: Clarendon, 1973) 5.
[54] Ibid., 8.

Peirce's third cosmological doctrine of agapism which implies that the cosmic evolution is driven by the purpose of love; second, his description of the universe as *God's great poem*; and third, his reference to the idea of God as the ultimate example of abductive reasoning. These all give the impression that the cosmological continuum, the motivational force behind it, as well as the most important ideas our minds produce, are all linked to the reality of a divine being. But there is an economy to everything and also to Peirce's philosophy, for he can not connect the loose ends of his philosophical system without invoking the reality of God as its ultimate systematic guarantor. That is, Peirce uses the doctrine of synechism to identify the evolutionary cosmos with the absolute, divine mind of a purposeful God of love. This then allows him to make the unambiguous statement that our capacity for knowledge "is proof conclusive that, though we cannot think any thought of God's, we can catch a fragment of His Thought" (*CP* 6.502). It is the doctrine of synechism, the doctrine of agapism, and his theory of abduction that make it plausible for Peirce to understand the philosophical system as essentially a religious system. Hence, these three also work in support of an integration of the faculty of reason and the experience of faith.

Of these three occasions to invoke God's reality, the first two are primarily cosmological, and the third primarily epistemological. Still, it is with the theory of abductive reasoning that Peirce links the cosmological and the epistemological. His argument is that abduction functions as rational guarantor of religious instinct. So, exploring abduction as epistemological guarantor of religious instinct, we find the principle of anticipation particularly applicable. Abductive reasoning turns out to follow the structure of anticipatory hope and in doing so also places itself at the core of Peirce's metaphysics. When we establish hypotheses, we have warranted hope to believe that there will be those hypotheses among them that are true representations of reality, for synechist resemblance of the human mind and God's mind implies that our minds are attuned to the truth about all of reality.

For Peirce, metaphysics gives the epistemological security of grounding the hopes that regulate our reasoning process. So, at the core of Peirce's metaphysics is the process of rational inquiry into the truth about all of reality, and not only does this process include the presence of hope, belief and faith as necessary parts of the right methodology; it also involves a kind of expectation that is more than merely a hopeful attitude about future knowledge. In other words, it is not enough for Peirce to have a static notion of metaphysics against which everything must be checked by a method of correspondence between ultimate truth of reality and relative truth of knowledge. Rather, the foundation of Peirce's metaphysics is the reality of anticipatory, warranted hope. This is a hope that anticipates what is certain to come but what can still never be fully obtained. In a word, Peirce's metaphysical realism is an adaptation of the principle of anticipation and a clear expression of the reality of anticipatory hope, not only as an epistemological principle, but *as a metaphysical principle also*.

Without simply invoking the handy help of anticipatory hope where reason reaches the limit of its capacity, my constructive approach to Peirce's position is based on the following thesis. In the theory of abduction, Peirce faces the task of formulating how the element of hope in knowledge has less to do with our inability to fully understand truth than it has to do with the nature of the truth there is to understand—including the truth about God's reality. In contrast, deciding in favor of a pragmatic correspondence theory of truth would be a serious obstacle in a context of considering Peirce's religious reflections in relation to his metaphysics. A pragmatic correspondence theory of truth would quickly translate into the use of an unfounded theological methodology that claims full access to the accurate truths about God but that would still lack convincing evidence of this accuracy. It would take the form of a simplistic adaptation of theism and would not reflect the full reach of Peirce's metaphysics and its systematic complexity. The key to his metaphysical realism is that the principle of anticipatory hope describes the structure of Peirce's epistemology as well as the structure of his metaphysics. Furthermore, this double applicability of the principle of anticipation is the key to a constructive theological reassessment of Peirce's alleged religious theism. Applying the principle of anticipation to the idea of God too, prepares us to make the case for a Peircean theology that avoids some of the weaknesses of traditional theism.

These constructive reflections tie back to the earlier conclusion that the significant systematic challenges that Peirce's philosophy manifests is in the tension between his two doctrines of synechism and tychism. Peirce's attempts to balance synechism and tychism are attempts to come to terms with the fact that all of reality is simultaneously stable and unpredictable. In my reading, it is the challenge of having to reconcile synechism and tychism that brings Peirce face to face with the inevitably anticipatory nature of his own metaphysical realism. He is forced to hold the philosophical system together by the principle of anticipation, for two equally strong reasons. First, he is convinced that the greater reality of the cosmic universe will not surprise and disappoint the hopes we erect by the help of logical principles. Second, he is convinced that epistemological hope is all we will ever have at our disposal in the pursuit of knowing the greater reality of the world in which we live.

The systematic tension in Peirce's philosophy is a significant reason for us to define regulative hopes as not just any kind of hopes, but precisely regulative, anticipatory hopes that lead the community of inquirers to true knowledge about a reality that continues to escape full comprehension. Moreover, we find ourselves forced to conclude that reality is structured by the principle of anticipatory hope because it is and will remain simultaneously stable and unpredictable. When Peirce asks metaphysics to define the most general feature of all of reality (i.e. the order of being as a whole), he also asks it to embody anticipatory, warranted hope. His contention, "Metaphysics consists in the results of the absolute acceptance of logical principles not merely as regulatively valid, but as truths of being" (*CP* 1.487), demonstrates that, in a certain way, the truths of being converge in the principle of anticipation. Reality is not reliable because it is stable, but because of its unpredictability; it can only be relied upon with caution. The inquirer's regulative hopes are conceived just as much by the reality to come as the reality that already is. Hence, not only is the epistemological structure of knowledge anticipatory but so is the structure of reality.

At this point, the notion of metaphysical voluntarism becomes relevant again. Whether or not the unpredictable element of reality is attributed to the creative influence of absolute chance at work in the universe (tychism), or to the free will of a divine mind, *the unpredictable is inevitable*. The free decision of a divine mind, just as well as a change of course caused by tychism, will always be an expression of something willed or some manner of volition that breaks into and disturbs a situation of stability. Volition always has the quality of disturbance whether it comes in the form of controlled will (divine decision, for instance) or uncontrolled will (unexplainable changes in natural processes, for instance). So, for the rational inquirer to invest regulative hopes in either the reliability of the universe or the reliability of a divine being is also to invest hope in the unpredictability of something over which it is impossible to have power because it is determined by the will of something, or someone, else.

If we narrow our focus to the investment of regulative hopes in the free will of a divine being, and remember that it is the responsibility of the faculty of abduction to formulate those hopes, it is interesting to find that one of the most central and difficult things for Peirce to define about abduction is *its dependence upon volition as facilitator of rational self-control*. Hence, it is somewhere in the theory of abduction that we must look for

Peirce's insight that the most important manifestation of volition happens in self-controlled rational activity. Paradoxically enough, abduction is also the most important means of accommodation to the will of God. With the problem of rational self-control in the process of abductive reasoning, we face the paradox of rational freedom. How can reason's most essential quality be the fact that it must counter volition with volition? Or, how is reason essentially reason when it decides, by an act of the will, to respond to the will of something, or someone, else? Somehow, rational self-control and divine volition have become each other's reflections. Human volition appears in response to divine volition and vice versa. Therefore, before we turn to a constructive reassessment of Peirce's theism, we now turn to the question of volition in the theory of abductive reasoning.

Rational Self-Control in Abductive Reasoning

Many argue that Peirce does not adequately clarify how to account for the inquirer's exercise of control in abduction, although he says that reasoning is "essentially a voluntary act, over which we exercise control" (*CP* 2.144). Still, it is clear that trying to reach some clarity, it is important to keep in mind that abduction consists of two distinct phases. Berit O. Brogaard reminds us of this when she says that "in the process of abduction we not only *form* a hypothesis, we also draw one relatively good hypothesis from an infinite population of mostly bad ones."[55] Because Peirce's theory of abduction continues to be a work in progress, several studies are devoted to mappings of its historical development. Among these studies, Anderson's is based on the same observation (that abduction is a two-part process), although he emphasizes the creative phase of hypothesis-*formation* and concludes that it "has both its logical and its psychological aspects as it lays the foundational hypotheses upon which deduction and induction must then work."[56]

Whether or not Anderson's conclusion is meant to indicate that both phases of abduction have logical and psychological aspects is unclear. It is clear, however, that Anderson introduces psychology as an element of Peirce's account of abduction when it comes to explaining the first appearance of the new and creative idea of a hypothesis. Interestingly, he then continues to note that many charges against the theory of abduction

---

[55] Berit O. Brogaard, "Peirce on Abduction and Rational Control," *Trans.* 35 (1999) 132.

[56] Douglas R. Anderson, "The Evolution of Peirce's Concept of Abduction," *Trans.* 22 (1986) 162.

"hinge on the claim that Peirce is confusing the logical with the psychological; that he presents abduction as an unresolvable paradox."[57] In any case, the question is whether Anderson suggests omitting the issue of the inquirer's rational control in the process of abductive reasoning or whether he suggests ascribing it solely to psychological mechanisms. Commenting on Anderson's study and the response it elicited from Robert J. Roth, Brogaard wonders about them: "both mention a possible connection between abduction and rational control, but both desist from exploring the issue in details."[58] Again, how does the inquirer control the process of forming and selecting hypotheses?

In response to Anderson, and with a desire not to see logic collapse into psychology, Brogaard argues that rational self-control in abduction is first of all based on Peirce's doctrine of synechism (the claim that all matter is effete mind) by which Peirce has already accounted for hypothesis-*formation*. Brogaard then turns to the abductive act of selecting one hypothesis out of the many and says that the "affinity of mind with nature requires an *awareness* or *attention* as the factor that completely links the experienced elements together in the inference."[59] This is her conclusive explanation and one that lets rational control rest on a principle quite identical to "Kant's answer to the question of how synthetic inference is possible,"[60] only reclassified by Brogaard as a synechist sensibility, or a cosmological awareness. But the difference between a Peircean idea of synechist sensibility and Kant's transcendental reference point for synthetic inferences hardly amounts to more than what Murphey determines one of degree: "Kant regarded the process by which the synthesis of intuition is made as susceptible of philosophic analysis whereas Peirce regards it as completely beyond the reach of consciousness."[61] Provided this is so, it is hard not to remain challenged by Peirce's focus on rational control as an event of inexplicable complexity, which in fact is the way he finally justifies retreating to psychology. This is to Peirce a discipline whose logic is

---

[57] Ibid., 161. This point is echoed by Murphey who takes the issue of psychology to be the main motivation behind the last of Peirce's successive revisions of his system: "The reduction of logic to psychology . . . has the effect of making the value of logic relative to a particular phase of development and so undercuts the entire architectonic theory"; Murphey, *Peirce's Philosophy*, 355.

[58] Brogaard, "Abduction and Rational Control," 132. See also Robert J. Roth, "Anderson on Peirce's Concept of Abduction: Further Reflections," *Trans.* 24 (1988): 131–39.

[59] Ibid., 148; italics mine.

[60] Ibid., 146.

[61] Murphey, *Peirce's Philosophy*, 370.

incomplete because "psychology tells us *that* such a synthesis occurred,"[62] not *how* it occurred.

Peirce's struggle to account for the metaphysical significance of volition is clearly reflected in his struggle to account for the role of volition in the process of abductive reasoning. As we have considered his disregard for the metaphysical significance of volition, a discussion of the role of volition in the process of abductive reasoning is an epistemological counterpart to the discussion of the metaphysical significance of volition.

In the following chapter, I suggest one way of constructing an interpretive reading of Peirce's philosophy so that the discussion of the rational inquirer's control in the process of abductive reasoning can take a new direction. This interpretation argues that abduction *is* anticipation, and that, through the process of abductive reasoning, the inquirer anticipates in the present what still belongs to the future and does this as a matter of controlling the rational process without having full control over it. Rational self-control is anticipation because it compels the inquirer to choose a specific direction into the future, not just any direction. As such, it anticipates the reality of the future as it *will be*, and this implies reliance on some objective element of reality as it is apart from the inquirer's own shaping influence upon it. This constructive reading includes an interpretive reading of Peirce's N.A. and results in the proposal of a Peircean theology of anticipation. My proposal rests on Peirce's claim that knowledge of God is the most significant instance of abduction. It draws inspiration from Pannenberg's theological metaphysics of anticipation. Additionally, it offers critical evaluations of Raposa's theosemiotic and Corrington's Peircean theology of divine potentialities, both of which are constructive and comprehensive interpretations of Peirce's philosophy of religion.

---

[62] Ibid., 370; italics mine. See also *CP* 2.141.

4

A Peircean Theology of Anticipation

THE experience of Christian hope is an experience of anticipatory hope. But what is anticipatory hope? It is to anticipate that one's hopes will be fulfilled because there is justified reason or a promise to do so. It is because of the promise of fulfillment that one anticipates the fulfillment of the promise. Anticipatory hope takes for real in the present what still belongs to the future, so to experience anticipatory hope is to know that promise and fulfillment converge and are inseparable. It conveys very specifically that a *future* reality has claim on the *present* moment, and that the actual content of the future is at work in the present. At the same time, however, fulfillment remains a reality of the future because it is no more than a promise and therefore not possible in any other form than promise. Hence, a person who hopes with anticipation lives on what is to come but also lives with its absence.

Because anticipatory hope contains a promise, it is different from both the hope of optimism and the hope of determination. It is *more* than hopeful optimism about the future because it is shaped by a promise that something specific is coming. We conceive some specific hope in response to the reality that the future holds its fulfilment for us, and when we receive some measure of its fulfilment, we set our hope on another—different or higher—object of future fulfilment. By the power of anticipation, this inner drive of hope pulls the future into the present and makes hope more than merely an acquired attitude of optimism or wishful thinking about whatever may come. In anticipatory hope there is something about the future that beckons the present forward and gives confident certainty that what is hoped for will in fact manifest. Optimism lacks this certainty; it is more of an attitude of readiness to receive and make the most of what happens.

At the other end of the spectrum, anticipatory hope is *less* than pursuing with determination what the future holds because hoping in a promise excludes actually having what the promise promises. The hope of determination is more akin to a desperate hope of wanting what the future holds. It does not permit the future to reveal itself through its own process of unfolding. To apply hope in a determined pursuit of future realities implies disregard for the propelling power a promise has of leading forward into a future that is still open. Applying hope with determination is a form of overconfidence that threatens the process of moving toward a future reality by virtue of promises about it. *Approaching the future with anticipatory hope is to find that uncomfortable middle position between actively pursuing the future and passively waiting for it; this is the only place a promise can live and survive as promise.* The hope of anticipation protects the fragile nature of promise and simultaneously explores its full potential.

Both rationality and faith are functions of anticipatory hope. This means that the rational inquirer as well as the Christian believer must live in the reality of what is to come and *also* accept the absence of its fulfillment. Through reflective and hypothesizing activities of the mind, the rational inquirer anticipates knowledge and understanding before actually having it. Through believing activities of faith in God's promises, the Christian believer anticipates God's gifts before actually receiving them. Observing the architectonic structure behind Peirce's systematic thought, it is significant to discover that it reflects this observation about the shared reliance of rationality and faith upon a hope of anticipatory nature. This observation is the basis of my proposal of a Peircean theology of anticipation.

My proposal relies on the earlier discussion of the function of hope within Peirce's philosophical system and now explores the role it plays in his philosophy of religion too. Peirce primarily invokes religious perception of God's reality because it is necessary in order for him to maintain systematic consistency. Exploring this further, I focus on the way hope informs religious perception of God's reality and conclude that, in the form of anticipation, hope runs deep within Peirce's philosophy as well as his religious writings and that *therefore*, anticipatory hope links these two parts of his work. With this conclusion I wish to challenge the view that Peirce's religious writings are barely more than a curios attachment to his philosophical writings. Moreover, understanding Peirce's theory of abduction as reflective of anticipatory hope can draw together two seemingly disparate parts of Peirce's work and—hopefully—also help unlock some of the more widespread discipline specific controversies between philosophy and theology. Because Peirce's theory of abduction is applicable to both disciplines, it is particularly effective in theoretical situations of reintroducing theological confidence in philosophical methodology as well as philosophical confidence in theological methodology.

As Peirce starts with Kant's critical philosophy, so does my argumentative demonstration of the role of anticipatory hope in Peirce's work. Kant's contention is, as we know, that rational inquiry always tries to answer these three questions: What can I know? What ought I to do? What may I hope? Inquiry can not be reduced to less than these three questions, but unless it wants to remain irresponsible speculation, he argues, it *must* be reduced to these three.[1] Last chapter's discussion of the nature of rational self-control in the process of abductive reasoning came to a halt at the stop-sign of inexplicability. That is, it concluded that the rational inquirer has control over the epistemological process, but not without engaging the ability to determine something as epistemologically true without yet knowing it for sure. It is in this sense that Peirce argues for the rational inquirer's engagement with the power of hope, which is another way of saying that Kant's third question—What may I hope?—is as central to Peirce's epistemology as it is to Kant's. Still, although Kant demonstrates that it is necessary to include the question of hope in critical philosophy, he does nothing more than to demonstrate this need. In contrast, Peirce moves on from demonstrating the epistemological need to rely on hope to actually struggling with the full formulation of a theory that makes hope an integral epistemological part of rational inquiry. With his theory of abduction, Peirce attempts to fulfill a need that Kant only demonstrated. As the discussion of this chapter will show, it is interesting to notice about Pannenberg that his primary frame of reference too is a struggle to respond to Kant's critical philosophy with systematic reflections that embrace both philosophy and theology. His contribution is to present an epistemology based on a metaphysics of anticipation. In my judgment, this is crucial in the present context because Pannenberg's discussion of anticipation in the context of post-Kantian metaphysics reflects fundamental theoretical

---

[1] The fact that Kant's question of hope is most often neglected, and the other two questions overemphasized has, in Peter Widmann's observation, resulted in three unfortunate developments. It has become a *carte blanche* for utopian speculations and an opportunity to introduce new theological categories (*existence* for example), in order to refute assumed access to any kind of absolute knowledge; or it has encouraged theologians to furnish systems of unsupported metaphysical postulates. See Peter Widmann, "Kants tre spørgsmål" [Kant's three questions], in *Teologi og modernitet* [Theology and modernity], ed. Peter Thyssen and Anders Moe Rasmussen (Århus: Aarhus Universitetsforlag, 1997) 22–33. With a discussion of Peirce's metaphysics in relation to Pannenberg's metaphysical reflections on the concept of anticipation, my proposal of a Peircean theology of anticipation responds to these unfortunate developments.

issues also at work in the way Peirce employs the notion of hope. The basis for my proposal of a Peircean theology of anticipation is this combination that Peirce and Pannenberg share, of fundamentally accepting Kant's critical philosophy and, in two different ways, creating a post-Kantian epistemology based on hope and anticipation.

As demonstrated in the previous chapter, Peirce's theory of abduction is central for his philosophical system but incomplete and in need of constructive interpretation. As previous chapters also demonstrate, attempts to make the theory of abduction complete must happen in the context of epistemology, metaphysics, and theist philosophy of religion. The present chapter combines these three in a constructive proposal of a Peircean theology of anticipation, and is structured as follows. It first discusses the epistemological significance of hope in Kant's critical philosophy in order to see how Pannenberg develops his theological metaphysics of anticipation in extension of Kant and intentionally avoids methods of metaphysical postulation. With some questions to Pannenberg, this discussion develops into a discussion of how Peirce's theory of abduction can take over where the critique of Pannenberg leaves off. Where Pannenberg leans toward a conceptualization of the lived life of faith in God's reality, Peirce relies boldly and directly on real encounters with God's reality as outcomes of an epistemological process. This deep involvement of God's reality with Peirce's architectonic system suggests that a Peircean theology must be formulated within the framework of theism. The chapter therefore turns to an evaluation of abduction's role in Peirce's religious thought and also of the *kind* of theological theism it supports. Following, therefore, a discussion of classical theism, are discussions of two current interpretations of Peirce's philosophy of religion in the context of theism. These two are, first, Raposa's theosemiotic (which relies on Duns Scotus' Scholastic realism) and, second, Corrington's Peircean theology of divine potentialities (which evaluates traditional theism very critically and proposes an eccentric Peircean adaptation of Schelling's theory of divine potencies). Responding to these two, I present some critical questions and give a third proposal, namely a Peircean theology of anticipation that interprets Peirce's argument for the reality of God in the light of anticipatory hope.

Using the notion of anticipatory hope as interpretive key to Peirce's theory of abduction enables a constructive interpretation of his N.A., indicative of a theology of anticipation. This proposes trajectories of attempts to do theologically what Peirce has already done philosophically. With reference to Peirce, it describes the relatedness of divine being and human beings as structurally anticipatory.

Beginning with Kant: What May I Hope?

Kant's famous list of questions covering the interests of reason—an interest Martin Buber has called the "cosmopolitan significance"[2] of philosophy—appears toward the end of his *Critique of Pure Reason*:

> All the interests of my reason, speculative as well as practical, combine in the three following questions:
>
> 1. What can I know?
> 2. What ought I to do?
> 3. What may I hope?[3]

Immediately following this list, Kant indicates a basic division of reason in two: speculative and practical. He describes the first of reason's three interests as merely speculative, the second as purely practical, and the third as both practical and theoretical. Considering his distinction between speculative and practical reason with the aim of determining Kant's own response to the question of hope, we note that he addresses their relatedness earlier in the *Critique of Pure Reason*. At that earlier point, Kant's contention is that the objects of hope are propositions of pure reason, or "synthetic assertions, which do not relate to objects of experience and their inner possibility."[4] Rather, the objects of hope are God's existence and belief in a future life after death. Most importantly, however, is his claim that these objects are also the sole means of reconciling practical and speculative reason. That is, "the two cardinal propositions of our reason—that there is a God, and that there is a future life"[5] are, for Kant, "propositions which are so very closely bound up with the speculative interest of our reason in its empirical employment, and . . . are *the sole means* of reconciling the speculative with the practical interest."[6] Kant asks his three questions because human rationality demands vindication for itself as well as for the trustworthiness of the two ideas it produces: immortality and God's existence. Together with the freedom of human will, these two ideas are unrelated to the realm of experience; but whereas Kant sees free will justified simply because it is a presupposition for moral action, immortality and God's existence remain unjustified. Still, human rationality produces

---

[2] Martin Buber, *Between Man and Man*, trans. Ronald Gregor Smith (London: Macmillan, 1965) 119.

[3] Kant, *Critique of Pure Reason*, A805–806/B833–834.

[4] Ibid., A743/B771.

[5] Ibid., A742/B770.

[6] Ibid., A743/B771; italics mine.

these two ideas, both of which escape rational examination because they persistently manifest outside the boundaries of experience. This is why the question of hope becomes a *necessary* third question for Kant, in addition to the two questions of theoretical and practical reason.

In Kant's universe, then, hope relates to religious, or theological, issues, but always in conjunction with theoretical and practical reason. That faith can never be concerned with unreasonable, irrational truth is the leading principle for the way philosophy and theology interrelate. Faith in God must be rational but, as Neiman argues, "This faith is regulative . . . not knowledge but a principle of action."[7] Neiman's argument represents the classic interpretive milieu of Kantian theology, which makes religious faith a matter of practical and moral behavior. Even though Kant indeed does suggest that religion should be a matter of morality, he is not as clear about the theological function of hope. Kant provides little more than a casual hint, in a letter to C. F. Stäudlin, that his book, *Religion within the Limits of Reason Alone*, contains the details of what the function of hope might be:

> My longstanding plan for my mandated work in the field of pure philosophy aimed at the completion of the three tasks: 1) What can I know? (Metaphysics) 2) What ought I to do? (Morality) 3) What may I hope? (Religion); which should finally be followed by the fourth: What is the human being? . . . —In the enclosed work: Religion within the Limits etc. I have sought to fulfill the third part of my plan.[8]

Without yet commenting on the fact that Kant has now added a fourth question to the previous list of three, we may wonder about Kant scholarship, as Curtis H. Peters does, why a "careful examination of the full range of Kant's views on hope is lacking in the literature. There is no work specifically devoted to the study of that theme in his philosophy. The topic is hardly touched upon in the journals."[9] Peters' own thesis is that

---

[7] Neiman, *Unity of Reason*, 177.

[8] Immanuel Kant, *Briefwechsel* (Hamburg: Meiner, 1986) 634; translation mine. In the original: "Mein schon seit geraumer Zeit gemachter Plan der mir obliegenden Bearbeitung des Feldes der reinen Philosophie ging auf die Auflösung der drei Aufgaben: 1) Was kann ich wissen? (Metaphysik) 2) Was soll ich tun? (Moral) 3) Was darf ich hoffen? (Religion); welcher zuletzt die vierte folgen sollte: Was ist der Mensch? . . . —Mit beikommender Schrift: Religion innerhalb den Grenzen etc. habe die dritte Abteilung meines Plans zu vollführen gesucht."

[9] Curtis H. Peters, *Kant's Philosophy of Hope* (New York: Lang, 1993), 16. Peters also observes that those who have paid attention to Kant's notion of hope have only done so very

Kant's writings actually do present something like a complete theory of hope; only, the pieces of it must be gathered from his moral philosophy, his philosophy of religion, his political philosophy, and his philosophy of history. Assembling Kant's insights on hope from these different sources must be subject to his "general *a priori* methodology,"[10] in that, as Peters says, "Reason provides a priori Ideas of a range of ideal conditions. These Ideas fill out the content of hope and are the basis for its rational justification."[11]

Peters offers his proposal in place of what he takes to be the unsatisfying move of simply relocating hope to the field of religion, which has the unfortunate repercussion of creating disregard for what first animated the appearance of the question of hope, namely how to vindicate human rationality and its ideas of immortality and God's existence. Nevertheless, interpreters of Kant's question of hope have gravitated toward this interpretation, which ultimately leaves God and the highest good classified as a postulate. In Lewis White Beck's evaluation, this is to say, "At most, the hope for it [the highest good] may be psychologically necessary to a semblance of morality . . . belief in its possibility may be a *legitimate accompaniment* of morality which is pure and autonomous."[12] Following Beck, religious hope can function as a means of becoming worthy of happiness, but not of obtaining it. Of course, this point can be supported by reference to Kant, who says that the "moral law of itself still does not *promise* any happiness, since this is not necessarily connected with observance of the law according to our concepts of a natural order as such."[13] If,

---

briefly and most often in association with interpretations of *Religion within the Limits of Reason Alone*, Kant's general philosophy of religion, or his moral philosophy. Interestingly, Peters also wonders why Albert Schweitzer (who is otherwise credited for initiating a philosophical application of historical time) omits the topic of hope in his study, *Die Religionsphilosophie Kants in der Kritik der reinen Vernunft bis zur Religion innerhalb der Grenzen der blossen Vernunft* [Kant's philosophy of religion from *Critique of Pure Reason* to *Religion within the Limits of Reason Alone*] (Freiburg: Mohr/Siebeck, 1899). Carl Braaten too, is puzzled about this same thing when he concludes that the debates "between Schweitzer, Cullmann, Bultmann, Dodd, Jeremias, etc., have not yet yielded an answer or answers to Kant's third question: What may I hope?—but only answers to the historical question: What did Jesus or the early church happen to hope?"; Carl Braaten, "Toward a Theology of Hope," *Theology Today* 24 (1967) 211.

[10] Peters, *Kant's Philosophy of Hope*, 16.

[11] Ibid., 141.

[12] Lewis White Beck, *A Commentary on Kant's Critique of Practical Reason* (Chicago: University of Chicago Press, 1960) 244; italics mine.

[13] Immanuel Kant, *Critique of Practical Reason*, trans. and ed. Mary Gregor (Cambridge: Cambridge University Press, 1997) 107.

however, we are to relate this understanding of hope to Kant's own fourth question—What is the human being?—and if we wish to take it seriously that he considers the third question encompassed by the fourth, then we must agree with Peters and remain on the lookout for a more persuasive interpretation of Kant's question of hope. To this end it is helpful with some reflections on the way Kant establishes a connection between hope and anthropology, and we now proceed to this.

The question of hope reappears in some of Kant's lecture notes on logic. Again, it is part of a list of questions, although this time one that concerns the more general range of philosophy which, he now says, can be reduced to *four* questions: "The field of philosophy . . . can be brought out by the following questions: 1) What can I know? 2) What ought I to do? 3) What may I hope? 4) What is the human being?"[14] Also, Kant immediately comments, in these lecture notes, that the question of hope is simply answered by religion. At the same time, he attributes the first three questions to the added fourth question, which asks about the nature of the human being, "Basically, one could ascribe all of this to anthropology."[15] That is, if we want to know what the philosopher's concern is, we find the answer by consulting the anthropologist.

Even though it is difficult to determine what exactly Kant intends for his anthropological question to accomplish, it is in our interest to explore its relatedness to the third question.[16] Reflecting on the philosophical weight Kant places on the question of anthropology, then, and discussing what might be defined as "the essential task of Rational beings gener-

---

[14] Immanuel Kant, *Gesammelte Schriften,* vol. 9 (Berlin, 1923) 25; translation mine. In the original: "Das Feld der Philosophie . . . lässt sich auf folgende Fragen bringen: 1) Was kann ich wissen? 2) Was soll ich thun? 3) Was darf ich hoffen? 4) Was ist der Mensch?") These were lectures given at the University of Königsberg where Kant first held a position as *privatdozent* (private lecturer) and later as professor of logic and metaphysics. In 1800, when he began to need editorial assistance, they were published, together with other lectures, by Gottlob Benjamin Jäsche. Their publication happened under Kant's supervision and was based on his manuscripts as well as students' lecture transcripts. The lectures themselves may have been composed years before their publication, and were, most likely, not accurately reproduced.

[15] Ibid., 25; translation mine. In the original: "Im Grunde könnte man aber alles dieses zur Anthropologie rechnen."

[16] Martin Buber suggests that Kant fails to achieve what his own philosophical anthropology requires. Buber's argument is that Kant has posed a question that his own philosophical method does not prepare him to answer. What Kant seeks to achieve, he argues, concerns the existential question of the "*wholeness* of man" (Buber, *Between Man and Man,* 120), which is something his "anthropology has neither answered nor undertaken to answer" (ibid., 121).

ally"[17] (the frame of reference for Kant's list of questions), Gene Fendt suggests the following. Kant's question of hope can be brought into play with anthropological considerations to argue that the essential nature of the human being is something that must be *actualized* according to a vision defined by hope. That is, in so far as Kant's question of what we may hope is "directed to that which does not yet exist . . . [it] adds the dimension of the future, of history and of the meaning of human life."[18] The challenge facing someone who seeks meaning in life through self-actualization, is no insignificant one, for he or she will have to accept, or even choose, a commitment to either "desiring or hating the implied *telos* of the task."[19] This, of course, also carries with it the very real possibility that a person may *not* be actualized, in which case hope necessarily gives way to its enemy, despair. Interestingly, Fendt appropriates an obviously intended Kierkegaardian dialectic of hope and despair as interpretive background for Kant's twofold division of rationality as practical and theoretical: Kant accentuates "the necessity of the connection between the 'essential interests of reason' and the passional dialectic of hope/despair."[20]

Turning next to Pannenberg's discussion of the concept of anticipation, this description of rational inquiry as an integration of the practical and the theoretical, combined with an indication of its anthropological significance, finds expression in a systematic approach to human life in the form of a theological metaphysics of anticipation that joins the life of faith and the life of reason in one.

Pannenberg's Theological Metaphysics of Anticipation

Pannenberg is a comprehensive systematic thinker whose ambition includes arguing for a reformulation of traditional metaphysics within the confines of the philosophical tradition from Kant to Hegel. This ambition is a bold response to the fact that metaphysics is a controversial issue in current philosophical theology. Pannenberg details the challenges that all post-Kantian metaphysics must be ready to tackle, if it desires to be taken seriously. These of course concern the preservation of the category of

---

[17] Gene Fendt, *For What May I Hope: Thinking with Kant and Kierkegaard*, American University Studies 5, 104 (New York: Lang, 1990) 44.

[18] Otfried Höffe, *Immanuel Kant*, trans. Marshall Farrier (Albany: State University of New York Press, 1994) 193.

[19] Fendt, *For What May I Hope*, 42.

[20] Ibid., 42–43.

human autonomy and self-determining subjectivity, which rests on the fact that all rational reflection must avoid foundational categories that lend themselves to different forms of transcendentalism, supernaturalism and religious metaphysics. Pannenberg therefore sets out to propose a metaphysics that does not fall prey to foundationalist metaphysics, simply because it is no longer a rationally credible enterprise to operate with postulated and foundational categories. At the other end of the spectrum, Pannenberg's proposal must also avoid the kind of generalist metaphysics that Dewey defines as "a statement of the generic traits manifested by existences of all kinds without regard to their differentiation into physical and mental."[21] The kind of metaphysics Pannenberg therefore wants to propose must meet the Kantian requirements for metaphysics and also refute the arguments that have created the very critical attitude toward metaphysics. His argument is that in order to formulate a theological metaphysics and also avoid the two extremes of generalist and foundationalist metaphysics, it is mandatory to be affirmative of divine as well as human freedom. The result is a legitimate post-Kantian metaphysics that relies on a metaphysical voluntarism that is operative through the principle of anticipation and thereby affirms the existence of a free divine being as well as the existence of free human beings. In a word, Pannenberg proposes a theological metaphysics of anticipation and thereby reintroduces the metaphysical discourse without retreating to pre-Kantian discourse.

The meaning of anticipation is best illustrated by the exact sciences. In fact, the scientific method *is* the method of anticipation, Pannenberg argues, in so far as it progresses by first forming hypotheses and then testing them in order to determine their truth value. The structure of anticipatory truth reflects that of scientific truth and is permanently questionable, just as the role of the scientist is to always doubt what is presently considered true. To take this point further, Pannenberg argues that the meaning of anticipation is contained in the fact that *every* possible assertion is anticipatory, or hypothetical, "in the sense that it reaches out toward or anticipates [*vorgreift*] empirical constellations by means of assertions, which then require confirmation or refutation through experience."[22] As

---

[21] John Dewey, *Experience and Nature* (1929; reprinted, New York: Dover, 1958) 412.

[22] Pannenberg, *Metaphysics*, 94. Much of Pannenberg's earlier work concerns conceptualizations of history as the place where God's historical revelation in Christ occurs. See his *Revelation as History* (New York: Macmillan, 1968). The primary body of his work is a comprehensive three volume systematic theology (*Systematic Theology*, 3 vols. [Grand Rapids: Eerdmans, 1988]), which is followed by an anthropological study that implements his work with history, revelation, their conceptualization, and the concept of anticipation;

Pannenberg makes a theological application of his theoretical definition of anticipation, it is no surprise to find that his "theological method involves the quest for points of contact in *all religions and all academic disciplines*,"[23] and that he expands his analyses into the proposal of something like a theological metaphysics of anticipation. The ability to reach out and consider true now what can only be established as true by an experience of the future—*this* is Pannenberg's structural definition of anticipation.

The following discussion of Pannenberg's theological metaphysics of anticipation first goes through a number of different ways anticipation is, historically, considered significant, beginning with Kant's definition of anticipation, and ending with Pannenberg's own. Secondly, it discusses how Pannenberg shows both conceptual knowledge and practical faith to be structurally anticipatory. Thirdly, two different critiques will question Pannenberg's suggestion that anticipation can be employed in a way that enables something like a synthesis of philosophy and theology. These critiques concern the question of whether Pannenberg gives priority to faith over conceptual knowledge or vice versa. Fourthly, I suggest a way Pannenberg could make up for his omission of a satisfying answer to the question of how he synthesizes conceptual knowledge and faith. I do this by reference to his attempt to show (on the authority of Kant's critical philosophy) that any knowledge—conceptual *and* faith based—can not possibly be anything but anticipatory. Fifthly, I turn to an elaborate description of the theological content of Pannenberg's thesis, acknowledging that, regardless of its weaknesses, it *is* very intriguing and relevant in the context of a constructive interpretation of Peirce's philosophy of religion.

Referring to Epicurus' use of πρόληψις, Kant claims that anticipation can not be attributed to empirical knowledge but only to *a priori* perception, or pure determination. Anticipations only concern *a priori* appearances of what is given *a posteriori* in experience: "All knowledge by means of which I am enabled to know and determine *a priori* what belongs to empirical knowledge may be entitled an anticipation."[24] What can never be *a priori* knowledge, then, is also what can never be anticipations; this is not perception itself but the *Materie der Wahrnehmung* (matter of

---

Anthropology in Theological Perspective, trans. Matthew J. O'Connell (Philadelphia: Westminster, 1985). In *Metaphysics*, Pannenberg brings together these main tenets of conceptualized history, Christian systematics, and anthropology.

[23] Philip Clayton, "Anticipation and Theological Method," in *The Theology of Wolfhart Pannenberg*, ed. Carl E. Braaten and Philip Clayton (Minneapolis: Augsburg, 1988) 127; italics mine.

[24] Kant, *Critique of Pure Reason*, A167/B209.

perception), or *Empfindung* (sensation). Perception is anticipation, but its object (matter) and the involved sensations are not. This means that the merely empirical, or the quality of sensation, as Kant calls it, can not be anticipated: "The *quality* of sensation, as for instance in colours, taste, etc., is always merely empirical, and cannot be represented *a priori*."[25] Note that Kant distinguishes between the *quality* and the *quantity* of empirical sensation. Quality refers to the merely empirical element of sensation, or that which can *only* appear *a posteriori* in experience. Quantity refers to the differing degree of intensity that experiential appearances can have. Heat illustrates the distinction. The radiation of heat fills a certain amount of space but will, in case its intensity decreases, still occupy the exact same amount of space and "without leaving the smallest part of this space in the least empty."[26] Anticipations can not ascribe any degree of intensity of empirical appearances, but they can justly ascribe the fact that appearances *have* this degree of intensity. This means, for Kant, that anticipations perceive nothing *a priori* about empirical appearances, save that they have *kontinuierlicher Zusammenhang* (continual coherence). When Kant then contends that anticipations refer to *a priori* perceptions only, it is not an accurate use of the notion of anticipation, Pannenberg concludes, because his anticipations are associated with pure determinations in space and time, in regard to shape as well as magnitude (i.e. degree of influence on the senses).[27] That is, Kant's anticipations are not concerned with the emergence of conceptual knowledge over time, but rather with *a priori* knowledge within time.

In his own study of anticipation, Pannenberg consults a number of different contexts in which anticipation is employed and considered significant. In the following I refer to these, plus examples from other sources. First, Gilbert van Belle mentions that prolepsis "can be defined in both rhetorical and grammatical terms."[28] Grammatically, it appears fairly often in the Greek language as "the anticipation of the subject (object) of the subordinate clause by making it the object of the main clause."[29]

---

[25] Ibid., A176/B218.

[26] Ibid., A175/B217.

[27] See ibid., A167/B209.

[28] Gilbert van Belle, "Prolepsis in the Gospel of John," *Novum Testamentum* 43 (2001) 335.

[29] A. Debrunner and F. Rehkopf, quoted in Gilbert van Belle, "Prolepsis in the Gospel of John," *Novum Testamentum* 43.4 (2001) 335. van Belle mentions Debrunner and Rehkopf's example of this grammatical use which is a reference to the "anticipation of the subject with verbs which can take the acc. and infinitive." (See van Belle, 335–336.)

Rhetorically, prolepsis is "the proleptic defensive anticipation of the opponent's argument"[30] (i.e. an anticipation of the antagonist's response before it is actually voiced). An opponent can be effectively disarmed by the rhetorical move of answering questions that he or she has not yet articulated, but, most likely, soon will. To these two uses of anticipation, Philip Clayton adds the artistic, where a future effect is present in the process preceding itself, like when "a soldier being killed is depicted in the same picture as being eaten by dogs."[31] This is an imaginative way of representing a future reality as if it takes place in the present. A fourth use of anticipation happens in liturgical theology. In liturgical praxis, James Lopresti suggests, "the ritual language of hope relate[s] to the life projects of individual worshipers."[32] He describes the religious cult as a practical embodiment of the conceptual meaning of prolepsis and a place where the yet ambiguous future takes form by facilitating the experience that "God is ever new and meets his people in unexpected ways."[33]

Finally, Pannenberg emphasizes the *systematic theological* significance of prolepsis by reference to the authority of Clement of Alexandria, who "interpreted faith as the anticipation or *prolepsis* of future salvation."[34] The connection Clement makes between the concept of prolepsis and the doctrine of faith situates anticipation dogmatically in a Christological context where Pannenberg employs it as a methodological device for conceptualizing the Christ event. As such, the doctrine of faith is, in Pannenberg's construction, conceptualized. This is to say that the one thing that is, as Josef Pieper reminds us, "primarily concerned with offering salvation, not with interpreting reality or human existence,"[35] is, in effect, expanded to include just that, reality and human existence. Pannenberg's addition to the list of anticipation's different uses is significant because it enables a theological application of a philosophical concept and turns it into a systematic principle. On this principle Pannenberg therefore places the whole responsibility of holding together the two discourses of philosophical metaphysics and Christian theology. In short, with the notion of prolepsis, Pannenberg

---

[30] H. Lausberg, *Handbook of Literary Rhetoric: A Foundation for Literary Study*, trans. M. T. Bliss, A. Jansen, D. E. Orton, ed. D. E. Orton and R. D. Anderson (Leiden, 1988), 383 (§ 855).

[31] Clayton, "Anticipation and Theological Method," 129.

[32] James Lopresti, "Rituals and Hopes," *Worship* 52 (1978) 348.

[33] Ibid., 358.

[34] Pannenberg, *Metaphysics*, 98.

[35] Josef Pieper, *In Defense of Philosophy: Classical Wisdom Stands up to Modern Challenges*, trans. Lothar Krauth (San Francisco: Ignatius, 1992) 113.

has found what he was seeking, namely a "robust ontological doctrine,"[36] as Clayton pointedly terms it.

Although Clement addresses the Christian doctrine of faith, Pannenberg expands the doctrine and argues that it is applicable to more than the Christian hope of heaven. It competently accounts for knowledge *also*:

> By interpreting faith as prolepsis, Clement characterized it as a knowledge that is already present before its final confirmation at the eschatological completion, namely, through anticipation. Faith and knowledge could thereby be seen as parallel in their structure, because the concept of anticipation brought the element of time into play in the understanding of knowledge itself.[37]

As this quote reveals, Pannenberg constructively concludes that there is a structural likeness between the philosophical concept and God's historical revelation. That is, he concludes that the epistemological event of knowledge and the event of faith in the historical revelation of God in Christ are strikingly comparable. To support this conclusion, Pannenberg invokes God's incarnation in Christ as the ultimate example of the principle of anticipation and then contends that we can *therefore* use it as argument for a metaphysics of anticipation. Moreover, contending that "the confused intuition of the Infinite . . . lies, prethematically, at the basis of all human consciousness . . . [as] a mode of the presence of God,"[38] Pannenberg seizes the opportunity to develop a systematic theology where conceptual metaphysics and historical Christianity are inseparable. He provides no argumentative support for the claim that the two events (the epistemological event of knowledge and the historical event of Christ) are comparable by virtue of their shared anticipatory structure, but the move is evidently well suited to argue for an interdisciplinary study of the notion of anticipation. His vision yields a frame of thought where the long and much desired synthesis of the philosophical and theological disciplines appears within reach.

Before exploring the details of Pannenberg's thesis, we should note that he is well assisted by Lothar Kugelmann's very detailed historical study of the different systematic theological appropriations of the concept of anticipation. Kugelmann's main argument is that, contrary to common analysis, we need to acknowledge the "superiority of history over the con-

---

[36] Clayton, "Anticipation and Theological Method," 129.
[37] Pannenberg, *Metaphysics*, 98–99.
[38] Ibid., 29.

cept"[39] in order not only to rehabilitate the dialogue between theology and philosophy, but also to *legitimize the method* Pannenberg employs in his argument for the structural likeness of knowledge and faith. Kugelmann's contention is that extensive analyses of Christian revelation (exegetical, dogmatic, systematic—as well as existential and phenomenological) will "examine the tenability of that thesis which is put forward as presupposition here, by seeking to emphasize the philosophical conceivableness and significance of anticipation."[40] Hence, the projected accomplishment of Kugelmann's study is two fold. It legitimizes the methodology Pannenberg uses for his constructive proposal of a theological metaphysics of anticipation and it serves as an encouraging incentive to, once again, revive the dialogue between theology and philosophy.

Considering anticipation in the context of Pannenberg's work, it is important to remember that his project rests on the methodological claims that epistemology and Christian faith are congruent. Although Kugelmann's study is impressive, it still does not offer a systematically qualified argument for just why it is that the shared structure of faith and knowledge can facilitate something like a synthesis of the two. At the most, his argument proves that they are *parallel in structure*. Hence, we are still left with the lack of a systematic reason for invoking the historical Christ event as the parameter by which to describe the event of conceptual knowledge. Kugelmann has accentuated what is an argumentative problem in Pannenberg's theological metaphysics, but he has not solved it.

Interestingly, this internal critique of Pannenberg's theological metaphysics can just as effectively be voiced in its reversed form, by pointing to an inordinate subordination of God's pneumatological presence to the altered notion of modern human subjectivity (rather than pointing to an inordinate use of God's incarnation in Christ as the interpretive parameter for conceptual knowledge). That these two critiques should be each other's reverted forms is a matter of the way they order knowledge and faith and determine which of the two should be subordinate in relation to the other.

This critique comes from Reinhard Hütter and relies on the distinction between *prolepsis* and *poiesis*. Pannenberg's use of *prolepsis* "includes

---

[39] Lothar Kugelman, *Antizipation: Eine begriffsgeschichtliche Untersuchung* [Anticipation: a concept-historical analysis] (Göttingen: Vandenhoeck & Ruprecht, 1986) 17; translation mine. In the original: "Überlegenheit der Geschichte über den Begriff."

[40] Ibid., 17; translation mine. In the original: "die Haltbarkeit jener hier als Voraussetzung geltend gemachten These prüfen, indem sie die philosophische Denkbarkeit und Bedeutsamkeit von Antizipation herauszustellen suchen."

forms of activity bound to the modern constitution of the subject,"[41] whereas *poiesis* refers to the actualization of the human subject by way of being shaped by "the reality of a distinct relationality"[42] (i.e. by communion with the triune God). Underlying this distinction is the question whether the human subject becomes a new creation because of God's pneumatological influence, or is actualized on its own account because it possesses an "inherently active logic of 'anticipation' and 'prolepsis.'"[43] In Hütter's opinion, Pannenberg agrees with the latter, and thereby promotes the unfortunate view that "the universal-historic perspective is a necessary consequence of the modern subject constitution [and] the . . . horizon in which the modern subject is able to conceive itself together with the unity of all that is real."[44] Hütter concludes that Pannenberg considers human subjectivity primarily historical and hardly argumentatively important in its spiritual relatedness to God—and that *this* unfortunate emphasis has grown into Pannenberg's impressive apologetic for the Christian revelation and a rendition of its theoretical plausibility. Pannenberg pays a high price, however, because this reduces the significance of the *eschaton* to a logical principle. His apologetic enterprise "integrates the eschaton into the logic of universal history, which in its own turn is dependent on the modern understanding of the subject."[45] In other words, Christian eschatology, and with it also the doctrine of the resurrection of all people, is required to comply conceptually with the parameter of the altered modern understanding of human subjectivity. Therefore, it loses the most significant aspect of its meaning. Pannenberg's "universal-historic horizon ultimately domesticates the 'future' by subordinating it to the anthropological structure of prolepsis, the universal-human disposition toward the future."[46]

---

[41] Reinhard Hütter, *Suffering Divine Things: Theology as Church Practice* (Grand Rapids: Eerdmans, 2000) 122.

[42] Ibid., 122.

[43] Ibid., 122. To this I would add another problematic issue in Pannenberg which relates to his statement that, at the time of the first Christian community, "Jesus' resurrection and the end of the world could be seen together as a single event [and to] that extent the eschatological future was nearer then than at any time since"; Wolfhart Pannenberg, *Jesus—God and Man*, trans. Lewis L. Wilkins and Duane A. Priebe (Philadelphia: Westminster, 1968) 108. In order, however, for Christians to participate in the redemptive work of God's pneumatological influence that Hütter refers to, it is problematic to say that there is one point in time where the eschatological future is more present than other times.

[44] Hütter, *Suffering Divine* Things, 121. "Modern subject" refers to the altered notion of human subjectivity that is the result of Kant's critical philosophy.

[45] Ibid., 121.

[46] Ibid.

Hütter basically argues that Pannenberg is caught in the web of his own project of conceptualization, which—unfortunately—also includes a conceptualization of the lived life of faith, and the relational knowledge of God.[47]

Whether one chooses to side with Hütter's critique of Pannenberg or its reversed version, it remains a fact that Pannenberg omits an argument for just why it is a logical implication that God's incarnation in Christ should be the ultimate expression of the principle of anticipation and that *therefore* knowledge is anticipatory too. He may still compensate for this omission, however, by following another argumentative route to show the structurally anticipatory nature of conceptual knowledge. This route is determined by his undivided commitment to analytical work with Kant's critical philosophy as the foundation and condition of all modern thinking, especially the altered notion of human subjectivity that it produces. The result is his metaphysical category of anticipation.

The Concept of Anticipation as a Metaphysical Category

As a result of Kant's critical philosophy, classical metaphysics is, in Pannenberg's assessment, irreversibly criticized. Its era is firmly closed, Pannenberg argues, and it is no longer an option to inquire conceptually and logically into the ultimate foundations of reality by engagement

---

[47] Another critique of Pannenberg is contained in the well-known accusations of his appropriation of Hegel's philosophy. For a full treatment of Pannenberg's appreciation of Hegel's contributions to modern post-Kantian theology, see: Wolfhart Pannenberg, "The Significance of Christianity in the Philosophy of Hegel," in *The Idea of God and Human Freedom* (Philadelphia: Westminster, 1973). Admittedly, there are striking similarities between Pannenberg and Hegel who both approach the disciplines of theology and philosophy with an attitude of seeking comprehensive and interdisciplinary outcomes. As for the notion of anticipation, one articulation of a Hegelian interpretation of Pannenberg's systematic application of anticipation is provided by Ronald D. Pasquariello. He comments about Pannenberg's system, "The presence of the ultimate negates the anticipation [and] . . . brings about the breakdown of the anticipation. However, this very breakdown projects a new context in which the ultimate is grasped in a new way, within an enlarged context, with a new meaning. This new context is itself an anticipation which is fated to run aground through the realization of its provisional nature in relation to the anticipated ultimate"; Ronald D. Pasquariello, "Pannenberg's Philosophical Foundations," *Journal of Religion* 56 (1976) 347. Other critiques concern Pannenberg's book *Anthropology*, the triadic structure of which seemingly parallels the structure of Hegel's *Phenomenology of Spirit*. Pannenberg's *Anthropology* could therefore be identified as something like a theological twin to Hegel's *Phenomenology*. See Roger E. Olson, "The Human Self-Realization of God: Hegelian Elements in Pannenberg's Christology," *Perspectives in Religious Studies* 13 (1986) 207–23.

of the language of substance.[48] Previously, philosophical monotheism and biblical monotheism were only latently in conflict and their compatibility therefore not questioned. Conceptualizations of ultimate truth, as provided by pre-modern philosophical metaphysics, were formally supportive of the theist notion of God as creator and sustainer of the world. It was the primary ambition of such pre-Kantian metaphysics to provide, once and for all, a final and comprehensive description of all reality, and to have a firm grip on reality that could function as a frame of reference for all future questions generated by the human mind. This was meant to secure the kind of fundamental knowledge of the world that would be invulnerable to the fluctuations of political, sociological, and cultural changes along with changes in theoretical fashion. Evidently, such a position is formally sympathetic of biblical monotheism and therefore protective of the connectedness of reason and faith.

The appearance of the philosophical rationalisms of Descartes and Kant questioned the reliability of reason and turned faith into a matter of individual needs and tastes. In Pannenberg's judgment, the serious repercussions of this change is that we now face the task of having to determine the degree to which truth claims are references to something objectively real, or merely to something subjectively constructed. The main motivation behind the mudslide disappearance of classical metaphysics is, Pannenberg argues, that no serious post-Kantian thinker can compromise the autonomy of human subjectivity. He therefore proposes, "Every conception of the absolute One must today prove its worth by showing itself to be not only the source and completion of the world but also the constitutive ground and highest good of subjectivity. . . . The Absolute must be understood not as standing in contradiction to the independence of . . . subjectivity, but instead precisely as the completion."[49] The absolute is only conceivable as a *relativized absolute*. By implication, the object of metaphysical reflection must be both the source and the goal of human autonomy, for the "Enlightenment has destroyed the principle of authority,

---

[48] This is why Pannenberg views the classical proofs of God's existence as no longer tenable options: "I hold that such claims were exaggerated and have been justly criticized. The history of the proofs of the existence of God within modern thought, from Descartes through Kant and Hegel, shows the necessity of extending reason to include the idea of God. It does not show that the existence of God . . . can be proved"; Pannenberg, *Metaphysics*, 19. The classical proofs concern rational logic more than divine existence.

[49] Ibid., 62.

and . . . the subjectivism of religious experience of a religion based solely upon the decision of faith . . . brings ruin to the truth of religion."[50]

For his assessment of post-Kantian philosophy and the view that all serious philosophy and theology is now irreversibly bound to consider the conditions for metaphysical reflection as determined by Kant, Pannenberg is greatly indebted to the work of Dieter Henrich. In *Metaphysics and the Idea of God*, where Pannenberg discusses the notion of anticipation most elaborately, Henrich's influence is explicitly noticeable, and in fact "more so than can be seen from the few references to him in the text."[51] A problematic thing about Kant is, Henrich argues, that he has "ascribed only a serving role to transcendental philosophy: *It is necessary*, in order to enable a defense of the most essential interests of humankind, all of which require that it is possible to justify the idea of freedom."[52] It is because of the irrevocable nature of Kant's transcendental philosophy that it becomes a theoretical necessity to supplement Kant's philosophy with Hegel's. Structurally, philosophical thought must consider the fact that a permanent deficit of Kant's theory is its lack of unity, which can only be overcome by attempting a full elaboration of the transcendental explanation of human autonomy and freedom, as found in Hegel. But, while the Kantian particularity lacks unity, the Hegelian unity lacks particularity, so within the tension of these two poles—Kant and Hegel—Henrich sees a rich and very complex *Kraftfeld der Motive* (power-field of motives) unfold as it tries to observe both extremes without succumbing to either.[53]

In our context, the most important implication of Henrich's position (and in turn Pannenberg's) is that his approach to the philosophical tradition framed by Kant and Hegel, German idealism, frees idealist thought from the classic metaphysical desire to provide an exhaustive world

---

[50] Pannenberg, "Christianity in the Philosophy of Hegel," 177.

[51] Pannenberg, *Metaphysics*, xiv.

[52] Dieter Henrich, *Identität und Objektivität: Eine Untersuchung über Kants transzendentale Deduktion* [Identity and objectivity: an investigation of Kant's transcendental deduction] (Heidelberg: Winter, 1976) 13; italics mine; translation mine. In the original: "der Transzendentalphilosophie nur noch eine dienende Rolle zuerkannt: *Sie ist notwendig*, um die wesentlichsten Interessen der Menschheit verteidigen zu können, die allesamt voraussetzen, dass sich die Idee der Freiheit rechtfertigen lässt."

[53] In Henrich's judgment, history itself confirms the theoretical tension between Kant and Hegel in so far as philosophies inspired by Kant have proved to stimulate the appearance of philosophies in reconsideration of Hegel, and vice versa. See Dieter Henrich, *Selbstverhältnisse: Gedanken und Auslegungen zu den Grundlagen der klassischen deutschen Philosophie* [Self-relations: thoughts and interpretations in regard to the foundations of classical German philosophy] (Stuttgart: Reclam, 1982) 175.

description by virtue of one single foundational principle while still preserving the idealist *vision* of such an exhaustive description. It is Henrich's emphasis on the irreducible disparity of human life (and his concern for *das bewusste Leben* (the conscious life) of not trying to reduce this disparity) that effects his metaphysical position of defining reality's most general feature by reference to humanity's persistent quest for final explanations *in union with* the impossibility of actually achieving such explanations. Henrich engages metaphysical reflection without compromising the conditions given with Kant's critical philosophy.

Pannenberg follows Henrich's lead and argues theologically that the new situation Kant's critical philosophy has created is the opportunity to reformulate Christian faith "with a new rigorousness and exclusiveness, *as the religion of freedom*."[54] At the same time, Pannenberg voices a caution and a need not to make the modern "principle of self-conscious subjectivity . . . the final basis for every discussion of metaphysics, as was the case in the entire tradition of German idealism."[55] Of course, this could be used as an answer to Hütter's critique that Pannenberg subordinates God's pneumatological presence to the processes of human consciousness and conceptualization.[56] As the following shows, however, Pannenberg's caution and desire to balance the possibilities and limits of a modern theology based on autonomous human subjectivity does not relieve his theological vision of the all-encompassing influence of the method of conceptualization.

Pannenberg's dual commitment to the Christian faith and the altered notion of self-conscious subjectivity makes it impossible to claim any explanatory and definitive conceptual foundation of reality. A conceptual construal can no longer provide credible descriptions of absolute reality, for the option of describing the absolute in terms of definitive and ultimate foundations no longer exists. Any notion of the absolute must be nothing less than the perfection and realization of human subjectivity. As Pannenberg concludes with an almost despairingly exclamatory voice, "This is no simple task."[57] Nevertheless, his response to the challenge of Kant's critical philosophy comes in the form of the argument that metaphysical statements must relativize their foundational dispositions and

---

[54] Pannenberg, "The Significance of Christianity," 177; italics mine.

[55] Pannenberg, "An Autobiographical Sketch," in *The Theology of Wolfhart Pannenberg*, ed. Carl E. Braaten and Philip Clayton (Minneapolis: Augsburg, 1988) 17.

[56] See 126–27.

[57] Pannenberg, *Metaphysics*, 62.

claim no more than hypothetical character: "Metaphysical reflection must instead take on the form of a *conjectural reconstruction* in relation to its object... Put more precisely, the philosophical concept will reveal itself to have the structure of anticipation."[58] *This* is the argumentative substance of Pannenberg's metaphysics of anticipation and the way he demonstrates the anticipatory structure of conceptual knowledge apart from invoking the historical event of God's revelation in Christ. Pannenberg has shown the concept to be—in and of itself—anticipatory, and he has done so by reference to the authority of Kant and the change he affected in how we define the abilities of human reason. One could therefore consider it a superfluous argumentative move that Pannenberg invokes the Christ event as interpretive parameter for an understanding of knowledge as anticipatory.

Again, whether one chooses to settle with a critique of Pannenberg that questions the parameter status of faith over conceptual knowledge, as formulated earlier, *or* of conceptual knowledge over faith, as Hütter argues, one critique still remains. Pannenberg omits a systematic and qualifying argument for how the comparable nature of conceptual knowledge and faith can facilitate something like their synthesis. In case my suggested argument that Pannenberg makes up for this omission is not satisfying, then a critique of his argument for the metaphysical and theological significance of anticipation is even less avoidable. Nevertheless, Pannenberg's thesis is intriguing, and we now turn to a more detailed description of his argument for the anticipatory quality of faith.

The Theological Environment of the Concept of Anticipation

Even though Pannenberg is "skeptical of the claim that with the notion of highest perfection we have already reached the idea of God,"[59] he is still confident that metaphysics and its concern for the Absolute One is a conceptual and structural parallel to the historical God of Christianity. In his illustration, the Christian doctrine of faith is a direct expression of the concept of anticipation. In fact, it is the *ultimate* expression of anticipation. Christ is the object of faith because he has claimed himself both the promise and the fulfillment of the kingdom of God and, most importantly, because he has provided self-verification by the event of his own resurrection. In Christ, the future of God's kingdom broke into history in its fullness, although this kingdom still awaits ultimate realization and remains an event of the future. God's incarnation in Christ is the promise

---

[58] Ibid., 94.
[59] Ibid., 28.

of a definitive coming of the kingdom of God at the end of time, but the kingdom of God is simultaneously and already fully at hand in Christ. The gospel of Christ is a proclamation of both the coming and the presence of God's kingdom.

One specific element points to the Christ event as most essentially anticipatory, Pannenberg argues, namely that Christ's message still has time to turn out nothing more than an intermezzo of embarrassment and a matter of religious zeal on the part of a few individuals. That is, the credibility of his proclamation about the kingdom still depends on whether or not the kingdom actually does manifests at some future point: "Without the definitive coming of the kingdom of God, the message of Jesus . . . remains a matter of religious enthusiasm."[60] It is because of this sobering reality about Christian statements of faith that Pannenberg considers them to "*always* contain a proleptic element. The fulfillment . . . in the appearances of the resurrected Lord, has become promise once again,"[61] because the cosmos is still in a state of awaiting the consummation of Christ's resurrection, which will only happen with the resurrection of *all* people. The fact that the crucifixion of Jesus is followed by his resurrection is the only available confirmation of his promise that the power of God's kingdom will resurrect all people on the final and apocalyptic *day of the Lord*. For Pannenberg, the Christian message is the proclamation of a promise that still awaits fulfillment, and the "truth of this anticipation hinges on the still-absent future. Only if that future actually arrives was it in fact already present in the life of Jesus."[62] In Pannenberg's view, then, it is insufficient for hopeful loans in the future to be repaid by mere fulfillment, even though the prefiguring resurrection of Christ is such a repayment of fulfillment. We can never consider the resurrection of Christ more than a promise. There is still a more substantial fulfillment to come, and this gives Christian faith its *anticipatory* quality, as opposed both to a determined pursuit of what the future does hold and an acquired attitude of optimism about the things it may hold. There is qualified reason to expect the fulfillment of promises that are most certainly given, but this expectation is permanently tainted by a threat of not actually experiencing their fulfillment. In a word, Pannenberg's theological metaphysics of anticipation defines both rational and believing hope as anticipation by pointing to the power *a future reality has over the present by means of a promise.*

---

[60] Ibid., 96.

[61] Pannenberg, *Jesus*, 108; italics mine.

[62] Pannenberg, *Metaphysics*, 96.

As already discussed, Pannenberg expresses a strong disconcert about the current lack of interest in metaphysics. Now, consider this statement from Peirce who is no less dissatisfied with his own contemporaries and their attitude toward metaphysics:

> The truth is that the minds from whom the spirit of the age emanates have now no interest in the only problems that metaphysics ever pretended to solve. The abstract acknowledgment of God, Freedom, and Immortality, apart from those other religious beliefs (which cannot possibly rest on metaphysical grounds) which alone may animate this, is now seen to have no practical consequence whatever. (*EP* 1.84)

For Peirce, metaphysics is considered invalid because no one considers God, freedom, and immortality to have practical consequences and therefore also do not consider metaphysics significant. Pannenberg's theological metaphysics of anticipation is one example of a constructive proposal in response to the kind of metaphysics a post-Kantian context requires. In Peirce, we find another thinker who proposes a metaphysics that tries to meet the requirements of post-Kantian theology and whose systematic thinking is guided by a desire for theological relevance. That is, both Pannenberg and Peirce pursue a formulation of the same *kind* of metaphysics. Approaching a discussion of Peirce's theist position, I aim to now demonstrate how Peirce's response to the lack of interest in post-Kantian metaphysics is successful in a way that Pannenberg's is not. Still, I wish to reach this goal by applying insights from Pannenberg's theological reflections on the notion of anticipation to Peirce's theism, theory of abduction, and the N.A. This application is precisely what makes Peirce's project stand out on its own and accomplish something Pannenberg does not. Peirce does not explicitly use the notion of anticipation, but to walk through his metaphysics, his theory of abduction and his argument for the reality of God is to walk through a philosophical system structured by anticipation—one that provides the theoretical background for the proposal of a Peircean theology of anticipation.

Peirce and Theism

Theism is faith in a God who is outside the world, who has created it, and who is in control of what happens in the world by the power of divine freedom and an ability to interfere in the course of worldly events. By way of affirming the difference between creator and creature, theism emphasizes that there is a radical difference between God and human beings.

Following the views of two influential contemporary theist theologians, Alvin Plantinga and Richard G. Swinburne, the most important thing about theism is, however, the belief that God interferes in the affairs of human life in accordance with the three divine attributes of goodness, omnipotence and omniscience.[63] We find these three qualities in the theist God, to the maximal degree, and in uncompromised form. A God with these qualities works to the unquestioned benefit of human beings; they have nothing to fear, but rather everything to believe. God's intentions are always good, God is always capable, and God always knows what is truly best, regardless of what merely seems best from a human perspective.

Historically, the notion of a theist God has proved a suitable parallel to the philosophical notion of an eternal and necessary divine being, and has consequently played a significant argumentative role in the ongoing conversation between the disciplines of philosophy and theology. Theism suggests identifying the philosophical God and the God of biblical faith. Because theology always will imply, if not consist of, theoretical reflections upon practical faith experiences, this identification is naturally attractive. By default, theology is in search of a theoretical understanding of its practical content, and this creates something like a gravitational pull toward conceptualization of faith.[64]

---

[63] Adhering to Plantinga and Swinburne's definitions of contemporary theism means leaving out other definitions. This includes F. D. E. Schleiermacher's theism which refers to the four divine attributes of eternity, omnipresence, omnipotence and omniscience. This choice of omission is made on the basis of the fact that, in the N.A., Peirce's few descriptive accounts of God gravitate toward an emphasis on the three divine attributes of God's goodness, omnipotence, and omniscience. The one example that will be discussed later in this chapter, is when Peirce asks this question: "Why does not this *Omniscient* Being see the need and interpose the *Omnipotent* and Supreme Authority to *meet the needs* prayed for?" (*CP* 6.517; italics mine). Here, I take Peirce to imply that a God who meets the needs of those who ask is a God of goodness.

[64] The drawing of parallels between a conceptualized and a historical God was perhaps most notably the case when Christianity first began to gain a following in the Hellenist world. (Aristotle's metaphysical idea of the *unmoved mover* is one example of a philosophical parallel to the historical, Judeo-Christian God of faith, and one easily transformed into a conceptualized version of the biblical God.) The Hellenist distinction between the divine and the human realms (between other-worldly and this-worldly, higher and lower, complete and incomplete, spirit and matter) makes Christian theism a suitable theological parallel. With its sharp distinction between creator and creature, it formally affirms the contrast between spirit and matter. Discussions of theism's advantages and disadvantages in contrast to a philosophical notion of the divine reappear up through history, especially in the works of philosophically oriented theologians (for example: Augustine, Thomas Aquinas, Schleiermacher, and Paul Tillich).

Theism is not without disadvantages, especially because significant characteristics of the biblical God must be compromised if the parallel between the philosophical God and the God of practical faith is upheld. Such compromise happens most easily by reducing the importance of God's redemptive and historical involvement in human lives. Most importantly, theism does not consider it *argumentatively* significant that God is moved by human suffering and practically involved in its elimination. Therefore, struggles with the reality of evil lead theists to argue that it is not, strictly speaking, a theological issue. Rather, "Such a problem, broadly speaking, is a spiritual or pastoral problem."[65] In contrast, consider faith, the incarnation, the sacrificial life, death, and resurrection of Christ which is the means of God's involvement in a world of human suffering and also the means of its removal. Christianity based on these things is more than theism in so far as it *adds* this to the divine qualities of goodness, omnipotence, and omniscience: the redemptive action of God who suffers with and for humanity as a way of making available a path to freedom from suffering. With a critical perspective on theism then, God's incarnation in Christ is not so much rational evidence of there being a God who is able and in control, real and existent, as it is the one thing that makes it practically possible to enter God's healing presence. Because Christ is considered the door to personal relatedness to God, more than he proves the intelligibility of faith in God, the practical effects of the Christ event simply are not argumentatively significant for the rational project of theism.[66] In

---

[65] Alvin Plantinga, *Warranted Christian Belief* (New York: Oxford University Press, 2000) 459. As a leading contemporary philosopher of religion, Plantinga addresses the theist question of whether Christian faith can be warranted and intellectually justified. See also Plantinga, *God and Other Minds: A Study of the Rational Justification of Belief in God* (Ithaca, NY: Cornell University Press, 1967); and Alvin Plantinga and Nicholas Wolterstorff, eds., *Faith and Rationality: Reason and Belief in God* (Notre Dame: University of Notre Dame Press, 1983). Richard G. Swinburne contributes significantly to rational theism as well. See Swinburne, *The Existence of God* (Oxford: Clarendon, 1979); and Swinburne, *The Coherence of Theism* (Oxford: Clarendon, 1993).

[66] Many judge this a serious theological breach. The tradition of liberation theology, for example, finds it necessary to provide a thorough redefinition of theology by articulating some serious points of critique against rationalist tendencies in traditional theology. Risking over-simplification, liberationists critique traditional theology for a much too heavy reliance on rational arguments for faith in the Christian God. They claim that these arguments result in theological indifference to the practical needs of those who suffer unjustly and whose sufferings go unrecognized. The different liberationist voices gravitate toward the one shared argument that theologians must develop a reflective awareness of God's actual involvement in the world—and then support it! As Gustavo Gutiérrez says in what has become a classic exposition of liberation theology, "In the last analysis, the true interpretation of the meaning revealed by theology is achieved only in historical praxis"; Gutiérrez,

conclusion, we can say that theism is a theological position committed to a negative and a positive cause. It defends itself against philosophical accusations of irrationality, and it advocates apologetically for faith in the good, omnipotent and omniscient God of Christianity.

Turning now to the way Peirce refers to the God of traditional Christianity, a first thing to notice is his frequent and clear referencing to biblical material, especially the teachings of Jesus and the gospel of John. His elaborations on the influence of divine purpose and love—which we have already encountered in his doctrine of agapism, for example—are clearly inspired by the gospel of John and its message that "as darkness is merely the defect of light, so hatred and evil are mere imperfect stages of αγάπη and αγαθόν, love and loveliness" (*CP* 6.287). Finding the essence of John's simple message to be that "in the law of love is the Christian faith" (*CP* 6.441), Peirce also says that this "may be regarded in a higher point of view with St. John as the universal evolutionary formula" (*CP* 6.441). Clearly, the connection Peirce makes here is one between evolution and Christian love, and this is, on his own account, also significant inspiration for his doctrine of synechism. That evolution is a higher form of Christian love translates almost directly into his cosmological teaching that the divine purpose that propels the evolutionary development of the universe is the simple love of God.

Most surprising, perhaps, is the fact that Peirce also relates the methodological principle of pragmatism to the teachings of Jesus. Pragmatism, he says, "is only an application of the sole principle of logic which was recommended by Jesus; 'Ye may know them by their fruits,' and it is very intimately allied with the ideas of the gospel" (*CP* 5.402 n.2). When Jesus says that knowledge of a person's inner state of being is available by looking at that person's actions and behavior, this expresses the logic of pragmatism. Bear in mind here Peirce's definition of pragmaticism, which "was originally enounced in the form of a maxim, as follows: Consider what effects, which might conceivably have practical bearings we conceive the object of our conception to have. Then, our *conception* of the effects is the whole of

---

A Theology of Liberation, trans. Sister Caridad Inda and John Eagleson (New York: Orbis, 1988) 10. Committed specifically to the cause of Black liberation, James H. Cone pointedly makes the same case: "God meets us in the human situation, not as an idea or concept that is self-evidently true. God encounters us in the human condition as the liberator of the poor and the weak, empowering them to fight for freedom because they were made for it"; James H. Cone, *A Black Theology of Liberation* (New York: Orbis, 1986) xix. Both of these statements support the much delayed call to end the endless discussions of rational evidence, correct abstractions, and theoretical descriptions of God. In my opinion, it is very difficult to refute the systematic legitimacy of the liberationist critique.

our conception of the object"⁶⁷ (*EP* 2.346). Then transplant this definition to the teachings of Jesus and the connection is that we can only know a person by also knowing what conceivable practical bearings the true inner state of his or her being has. It is important that Peirce does not advocate for a causal relatedness of thought and action, for "*praktisch* and *pragmatisch* were as far apart as the two poles, the former belonging in a region of thought where no mind of the experimentalist type can ever make sure of solid ground under his feet, the latter expressing relation to some definite human purpose" (*EP* 2.333). Rather, his theory is that "a *conception*, that is, the rational purport of a word or other expression, lies exclusively in its conceivable bearing upon the conduct of life" (*EP* 2.332). Pragmatism concerns the "inseparable connection between rational cognition and rational purpose" (*EP* 2.333), not a practical consequentiality between belief and action. Pragmatism is, he holds, a methodological principle of logic that is repeated in the logic of Jesus' teaching.

Despite Peirce's frequent references to biblical texts, he still applies them rather casually. It is not clear how his use of biblical material translates into systematic, theological language, and although most research agrees that Peirce advocates for a theist position, other positions are potentially applicable. For instance, Hookway suggests that Peirce's religious optimism is more like an expression of pantheism. Our confidence in the process of purposed evolution, he says, "reflects a Pantheistic tendency in Peirce's thought which is present in his claim that we can directly perceive God."⁶⁸ The first possible option, then, is that Peirce is a religious pantheist. Secondly, one could argue that he is a speculative mystic. His claim is that only the religious experience enables a solution to the tension between theoretical reasoning and practical faith. This presumes a mystic union with the divine as facilitator of the religious experience. Peirce's fascination with Eastern mysticism supports this view. All the same, his mysticism may not go beyond the point of fascination: "Peirce was a Western rather than an Eastern mystic; he envisaged remote goals and impossible ideals not as objects of pure contemplation but as limits to the accomplishment possible of approach by means of the scientific method."⁶⁹

Thirdly, we must also consider Peirce's espousal of other religious traditions. He finds no reason to discriminate between religions, and because the universal formula of love "was anticipated by the early Egyptians, by

---

⁶⁷ Italics mine.

⁶⁸ Hookway, *Peirce*, 280.

⁶⁹ Feibleman, *Interpreted as a System*, 16.

the Stoics, by the Buddhists, and by Confucius . . . it was anticipated from primitive ages. The higher a religion the more catholic" (*CP* 6.442). Had Peirce lived in the more pluralist religious atmosphere of today's America, I wonder if he would consider it non-discriminatory to regard Christianity as superior to other so-called "primitive" world religions as confidently as he does. Had he lived today, he may not even have chosen Christianity as the *higher* religion to which all others lead. My point is that his application of Christian terminology is general enough to fit other religious traditions, perhaps with some moderate alterations, and that his theological position is in fact more generally religious than specifically Christian. In today's context, it is unlikely that he would consider his religious thoughts so naturally in tune with the Christian tradition as opposed to other traditions (for example the ones he lists as more primitive than Christianity). In my judgment, however, the likelihood of Peirce's loose relatedness to the Christian doctrines is interesting for the following reason. His commitment to the method of abductive reasoning betrays his generally religious attitude of faith because Christian faith in particular—more than any other religion and by virtue of its commitment to the incarnation—hangs on the principle of abduction. Considering earlier conclusions (that both the incarnation and Peirce's theory of abduction give *qualified* reasons to take for real in the present what still rightfully belongs to the future), we see how it is the anticipatory quality of abductive reasoning that makes Peirce's theory of abduction supportive of Christian faith and not other faiths.

In any case, the different possible interpretations of Peirce's religious position can not alter the fact that theism is most commonly attributed to him, and that he gives reason to look favorably on this interpretation. Therefore, we now turn to two constructive interpretations of Peirce's theological position, both of which present themselves as alternatives to traditional theism, and still consider Peirce's position theist.

A Peircean Theosemiotic: Michael Raposa

As Peirce espouses both the philosophical and the theological discourse, it is no surprise that his religious writings appear theist. Nor is it a surprise that they paint the picture of a complex religious position, which, of course, relates to the fact that Peirce does not develop a philosophy of religion systematically. This lack of systematics is also the reason Peirce's employment of religion is often written off as an obscure appendix to the work of an otherwise genius philosophical thinker. Many consider his religious position in grave need of constructive assistance. Such is, for example, Raposa's opinion, when he argues for the necessity of developing "a systematic account of his [Peirce's] philosophy of religion,"[70]—and then offers an elaborate rendition of Peirce's religious beliefs in order to ascertain their function and importance in his philosophy as a whole. Raposa's proposal is "to suggest the sort of text that Peirce might have written,"[71] had he completed the task of finishing what he himself called a poor sketch of an argument for the reality of God. Raposa proposes that if Peirce's argument for God's reality were to be completed, then it should argue that faith is a semiotic process, involved in the grander process of cosmic semiosis and reliant on the perceptive faculty of abduction to facilitate knowledge of a theist God.

Raposa suggests that if it is to be taken seriously that Peirce intends for an evolutionary cosmology to be the theoretical background for his philosophical system, and if his relentless commitment to the scientific method of inquiry is to be observed, it is most accurate to interpret his theological position as a *theosemiotic*. Together with everything else, the human mind is implanted in the divine Absolute Mind of the cosmic continuum and therefore naturally inclined to acquire knowledge of God, most especially the fundamental knowledge of God's reality. The Absolute Mind embodies God's divine purpose of love; it is "a great symbol of God's purpose" (*CP* 5.119) and appears like "a great poem" (*CP* 5.119)—God's great poem—in a way similar to conceiving of a universe that can be traced back to a final cause. As Raposa argues, the evolving cosmic thoughts of Absolute Mind (which are identical with the laws of nature) weigh so heavily in upon the human mind that they produce intimate experiences of God's love: "The final causes that effect the development of the universe represent Love's teleology, a selfless, cherishing Love that Peirce, like the author of the fourth gospel, identified with the very being of the Deity."[72]

At first, and by way of abductive reasoning, the human mind instinctively has hypothetical knowledge of *God's great poem* (the universe) in different encounters with it and is then compelled to unpack this knowledge by the help of deductive explanations and inductive testing. This process is the semiotic process, and as the human mind goes through it repeatedly, in a continual string of encounters with parts of the universe, it is quite literally impossible not to have an encounter with the idea of the reality of

---

[70] Raposa, *Peirce's Philosophy of Religion*, 4.
[71] Ibid., 3.
[72] Ibid., 144.

God. The process of semiosis will necessarily yield the idea of God who is the final cause behind everything else and, in Peirce's poetic language, the author of the universe. That is, because the human mind is implanted in the divine mind and the reality of God, it is impossible that it should not encounter this idea (i.e. that it should not at some point have the thought, "God is real"). Peirce's contention that mind is not something in us, but that we are in it, is the reasoning behind his confident belief that the hypothetical inference "God is real" belongs to the most reliable hypotheses the human mind can produce. As we shall see, Peirce adds to the argument that even though this hypothesis is among the vaguest, it is not the least less reliable.

Raposa concludes, then, that a Peircean theosemiotic conveys a developmental theism of continued semiotic self-modification which relies on the principles of rational inquiry and scientific methodology as embodied in the theory of abduction. This means that a Peircean theosemiotic is a theological interpretation of the relationship between God and human beings, facilitated by *the religious experiences that abductive reasoning produces and that follow the pattern of semiosis*. The epistemological key is, of course, that religious experiences of encounters with God come in the form of direct and irrefutable knowledge of God's reality, even in its vagueness. As Raposa says, classifying the theist method of knowing God with the method of abductive reasoning, "Peirce's theory of inquiry supplies the rubric for what is, in essence, a complex theological method."[73] Peirce's epistemological rubric is therefore also an interpretive and systematic rubric for his philosophy of religion. In Raposa's interpretation, this means that Peirce's theology is based on a theist faith rooted in the hypothetical inferences of abductive reasoning and reflective of the process of cosmic semiosis.

Some Critical Questions to Michael Raposa

Aiming to fill out the poor sketch Peirce provided of a philosophy of religion, Raposa does more than propose a theosemiotic in the form of an epistemological theory. His interpretive project also includes a systematic analysis of Peirce's philosophy in order to determine his religious position more broadly as an integrated part of his philosophy. To this end, Raposa's exegetical analysis of the doctrine of synechism "is the key to understanding the religious dimension of Peirce's thought."[74] In Raposa's assessment,

[73] Ibid., 144.
[74] Ibid., 41.

the doctrine of synechism explicates the way in which "God's relationship to individuals in the world might be roughly compared to that existing between a continuum and its topical singularities."[75] Raposa reconstructs Peirce's entire philosophy of religion on the basis of the epistemological and theist functions of Peirce's semiotic, together with his metaphysical reflections on synechism, Absolute Mind, and evolutionary love. He concludes that Peirce is a theist of the panentheist kind: God is creator of the universe, independent of it, but still continuous with it. It is, Raposa argues, Peirce's doctrine of tychism that signifies his philosophy of religion as panentheism and distinguishes it from pantheism. In Raposa's interpretation, tychism "is an essential ingredient of Peirce's evolutionary cosmology"[76] but, although it is the doctrine of absolute chance, it still works toward the unfolding of the synechist continuum. Hence, Peirce's doctrine of tychism, the fact that there are "deviations from the regular uniformities of the world" (*CP* 6.512), is encompassed by his doctrine of synechism. This happens in the sense, Raposa explains, that "the very laws of nature, if not robbed of their ideality and their evolutionary character, presuppose such deviations"[77] as provided by tychism. Synechism encompasses tychism. So, "chance begets law; continuity presupposes spontaneity; synechism entails tychism,"[78] and Raposa thus demonstrates that one can not analyze Peirce's doctrine of synechism in isolation from, or even in opposition to, his doctrine of tychism. Tychism lives to support synechism. In a word, Raposa understands Peirce's philosophical system as primarily an expression of his doctrine of synechism which includes tychism and is backed by an evolutionary cosmology.

I question the degree to which Raposa understands tychism as an integrated part of synechism because this understanding underemphasizes tychism's systematic role as *disruptive* and essentially in opposition to synechism. I base my critique on the implicit influence the later Schelling's philosophy has on Peirce's thinking and argue that Peirce's philosophy embraces the tension between synechism and tychism as oppositions. Tychism is significantly more disruptive, unpredictable and unruly than a harmonious evolution of the synechist continuum allows. Not only do tychist impulses disrupt the continuum, but they also disrupt the harmony of its evolutionary process. Systematically, the disruptive reality of

---

[75] Ibid., 51.
[76] Ibid., 32.
[77] Ibid., 31.
[78] Ibid., 32.

tychism reinforces an interpretation of Peirce's philosophy of religion as structurally anticipatory in so far as anticipation involves the notion of a permanently unpredictable future more than a future that unfolds as an evolving and developmental process.

Reading Raposa's argument for a theosemiotic suggests that the cosmic semiosis is an evolutionary process of unfolding God's divine being as love. From a human perspective, our hypothetical inferences (determined by abductive reasoning), reflect this process of cosmic semiosis and link us to it. We establish and test hypothetical inferences through a semiotic process whose ultimate goal is to experience God's love, which is to experience the very being of God. This way we grow in the knowledge of divine love and participate in the evolutionary development of the cosmic continuum so as to be satisfied in our longing for harmony, meaning, and integration.

Even though Raposa emphasizes that "some of the essential features of tychasticism are preserved in Peirce's theory of evolutionary love,"[79] I question the extent to which he still relies on divine love as "an ordering love, seeking no simple uniformity or regularity but a general harmony, the continuity of all things."[80] Again, I base my critique on Peirce's implicit reliance on the later Schelling's philosophy, in particular Schelling's reflections on the concept of God. My argument there was that, in order to give Peirce's doctrine of tychism full credit, one must subscribe to a personal God who initiates the disruptive, the unpredictable and the impulsive. Tychism defined in opposition to synechism need not reflect "the randomness of pure chance,"[81] as Raposa suggests. Rather, within God, who is love, is also the impulse of pure freedom to initiate anything at all, because everything else—including everything else about God—is subject to God's freedom.

What Raposa notices as an *epistemic blindness* in Peirce's thinking is a problem that supports my argument. This blindness refers to a clear discrepancy in Peirce's system. On one hand, he teaches that we all have direct perceptions of God (by virtue of identification with God and participation in the Absolute Mind). On the other hand, however, is the disturbing fact that many individuals simply have no such perceptions. Hence, as Peirce says, "the question arises how it is possible that the existence of this being should ever have been doubted by anybody" (*CP* 6.162). Raposa's response

---

[79] Ibid., 78.
[80] Ibid.
[81] Ibid.

to this question is, in effect, the thesis of his book, *Peirce's Philosophy of Religion*, that although Peirce did not provide a direct or satisfying answer, "the entire Neglected Argument, and in particular the prescribed activity of Musement, can be interpreted as a proposed 'remedy' for this [epistemic] blindness."[82] In my judgment, Peirce's N.A. indeed is a likely candidate for a possible response to his own question, but the way Raposa turns this into a cosmic theosemiotic relies too much—again—on synechism's ability to absorb the impulsive and disruptive power of tychism. Yes, the human mind is attuned to the Absolute Mind because it literally lives within it, but the Absolute Mind of God as well as (by implication) the human mind can at any point experience a release of volitional power and therefore behave in unpredictable ways. Divine being and cosmic continuity may surprise by a sudden influence of tychism, and so may the human mind. In response to Raposa, I therefore argue that Peirce's relatedness to the philosophy of the later Schelling suggests a stronger systematic emphasis on Peirce's doctrine of tychism and thereby provides a convincing explanation of Peirce's epistemic blindness. In short, it connects the epistemic blindness to Peirce's doctrine of tychism. In plainer language, this means that some individual minds do not perceive God because impulse, volition, or unpredictable occurrences determine it to be so. Such things originate in God's Absolute Mind or in the human mind, but are always disruptive enough to thwart the harmony of the evolutionary process of growth in the knowledge of God.

A Peircean Theology of Divine Potentialities: Robert Corrington

With a critical consideration of traditional theism in the context of exploring the possibilities of a constructive Peircean theology, another interesting alternative to traditional theism is provided by Corrington. His Peircean theology draws significantly on Schelling's theory of God's three potencies. Although Corrington's theological construction is fueled by a very critical assessment of the "patriarchal tyranny of the three Western monotheisms,"[83] it is in fact much more constructive than critical. Focusing on a positive alternative to monotheism, Corrington proposes a religious metaphysics which is rooted in a deep religious consciousness and supposedly pre-dating all categorial classifications. Employing something like a semiotic naturalism, Corrington engages a meditative theology whose

---

[82] Ibid., 40.

[83] Robert S. Corrington, *A Semiotic Theory of Theology and Philosophy* (Cambridge: Cambridge University Press, 2000) x.

object is the movement of the cosmic potencies that reside at the deepest level of the universe. His goal is for individuals to become aware of these divine and natural movements of the cosmos. Such a religious consciousness of the individual is only possible, however, in so far as it is embedded in the deep unconscious of the universe itself. That is, in order to awaken one's religious consciousness, it is not enough to establish a living contact with the unconscious life of one's own being; rather, it is necessary also to tap into the pre-categorial movements of the soul of the cosmos and to join a collective experience of the universe. What could be called a religious process of individual selving (becoming a self) is a partaking in the process of cosmic selving, or, in Corrington's terminology, *natura naturans*. This process is a deeply religious experience of melting into the self-renewing, or self-othering, emergence of nature. Because "the human unconscious has shown itself to be the gateway to the underconscious of nature, to the potencies of *nature naturing*,"[84] one has to allow oneself to sink into the underconscious of the universe. This is the central theme of Corrington's proposal of a religious metaphysics in replacement of traditional forms of theist metaphysics.

Although Corrington's metaphysics relies on Peirce's semiotic theory, its religious frame is determined by insights from Schelling's teaching on God's divine potencies. Corrington's argument is that Peirce uses "the potency theory, via his infinitesimals, to explain aspects of novelty and growth"[85] (i.e. the notion of absolute chance, or tychism), by reference to the underconscious pulsation of the universe which brings forth the new and the unexpected. Schelling's divine potencies are, Corrington says, "more like Peirce's infinitesimals; namely, as prespatial, pretemporal, and presemiotic powers awaiting a sudden entrance into the world of orders;"[86] they are the "underlying unruly ground"[87] of all reality. In short, amalgamating Peirce's semiotic and Schelling's theory of God's three potencies, Corrington constructs a semiotic cosmology of religious dimensions, in support of a metaphysics "which speaks of the holy or numinous that represents a fully natural process of sacred semiotic folds impacting on the human unconscious."[88]

---

[84] Ibid., 245.
[85] Ibid.
[86] Ibid.
[87] Ibid., 85.
[88] Ibid., 61.

Some Critical Questions to Robert Corrington

There is one particularly problematic aspect of Corrington's application of Schelling's potency theory to Peirce's semiotic, namely that Schelling's account of the principle of volition and divine freedom goes largely unmentioned. For Schelling, the potencies are permanently subject to the reality of pure volition, the absolutely free will of God, or the divine *purus actus*—which is precisely not a potency, but simply and purely volition. If Corrington is to apply the full insight of Schelling's model, and if he wants to explain the self-emergent universe as grounded in something like Schelling's three potencies, then I miss an account of the reality of pure volitional freedom, to which the potencies must show permanent submission.

Addressing the issue of volition, Corrington argues that when the unconscious emerges in the process of *natura naturans*, it only *appears* to happen by virtue of deliberation, choice, volition, and the pursuit of ends. Deliberation has no reality in and of itself. For Corrington, the difference between ends and origins is intentionally blurred, for "ends are always and already consummated,"[89] which is to say that will, choice, and deliberation are only eruptions of dormant powers awaiting the opportunity to emerge. In its stage of emergence, a deliberately chosen end is already consummated and thereby part of its own origin. Thus, the novel is always potentially there, either as dormant, awakening, or actually erupting, and as erupted it is already part of the eternal reality and unity of all there is. Hence, novelty is barely more than a matter of perception, and a matter of where in the evolutionary process one's attention is focused, for evolving process in and of itself is in fact the best description of the cosmic whole.

By virtue of its constructive nature, Corrington's religious metaphysics need not, of course, observe its inspirational sources in detail, and he makes no promises of attempting to do so. Still, the need for a more comprehensive account of the creative impulses of the universe remains unmet. In Schelling's own speculative metaphysics and the argumentation behind it, it is important for him to demonstrate why it is systematically necessary to acknowledge the need for a metaphysical principle of volition in order to facilitate freedom from the restrictive and repetitive movements that a system of triadic relatedness inevitably produces. In critique of Hegel, this is the logical conclusion that marks the transition from Schelling's earlier to Schelling's later philosophy (i.e. from a system of cosmic naturalism to

---

[89] Ibid., 205.

a system of metaphysical voluntarism[90]). It is precisely his theory of the three divine potencies that becomes a response to the need for a system of complete identity of mind and matter to be emancipated from its own inner circularity. In my judgment, the ambition of Schelling's earlier work is not unlike that of Corrington's religious metaphysics with its doctrine of a self-emerging cosmic universe. Therefore, Schelling's concern about a Hegelian-fashioned absolutism is not unlike the concern one might have about Corrington's religious metaphysics. Unless the eternal process of divine self-transformation and cosmic evolution is conceived in submission to the reality of pure initiation, free will, and volition, it is indeed best likened to a worm incessantly eating its own tail, gaining neither death nor life, because its tail keeps growing back. As Schelling concludes about systems of undisturbed identity of mind and matter, its *inner life* needs emancipation.[91] In regard to Peirce's philosophical system, the same conclusion is already drawn there too, namely that the doctrine of synechism is always in tension with the doctrine of tychism because a supposedly undisturbed identity of mind and matter will always be disrupted by the disturbing reality of chance events.

Once again, we have returned to the conclusion that a Peircean theology must involve an account of the metaphysical significance of volition. Hence, moving next to a constructive formulation of such a theology, we turn to a discussion of the possibility of arguing for a Peircean theology of anticipation.

A Peircean Theology of Anticipation

In the following I explore a constructive interpretation of Peirce's theological position as an alternative both to a Peircean theosemiotic and a Peircean theology of divine potentialities. This alternative relies on conclusions from chapters two and three, with the purpose of letting these conclusions

---

[90] What is traditionally described as Schelling's earlier philosophy covers the time period from his *Ideen zu einer Philosophie der Natur* [Ideas for a philosophy of nature] (1797) to the work that has gone down to history under the name of *Identitätsphilosophie: Darstellung meines Systems* [Philosophy of identity: an account of *my* system] (1801). During these few years, Schelling slowly distances himself from the subjective idealism of J. G. Fichte (whom he both admires and critiques), and finally breaks away from him by launching his own philosophic system, *Natur- und Identitätsphilosophie* [Philosophy of nature and identity]. This early period of Schelling's thought is characterized by the attempt at a systematic demonstration of his conviction that mind and matter, freedom and necessity, are only different aspects of the same entirety. See *Justifying Speculative Metaphysics*, 67ff.

[91] See *Schelling's Theory of God's Three Potencies*, 63ff.

merge with the argument that Christian hope is most appropriately defined as anticipatory hope. In other words, I propose a Peircean theology of anticipation by merging Peirce's theory of abduction (identified as an embodiment of the principle of anticipation, and set in the frame of metaphysical voluntarism) with the notion of anticipatory, Christian hope.

Theism, perhaps in the form of a theosemiotic, may be an accurate reflection of Peirce's religious position, but if we want to explore the theological possibilities of Peirce's insights, there is still more to be said. Considering abductive reasoning to include the religious experience of belief in God's reality, Peirce offers the beginning of an alternative position to classical theism as well as to a Peircean theosemiotic. Following the earlier conclusion that Peirce must consider the metaphysical significance of the principle of volition together with its role in the process of abductive reasoning, then we must say that the notion of will, choice and deliberation has direct bearings on how we determine the nature of a Peircean theology. Keeping in mind the intimate relatedness of volition and anticipation helps support a Peircean theology in the form of a theology of anticipation. In any case, it is my contention that we now have an argumentative cluster strong enough to support a Peircean theology of anticipation. Therefore, we now turn to Peirce's argument for abductive reasoning as guarantor for the religious experience of God's reality, with particular view to the way this argument embodies the principles of volition and anticipation.

Abductive Reasoning as Guarantor for Religious Experience

Peirce detests denominational "formulas invented to exclude some Christians from communion with others" (*CP* 6.445), but he just as passionately believes that true religion is based on an instinctive, true encounter with God's reality. This manner of encountering God is simply a higher and more reliable source of knowing God than reliance on any one—among all the many—existing opinions about God. Furthermore, an instinctive and true encounter with God's reality is only possible when it is truly abductive. It involves the one God before whom all believers fall down in adoration, and it has nothing to do with the God of denominational or individual creeds, "whether it be that of Trent, Lambeth, Geneva, or what" (*CP* 6.450). For Peirce, the truly religious experience of God's reality is means of avoiding the impasses of unnecessary denominational disputes. The problem is, however, that experiential encounters with God are short-lived in their purity because they immediately turn into objects of interpretations that increase both in number and complexity, resulting in what we know and struggle with as denominational differences—and ultimately even religious wars. Hence, considering Peirce's references to various traditional conceptions of God should only happen in so far as they are "functions of instinct,"[92] as Anderson formulates it. This echoes the earlier thesis that Peirce might not be as directly interested in an argument for the specifically Christian God's reality as for the religious experience as such. Therefore, if we want to understand and evaluate Peirce's theological position, we must assume a narrow focus on his method of the religious experience, which involves his theory of abduction and the discipline of what he calls Musement. Lacking the religious experience, Peirce says, should make a person "wait quietly until such experience comes. No amount of speculation can take the place of experience" (*CP* 1.655). The alternative to speculation is engagement with the discipline of Musement, and when the religious experience of God's reality manifests, then one is a witness to the ultimate instance of abduction. The extent, therefore, to which Peirce's experiential method of religious experience and his theory of abduction might support, compromise, or revoke his theism is an interesting question to pursue. First, though, to the discipline of Musement.

Musement

Quietly waiting for an encounter with God is not a passive state of being but involves a very real exercise of pursuing God in something like meditative expectation or mental play with ideas that avoid presumptuous and strenuous reasoning. Explaining the significance of this mental play in the pursuit of a religious encounter with God, Peirce gives the admonition to "push off into the lake of thought, and leave the breath of heaven to swell your sail" (*EP* 2.437). Doing this, he explains, is to follow "certain lines of reflection which will inevitably suggest the hypothesis of God's Reality" (*EP* 2.439). Asking us, therefore, to join in a playful meditation on the extraordinary vastness of the universe, perhaps during a leisurely walk at night, looking "at the stars in the silence, thinking how each successive increase in the aperture of a telescope makes many more of them visible" (*CP* 6.501), Peirce argues that if we "drink in such thoughts . . . without any special purpose . . . The idea of there being a God over it all of course will be often suggested" (*CP* 6.501). And this is where the Pure Play of Musement begins to take effect in a person's mind by allowing the idea of God to sink in, for "the more he considers it, the more he will be enwrapt with Love of this idea. He will ask himself whether or not there really is a

---

[92] Anderson, *Strands of System*, 139.

God. If he allows instinct to speak, and searches his own heart, he will at length find that he cannot help believing it" (*CP* 6.501). Although Peirce feels "half-inclined to call it reverie with some qualification . . . for a frame of mind so antipodal to vacancy and dreaminess, such a designation would be too excruciating a misfit" (*CP* 6.458). Peirce informs us that the term Musement is equivalent rather to speculation in the form of *deep thinking*, a term he borrows from Friedrich Schiller's aesthetics, more specifically his notion of *Spieltrieb* (play instinct). So, Schiller's understanding of this instinct, inner drive, or something like a natural force of playfulness, is exactly what Musement embodies when it accounts for the mind's quiet ability to play with ideas that hardly exist but then gradually emerge and become conscious to the Muser when he or she allows this instinctive and fragile playfulness to take its course.

Peirce of course refuses pursuing experiences of God with a presumptuous attitude. It is simply not possible to provoke an encounter with God, for it must happen in a certain kind of detached expectation which is free to receive any idea that may or may not come. An idea that wishes to emerge can do so, and the Muser is ready to acknowledge it. Subsequently, he or she is then free to reason deductively about the logically possible implications of this idea, or to test its validity inductively. The power of Musement to bring about an encounter with the reality of God is precisely its lack of a specific purpose and so Musement is most likely to start with some experience, or "*petite bouchée* with the Universes [in] the form of æsthetic contemplation, or that of distant castle-building (whether in Spain or within one's own moral training)" (*CP* 6.458). When the Muser conceives the idea "God is real," one can describe Musement as a mental dream catcher that does not produce a full-blown conception of God unless it is also assisted by deductive and inductive reasoning.

Describing this deliberate discipline and rational application of Musement, Peirce concludes that the hypothesis "God is real" is the most astonishingly plausible abductive hypothesis that Musement can produce. In spite of its imprecise nature, "the Plausibility of the hypothesis reaches an almost unparalleled height among deliberately formed hypotheses" (*CP* 6.488). Before we know it, we have faith. The reverence Peirce has for God is reverence for belief and instinctive faith in its most raw and unspoiled form; the paradox Peirce thereby affirms is that instinctive knowledge of God exhibits the highest possible degree of persuasiveness *by virtue of its vagueness*. In fact, Peirce continues, the result is a religious experience that makes it so hard "to doubt God's Reality, when the Idea has sprung from Musements, that there is great danger that the investigation will stop at this first stage, owing to the indifference of the Muser to any further proof of it" (*CP* 6.488). There is no reason to feel satisfied with the experience itself, however, for the hypothesis of God's Reality is logically connected with an epistemological theory, and more precisely the theory of abduction. The vague hypothesis of God's reality is nothing less than an "instance of Retroduction, undeniable as this character is" (*CP* 6.488),[93] and it should have utmost attention from anyone concerned with philosophical epistemology and the role it plays in theological reflection. The way, then, that Musement relates to abduction and has a place in theological reflection is the following. In the process of formulating and suggesting a hypothesis in response to some surprising fact, there may not be the immediate presence of a convincing hypothesis, and then the Pure Play of Musement must be activated in search of such a hypothesis. Theologically, this is to say that the *surprising fact* of an experiential encounter with God comes *after* one has initiated and engaged the discipline of Musement. Even then, the encounter is distinctly vague because the attributes of the God one encounters, are distinctly vague. God's reality is, in other words, only real in its *expected*, or its anticipated, form.

Anticipating Divine Reality: Vagueness as Hope

As Peirce's description of Musement indicates, the abductive idea of God's reality is exceptionally paradox in nature because it is both vague and reliable. And so it should be. True, we are allowed to "attach traditional attributes to God . . . [but only] as long as we understand them to have an appropriate vagueness themselves."[94] To the extent, then, that Peirce defends God's vagueness, the traditionally theist claim to God's "omniscience, omnipotence, and infinite benignity" (*MS* 843.12) must be compromised. And so must the traditionally theist arguments for God's existence, which is not unrelated to the fact that Peirce continually refers to the argument for God's reality, rather than the argument for God's existence. It is not that Peirce makes theist argumentations redundant, but he resolutely subjects them to the fact that the "hypothesis of God is a peculiar one, in that it supposes an infinitely incomprehensible object [and still also] supposes its object to be truly conceived in the hypothesis" (*CP* 6.466). What divine omniscience, omnipotence, goodness, and divine existence are, we can not know, except by hypothetical approximation. We can also employ analogical terms because they retain sufficient vagueness, and because the logic of

---

[93] Peirce uses the term retroduction synonymously with abduction.
[94] Ibid., 139.

abduction is built on resemblance: "The mode of suggestion by which, in abduction, the facts suggest the hypothesis is by resemblance—the resemblance of the facts to the consequences of the hypothesis" (*CP* 7.218).

Just as Peirce argues that "inexplicabilities are not to be considered as possible explanations" (*CP* 6.173), he also argues, as already indicated, that God's vagueness assures God's indubitableness, and that the pursuit of conceptual precisions increases the methodological risk of appropriating false perceptions: "To render any vague proposition more precise is to problematize it, to specify the predictions that can be derived from it, thus making it vulnerable to falsification."[95] The more one wants, the less one gets, and this applies to the proposition "God is real" in a particularly strong way.

Peirce's doctrine of God's vagueness is perhaps best understood in relation to the logic of his semiotic: "A sign is objectively *vague*, in so far as . . . it reserves for some other possible sign or experience the function of completing the determination" (*CP* 5.505). God is such an objectively vague sign, permanently indeterminate and vague. But as we keep in mind that Peirce applies the process of semiosis to the doctrine of synechism and that he identifies semiosis as the structural movement of the cosmic continuum, statements pertaining to the ultimate reality of the cosmos are vague too. That is, in theological *and* metaphysical terms, there is no escaping the vagueness of conceptual statements of one's object, if the pursuit is of true statements. In our constructive context, Peirce's logic of vagueness is yet another element that works in support of the thesis that his metaphysics, and now also his theology, involves the principle of anticipation. That a metaphysics of anticipation is compatible with Peirce's philosophy of religion, and thereby solidifies the plausibility of a Peircean theology of anticipation, hangs on his application of the logic of vagueness, not just to God but to all of reality. *The present moment contains the reality of God and all of reality only vaguely, but not therefore less indubitably, and within the very vagueness of divine and cosmic reality lies the promise of their indubitableness.* Even though "the inquirer is unable definitely to formulate just what the explained wonder is" (*CP* 6.469), the paradox that vagueness embodies indubitableness turns such a hypothetical explanation into a reliable promise. There is qualified reason to trust that what is only vaguely believed to be real rests on more than wishful thinking about its potential future reality; it rests on the anticipatory hope that its future

---

[95] See Raposa, *Peirce's Philosophy of Religion*, 131.

reality is, in fact, already real and present prior to its actualization. The promise of its future reality enables its anticipation.

Returning to Peirce's emphasis on the religious experience, the certain and anticipated reality of God always comes to the Muser in the form of an ever growing sensation that can not let go of God's vagueness, for religious knowledge is experiential and therefore inseparable from the fact that "emotion *is* vague, incomprehensible thought, [which] is why the highest truths can only be felt" (*MS* 891). Musement is a form of anticipation that has at its very core the experiential encounter with God, and this encounter may produce puzzling and paradoxical statements about God, but does not therefore make God less real. Therefore Peirce classifies "the *vague* . . . as that to which the principle of contradiction does not apply" (*CP* 5.505). The sense of contradiction that it involves to take for real in the present what is only to be real at some point in the future is simply of no logical significance for the person who is experientially related to that reality, be it of cosmic, divine, or any other nature. The vagueness involved in this contradiction is the very thing by which reality is qualified as real.

The Anticipatory Nature of *The Neglected Argument for the Reality of God*

The Neglected Argument for the Reality of God is technically fashioned as a nest of three: the humble argument, the neglected argument, and an unnamed but still explicated third argument. The humble argument, Peirce says, is "open to every honest man, which I surmise to have made more worshippers of God than any other" (*CP* 6.486). Perhaps because it is "that entirely honest, sincere and unaffected, because unprepense, meditation upon the Idea of God, into which the Play of Musement will inevitably sooner or later lead, and which, by developing a deep sense of the adorability of that Idea, will produce a truly religious Belief" (*CP* 6.486). This first of the three arguments is simply the product of the discipline of Musement. It comes in the form of a quietly emerging belief in God and has a strikingly irrefutable plausibility. The second argument has received its name because "the caste of theologians" (*CP* 6.3)[96] has neglected the force of the first argument and therefore refrained from formulating a proper "apology—a vindicatory description—of the mental operations which the Humble Argument actually and actively lives out" (*CP* 6.487). That is, the second argument (the neglected argument proper) unfolds in

---

[96] This term is used in a context where Peirce criticizes the negative influence of theologians on the discipline of metaphysics.

the form of an objective description of the mechanics of the humble argument, but without "going into original logical researches" (*CP* 6.484), and therefore without trying to explain and logically qualify the humble argument. The third (unnamed) argument, too, relates to the humble argument. Not apologetically but as "a study of logical methodeutic, illuminated by the light of a first-hand acquaintance with genuine scientific thought" (*CP* 6.488). The third argument, then, identifies the humble argument as an example of retroduction, or abduction, and explains how the humble argument is "nothing but an instance of the first stage of all such work" (*CP* 6.488) (i.e. scientific inquiry). In short, Peirce's nest of three arguments for God's reality means to serve the purpose of developing a rationally qualified argument for God's reality, rather than just remaining satisfied with the practical belief in God, as already acquired through Musement. Still, the humble argument is "the innermost of the nest" (*CP* 6.483), and unfolds as a rationally substantiated elaboration of Musement.

Introducing the N.A., it is important for Peirce to emphasize the distinction between an argument and what he classifies as argumentations: "An 'Argument' is any process of thought reasonably tending to produce a definite belief. An 'Argumentation' is an Argument proceeding upon definitely formulated premisses" (*CP* 6.456), to which belong the more traditional conceptions of God and theist arguments for God's existence. In order to have an argument, one does not need to argue deductively (by necessity) or inductively (by testing). Any possible thought process will do, if only it results in a belief of definite nature—including, therefore, plausible hypotheses, which qualify as arguments without further ado. That Peirce favors the argument, as opposed to argumentations, reflects the fact that he takes "the liberty of substituting 'reality' for 'existence'" (*CP* 6.495). This matter, moreover, relates back to his theory of the three categories. As he says, "I myself always use *exist* in its strict philosophical sense of 'react with the other like things in the environment.' Of course, in that sense, it would be fetichism to say that God 'exists'" (*CP* 6.495). For Peirce to argue for God's existence would reduce God to the category of Secondness, or the realm of brute reaction, and this would not only rob God of intelligibility, or Thirdness. It would also exclude experiences of God from occurring throughout the full expanse of the universe, which, of course, embodies all three categories. Also, how can Musement be what it is and not be open to all categorial aspects of reality?

Peirce strives to keep traditional arguments for God's existence at a distance by setting abduction down as the cornerstone of his argument, thereby refusing to claim God's reality by deductive and inductive reasoning in isolation from experiential reasoning. For, as he quite simply asks, "Where would such an idea, say as that of God, come from, if not from direct experience?"[97] Peirce's uncomplicated reliance on the experiential mode of happening upon rationally qualifiable ideas explains how an argument, as opposed to an argumentation, is fundamentally dependent upon the practical exercises of Musement and only subsequently carried out during the process of abductive reasoning. So, even though abductive reasoning can never exceed hypothetical plausibility as its level of rational certainty, it is the irrefutable plausibility of the abductive hypothesis that makes it more reliable than purely rational proofs are certain. With this move, Peirce demonstrates how the deductive and inductive modes of reasoning (which traditional argumentations limit), must be *functions* of abductive reasoning, not superior to it. He summarizes, "all I have been saying is not preparatory to any argument for the reality of God. It is intended as an apology for resting the belief upon instinct as the very bedrock on which all reasoning must be built" (*CP* 6.500). The important thing about the experiential is, as Hermann Deuser also explains, "that God's reality (of the concept of God or of the idea of God) is rightly conceived only when related to the experiential situations, in which that becomes evident, which reason alone can generate as mere abstraction."[98] Keep in mind, however, that Peirce launches the N.A. in order not to leave instinctive and experiential faith on its own (which would leave faith eventually succumbing to simplicity). To say that rational faith, or abstractions of experiential

---

[97] Some contend that Peirce's argument uses elements from traditional arguments for God's existence. For example, Donna M. Orange argues that Peirce's humble argument "closely resembles the argument from design" (Orange, *Peirce's Conception of God: A Developmental Study*, Peirce Studies 2 [Lubbock, TX: Institute for Studies in Pragmaticism, 1984] 78), and that the N.A. proper can easily be seen as a variation of "Anselm's ontological argument which required the existence of God in order to think the concept of God" (ibid., 78). Also, she continues, the fact that Peirce employs the word "God" as definitely "signifying *Ens necessarium*" (*CP* 6.452) is hardly probable without first "thinking of the 'third way' of the *Summa Theologiae* (1a, qu. 2, art.3), the argument from the being of contingent beings to that of a necessary one" (Orange, *Peirce's Conception of God*, 79). In my judgment, however, it is as difficult to deny the differences as the similarities between Peirce's argument and traditional ones, because of his diligent integration of the experiential.

[98] Hermann Deuser, *Gott: Geist und Natur: Theologische Konsequenzen aus Charles S. Peirce's Religionsphilosophie* [God: spirit and nature: theological consequences of Charles S. Peirce's philosophy of religion] (Berlin: de Gruyter, 1993) 28; translation mine. In the original: "dass die Realität Gottes (des Gottesbegriffs oder der Gottesidee) erst richtig gedacht wird bezogen auf die Erfahrungssituationen, in denen evident wird, was das Denken allein nur als Abstraktion erzeugen kann."

belief, is *merely* a function of instinctive faith, is for him just as erroneous. Experiential faith, and experiential reasoning with it, should not be left to itself, but nor should we attempt to argue deductively and inductively without situating those rational efforts directly on the experiential.

One of the incentives behind the present study of Peirce's religious writing is to explore how his theory of abduction needs to unlock some of the problems encountered in the ongoing attempts to reconcile the disciplines of philosophy and theology. Based on the discussion of Musement and Peirce's N.A., I suggest some constructive conclusions in response to this incentive. Peirce's way of assimilating experiential reasoning into purely rational and abstractive reasoning has direct bearings on a possible integration of practical theology and the theoretical disciplines of philosophy and science. The reason is his claim that experiential faith in God should rank with the theoretical—and the fact that, for Peirce, experiential faith is a fundamentally necessary requirement in order even to get the rational enterprise started in the first place. Furthermore, by placing the humble argument in his triadic epistemological scheme, as the third kind of reasoning (abduction), Peirce invites experientially established belief in God into the world of his philosophical architectonic. Even though he argues that God is "*Really* creator" (*CP* 6.452),[99] his argument is not straightforwardly for belief in the God who has created that upon which scientists and philosophers reflect. This would be more like a call for them to humbly ascribe their own existence to the creator of the universe. Although he does affirm that God is "Really creator of all three Universes of Experience" (*CP* 6.452),[100] Peirce's argument is rather that belief in God is but one instance, among all possible instances, of abduction. There is absolutely no legitimate reason to exclude experiential belief in God from the class of rational arguments, for just as any hypothetical knowledge is rationally valid knowledge—if it is plausible—so is hypothetical knowledge of God. In other words, if one were to exclude instinctive belief in God from the realm of reasoning, the very foundation of the rational enterprise itself would be eliminated too. *Philosophical reflection can always be undertaken on its own, and without giving any thought to the reality of God, but it can not therefore close the door to practical faith in God's reality without closing the door to itself.*

---

[99] Italics mine.

[100] This reference to the three universes of experience appears at the beginning of Peirce's N.A. Obviously, he refers to the phenomenological categories of Firstness, Secondness, and Thirdness and insists that God can be experienced in all three categorial realms (or *universes*).

Another incentive behind the present study of Peirce's religious writing is to inquire about the extent to which it supports a position of theism. In order to suggest what the result of this inquiry might be, we first reconsider some of the conclusions from the comparison of Peirce and the later Schelling. One focal point of this comparison was Peirce's struggle to integrate the philosophical and the religious components of his architectonic. We concluded that this struggle relates to Peirce's unrecognized acknowledgement of the systematic importance of the principle of volition. Peirce does not address this importance exhaustively. Nor does he glean from his sporadic readings of Schelling's philosophy that *he* has already acknowledged the importance of volition. As already commented, this blind spot is probably related to Peirce's ignorance about the shift in Schelling's philosophy that separates his earlier writings from the later. A shift that occurs exactly because Schelling faces a systematic need to acknowledge the metaphysical significance of the principle of volition, and because he resolves to integrate it.

Evaluating the theist nature of Peirce's N.A. by reconsidering Schelling's later work becomes even more relevant if we add a reconsideration of the systematic tension in Peirce's philosophy between synechism and tychism (i.e. his struggles to account for the reality of absolute chance (tychism) in a universe whose permanence is secured by the doctrine that everything is continuous (synechism)). Although tychism is, of course, conceivable apart from any influence of volition, the reverse is inconceivable. Anything volitional involves tychism, for there can be no continuous past to something that finds its beginning in an instance of volitional initiation. The moment something is motivated by pure will and initiation, there will be occurrences it is impossible to account for by some preceding, causal relatedness or evolutionary development within the cosmic continuum. In Peirce's architectonic system, tychism functions as a doctrinal designation of the metaphysical reality of volition.

Using the insights drawn earlier from Schelling's theory of God's three potencies, clarifies the tension of synechism and tychism in the N.A. and how this tension involves the principle of volition. For Schelling, God's will in its purity is hidden behind God's reality. It is truly a principle above everything else, even above the part of God that consists of the divine potencies. God's will is *not* a potency, but the motivational power behind and beyond the potencies, so that even when God's divine potencies manifest to human experience, God's will is not experienced as will, because divine volition is never a will to anything specific. This means that God's will can only be experienced indirectly (i.e. by an encounter with the erupting or emerging potencies). But even then it is the triad of the potencies that one encounters, not the initiating power behind them. We can experience the potencies as they manifest, but the motivational power behind them escapes us.[101]

Considering such relatedness of will and potency in the context of Peirce's N.A., it appears to me that for him, just as for Schelling, it is impossible to relate directly to the volitional part of God, even—and perhaps especially—in the midst of experiencing an irrefutably plausible knowledge of God's reality. The Muser simply experiences unquestionable faith. Not faith in a God with the will to something specific, but a God who has made the volitional effort to reveal the highest point of view. This highest point of view is, as we recall, that of simple, divine love. Reference has already been made to the part of Peirce's N.A. where he describes the divine purpose that propels the evolutionary development of the cosmos as nothing but the simple love of God. In this new context, my point is that as God's will sets in motion a manifestation of God's divine reality—and as the Muser is in a position to receive it—God's will shows itself a necessary ingredient for a revelation of God's love. But, this new context also reveals God's love as nothing but a simple *falling into place* of the intended and purposed order of the universe, and this includes a natural, even necessary, relatedness of divine and human.

Theologically, Peirce's N.A. introduces us to a God of love who is in need of something to facilitate self-manifestation, and divine volition provides this power of initiation. The N.A. ultimately is no specifically theological argument, but rather an elaborated argument for why the theory of abduction should *not* be disregarded as a philosophical qualifier of religious instinct and knowledge of God. This makes it no surprise to find that what we consider theological insights drawn from Peirce's religious writing are deeply embedded in his philosophical architectonic. The N.A. embodies the doctrine of synechism and tychism, and attached to tychism also the principle of volition. Tychism explains the effortless and spontaneous growth of religious belief and turns out to insist that Musement makes room for God to manifest. Paradoxically, however, what Musers are then in a position to receive is faith in the God of the divine continuum, which is to say that they find themselves irrevocably *related* to God by faith. This relatedness is alone possible because of divine volition. Hence, the essential complexity of Peircean faith is this: the Muser who enters a state of faith

---

[101] The insight from Schelling that God's potencies only relate indirectly to God's reality in its entirety (i.e. including God's divine will) is the element Corrington does not emphasize in his constructive suggestion of a Peircean theology of divine potentialities.

does not experience a volitionally imposing God (of tychism), but rather a synechist God of love. At the same time, he or she can not possibly have faith without God also embodying divine tychism. This way, God is more real than existent, because divine volition enables a person to experience God as a synechist reality. Again, this reflects the fact that Peirce argues for God's reality, not for God's existence.

Now, what can these insights say about the condition of the *Muser* as far as volition is concerned? Peirce emphasizes that effective Musers do not engage their will, but rather assume a posture of purposeless indifference. They meditate "without any special purpose" (*CP* 6.501). A Muser's volitional faculty is only supposed to be engaged for the purpose of holding itself back; otherwise, God can neither initiate self-manifestation, nor be experienced. In other words, engaging divine volition presupposes *dis*engagement of human volition. In a certain sense, then, Musement is both a controlled and an un-controlled rational exercise. It is controlled play with the spontaneous, and in fact a way for an earlier question to reappear, namely the question of the role of volition in the process of abductive reasoning. We shall now give this question some thought by reintroducing it in a theological context.

Peirce can make Musement the foundation of the N.A. because he has already argued that abductive knowledge is warranted only by plausibility. The reason Musement can be trusted is that the knowledge of God that it produces is qualified by a logic of plausibility, not a logic of necessity. The warranty of abduction as well as that of faith in God hangs on the qualifying instincts of plausibility. Now, in so far as abduction is an instance of anticipation, we can identify Peirce's N.A. as an instance of anticipation too. First, anticipation considers plausible in the present what can only answer to its own plausibility if and when the future will reveal it to be not only plausible, but also true. It relies on a reality that still belongs to the future, and that therefore can not possibly be more than plausible in the present. With the N.A., the experience of faith in God is anticipatory because it is conditioned by the humble activity of Musing reliance on God's reality without knowing it and without having experienced it. The experience of faith in God also embodies the reality of a promise in the form, I suggest, of the intended order of the universe. This promise is the love of God, with whom it is cosmically natural to relate. This defines the present moment of faith by the spontaneous emergence of belief in a God who is known as a divine reality, rather than a volitionally imposing being. This is nothing other than anticipatory hope: a qualified reason to believe in a God whose full revelation still belongs to the future. With this,

I suggest that the element of promise that anticipation always includes is, in Peirce's N.A., secured by the implied doctrine of synechism. The reason someone will actually assume a posture of meditative Musement, as well as the reason why faith in God will eventually emerge, are both contained in the doctrine that everything is continual and that therefore relatedness of the divine and the human is cosmically natural. Now, a theology of anticipation defends this relatedness to God as always and still inherently a promise of fulfilment regarding the future. Such reliance upon the future is, moreover, secured by the involvement of the doctrine of tychism in the N.A., because the spontaneous, the unpredictable, the mystery, and the hiddenness of God are core realities of relatedness to God. No encounter with God, nor any implied experience of faith in God's reality, can be *more* than anticipatory, simply because no one can possibly have sufficient means of predicting—or of having *ontological knowledge* about—the future and what it may or may not reveal about God. Because there is divine volition behind and beyond the synechist harmony of the universe (which includes the naturalness of the human and the divine in relationship), some aspect of God is always inaccessible to human beings. Theologically, these reflections mirror a situation where God can only be partially experienced in the present, but where that in no way compromises the reliability or scope of a person's faith. In fact, it is faith in its simplest and unadulterated form that is most reliable and unshakable. The dominating experience is one of simply knowing God to be real without knowing, understanding, or experiencing God's particular will in any given situation. Now, this is not to say that God's particular will about certain things can not be known, pursued, or expected to manifest. Quite the opposite. After all, believers are often engaged in a frustrating struggle to decipher God's immediate and particular will and then in hindsight find that simple faith in God took them down the path of that concrete will, even though they did not understand it as such. It is engagement in the activity of Musement long and indifferently enough that allows the instincts of faith to lead a person down the path of God's very specific will. Peirce's post-Musement activities of deductive and inductive reasoning should establish this as true.

These reflections help us briefly evaluate Peirce's theism. If Peirce is a theist, then he is hardly a traditional theist. Because of a consistently nudging possibility of experiencing God's reality, God and human beings are more fundamentally related than fundamentally different. Traditional theism emphasizes their difference at the expense of their relatedness. For Peirce, rational inquirers go through a process of experiential training that involves exercising the skills of abductive reasoning; this prepares inquirers to enter the receptive posture of Musement. Traditional theism is much less concerned than Peirce with the relational and experiential foundation of knowing God, and it does not match Peirce's level of investment in explanations of how important experiential faith is for processes of reasoning itself. Contrary to what one might think, however, Peirce's system does not compromise the freedom of the theist God. Freedom is an integrated part of the rational process itself in a way it is not, for the traditional theist position. Admittedly, in Peirce's theology, there is not as deep a gulf between God as creator and human beings as creatures. The Peircean God is less distant, and certainly the doctrine of synechism ensures this. But in so far as Peirce also upholds the doctrine of tychism, his theology does not compromise God's volitional freedom. In fact, the power of volitional initiation has a prominent status in the way God relates to human beings, even though Peirce's volitional God is less distant, less unpredictable, and less hidden than the traditional theist God. Paradoxically, God is *more* of all of these things for Peirce. That is, the traditionally theist attributes are critical elements of the relational and experiential way of knowing God intimately; they are the vehicles of intimate relatedness to God. A Peircean God must be distant, unpredictable, and hidden, but must be these things in a non-frightening way because it is an intimate acquaintance with God that enables Musers to prepare for encounters with the God who produces in them an unassailable belief in "His Reality and His nearness" (*CP* 6.486). Musers do not have direct experiences of a majestic God whose encountered attributes are omniscience, omnipotence, and pure goodness. Rather, they enter a realm of experiential relatedness to a God with these attributes remaining permanently veiled, mostly incomprehensible, and definitely *vague*. It is no surprise, therefore, to find the following three questions and their answers immediately following the N.A. in a chapter consisting of a list of questions and answers about Peirce's personal belief in God. First, Peirce asks himself, "'Do you believe Him to be omniscient?' Yes, in a vague sense" (*CP* 6.508), he answers. Then he asks, "'Do you believe Him to be Omnipotent?' Undoubtedly He is so, vaguely speaking" (*CP* 6.509). Finally, in a section on the issue of prayer, we find his question about the pure goodness of God: "Why does not this Omniscient Being see the need and interpose the Omnipotent and Supreme Authority to meet the needs prayed for?" (*CP* 6.517). As his lengthy and complex answer indicates, that too is only vaguely clear.

I propose that interpreting Peirce's N.A. as essentially anticipatory supports a Peircean theology of anticipation. In conclusion, therefore, it is tempting to voice some caution about Peirce's critical view, as Donna M.

Orange does when she comments, "Many have been misled . . . by the attempts of theologians to make vague beliefs precise."[102] This final constructive chapter has argued that it is, very precisely, the *anticipatory quality* of God's presence that translates into such passages as when Peirce curiously observes about the hypothesis of God's reality that "the Plausibility of the hypothesis reaches an almost unparalleled height among deliberately formed hypotheses" (*CP* 6.488). It is the experience of God's presence—again, "His Reality and His nearness" (*CP* 6.486)—that turns into a function of promise and becomes the real and substantial reason for investing one's hopes in the plausibility of one's instinctive beliefs. Moreover, it is reality's anticipatory quality that motivates "the dark laboring, the bursting out of the startling conjecture, the remarking of its smooth fitting to the anomaly, as it is turned back and forth like a key in a lock, and the final estimation of its Plausibility" (*CP* 6.469). Struggling to formulate his theory of abduction, I say that Peirce, albeit reluctantly, admits to the preaching of "a sort of logical gospel" (*CP* 6.482), of anticipation. A broader theological application of this "logical gospel" results in a theology of anticipation that builds on the metaphysical contention that all of reality is structurally anticipatory. Perceptive relatedness to the phaneron *and* to God is to experience reality breaking into the present with a promise of ultimate future realization. As Peirce tells us, such an experience always contains an element of utter surprise—but luckily so, for this compels our inner detective to exercise the kind of self-control that leads us to the right explanation. It does not lead in just any direction possible, but always in the right direction, and it is a direction that must be chosen in order to manifest. This is an argument that only the theologian can make, and one that leads more than it misleads, within Peirce's architectonic system.

---

[102] Orange, *Peirce's Conception of God*, 85.

5

Conclusion

How does the narrative of Abraham's faith and life with God belong in the context of a study of Peirce's philosophy? The argument of this book does not aim to apply Old Testament theology to Peirce's philosophy of religion. But, it does aim to give relevance to the involvement of suffering in the life of anticipatory hope. It also aims to demonstrate the applicability of Abraham's experience of such suffering in the context of Peirce's philosophy and epistemological reflections on religious encounter with God. So, Where did this study start? Where did it go? Where did it arrive? Bringing closure to this book's argument, and hopefully also inspiring new dialogue about Peirce's philosophy and the Christian believer's experience of hope, these are three final questions to answer.

Where did this study start? It started with a discussion of the nature of anticipatory hope. Originally inspired by the question of suffering and how to endure it as an integrated part of hope, it began where most experiences of suffering tend to settle, namely with Kant's question: What may I hope? Reflecting on this question, it started with discussions of the notion of anticipation. Both as Kant defines it and as it has been applied and interpreted by other thinkers, in different contexts and for different purposes. Most significantly, however, was the examination of the way Pannenberg conceptualizes anticipation and ambitiously elaborates on its philosophical and theological significance. He does this in pursuit of the vision of reconciling the disciplines of philosophy and theology and of proposing a theological metaphysics of anticipation, an issue this study examined also. As these examinations came to an end, some questions to Pannenberg were still left unanswered. And so we were braced by unanswered questions about the nature of anticipatory hope and ready to embark on a more analytical journey through the philosophy of Peirce, with the goal of searching his thought for answers to them. That is, we knew roughly what we were looking for, and wanted to explore the extent to which Peirce's writings provide it. The leading desire was to find an elaborate philosophical qualification for a systematic theological description of anticipatory hope as it is experienced through faith in the Christian God. With this search, the study began to go somewhere and left the preliminaries behind.

Where did this study go? Here, I first want to express some puzzlement about the fact that Pannenberg has not incorporated or deliberately relied upon Peirce's work. Peirce and Pannenberg generally share the same systematic ambition and both follow the overarching vision of establishing a synthesis between the disciplines of philosophy and theology. What is more, both of them are looking to demonstrate that the scientific and philosophical methods are similar, if not identical. Doing this, they also both claim to demonstrate that the experience of coming to know God is no different than the experience of gaining scientific knowledge—or, in effect, the experience of gaining any knowledge at all. Also, both Peirce and Pannenberg conclude that the rational pursuit of knowledge follows a structure of anticipation, and in their metaphysics this conclusion leads both of them to use anticipation as a structurally primary and leading principle. Pannenberg uses it directly; Peirce uses it indirectly as an integral part of his theory of abduction. So, when Pannenberg's discussion of metaphysics turns into the argument that post-Kantian metaphysical discourse must take the form of a conjectural reconstruction in relation to its object—why does he not seek inspirational counsel in Peirce's work, and especially in his theory of abduction? With its reliance on the notions of regulative hopes and anticipation, would not Peirce's theory of abduction be a sufficiently substantial proposal of a possible frame of thought for legitimate post-Kantian metaphysical reflections? And would not Peirce's N.A. be an obvious candidate for Pannenberg to incorporate, or at least consider, given the fact that he openly seeks to establish a theological metaphysics? A possible reason why Peirce's work goes largely unmentioned by Pannenberg could be the magnitude and ambitious nature of both of their systematic projects. Peirce projects a system as comprehensive as Aristotle's, and Pannenberg conjectures a metaphysics that would "need to be thought through in an exercise at least as elaborate as Whitehead's *Process and Reality*."[1] One of Pannenberg's self-evaluating remarks reflects this level of ambition when he considers Hegel's evaluation of modern theology of such extent "that theology has to be developed on at least the same level of sophistication as Hegel's philosophy."[2] This of course implies

---

[1] Allan Galloway, *Wolfhart Pannenberg* (London: George Allen & Unwin, 1973) 97.

[2] Pannenberg, "An Autobiographical Sketch," 16.

precisely a theology of anticipation which is able to integrate the disciplines of philosophy and theology. This suggestion is also an accomplishment in so far as it enables an integration of the disjointed parts of Peirce's own work and it thereby helps reducing the split between his philosophical and his theological writings. On the matter of Peirce's commitment to the theological discourse, this split has caused significant interpretive ambivalence among Peirce scholars and is, in my opinion, not always productive in discussions of the systematic nature of Peirce's work.

So, what is a Peircean theology of anticipation? And what does anticipation mean now, at this point of concluding our constructive study of Peirce? Anticipation still means taking for real in the present what permanently belongs to the future. But with the insights about the importance of volition and tychism for Peirce's philosophy, there is another aspect to emphasize. Going back to the vocabulary used in the N.A., Peirce here develops the notion of Musement in order to describe the way experiential encounters between God and the human being happen in a manner that brings synechism and tychism into play—which is exactly what happens in anticipation. Stay with the example of the Muser's encounter with God and the anticipatory nature of it. Anticipation of God's reality is only possible if there is something like ontological (and synechist) continuity between a person who exists only in the present moment and God who exists apart from the person, outside the person, and who therefore always remains a reality of the future, for that person. But this description of ontological continuity between God and the human being has already betrayed itself by the involvement it presupposes of (tychist) freedom—on the part of both God and the human being—to decide on some self-controlled activity that brings disruption to the harmonious continuity they enjoy with each other. Yes, the Muser chooses to anticipate God's reality by taking for real in the present the reality of God that always belongs to the future. But the Muser also has to suffer the absence of God who is anticipated because God can, at any given point, choose *not* to respond to any one believer's anticipation.

The principle of volition is at the heart of anticipation and therefore at the heart of a theology of anticipation. It is the core principle of relatedness between the anticipat*or* and anticipat*ed*, which includes the ultimate expression of relatedness between God and human beings. Anticipation is particularly well suited to describe relatedness between one who receives a promise about the future and one who gives the promise—precisely because the receiver, after believing the promise, must endure the suffering which is always involved in the experience of knowing by promise, namely the suffering that is to lack its fulfilment.

This conclusion may remind the reader of the biblical narrative of Abraham. If so, the interpretation of Abraham's life with God, with which this book first started, will have fulfilled its intended role. Incidentally, this role was to anticipate the conclusion of this constructive study of C. S. Peirce.

Bibliography

Works by C. S. Peirce

Collected Papers of Charles Sanders Peirce. Edited by Charles Hartshorne, Paul Weiss, and Arthur Burks. Cambridge: Harvard University Press, 1935, 1958.
The Essential Peirce. Edited by Nathan Houser and Christian Kloesel. Bloomington: Indiana University Press, 1992.
Writings of Charles S. Peirce: A Chronological Edition. Edited by Max Fisch et al. Projected in 30 vols. Bloomington: Indiana University Press, 1982– .
"Uniformity." In *The Dictionary of Philosophy and Psychology*, edited by James Mark Baldwin, 2:727–31. New York: Macmillan, 1901–1905.
"Guessing." *Hound and Horn: A Harvard Miscellany* 21 (1928) 267–83.
The Charles S. Peirce Papers. Microfilm edition. Harvard University Library, Photographic Service, 1966.
The New Elements of Mathematics by Charles S. Peirce. Vols. 1–4. Edited by Carolyn Eisele. The Hague: Mouton, 1976.
Peirce on Signs: Writings on Semiotic by Charles Sanders Peirce. Edited by James Hoopes. Chapel Hill: University of North Carolina Press, 1991.
Semiotic and Significs: The Correspondence between Charles S. Peirce and Victoria Lady Welby. Edited by Charles S. Hardwick. Bloomington: Indiana University Press, 1977.

Other Works

Abbot, Francis Ellingwood. *Scientific Theism*. London: Macmillan, 1885.
Alves, Rubem A. *A Theology of Human Hope*. Washington, DC: Corpus, 1969.
Anderson, Douglas R. "The Evolution of Peirce's Concept of Abduction." *Trans.* 22 (1986) 145–64.
———. *Strands of System: The Philosophy of Charles Peirce*. Indiana: Purdue University Press, 1995.
Apel, Karl-Otto. *Charles S. Peirce: From Pragmatism to Pragmaticism*. Translated by John Michael Krois. Amherst: University of Massachusetts Press, 1881.
Arendt, Hannah. *The Life of the Mind*. 2 vols. New York: Harcourt Brace Jovanovich, 1978.
Aristotle. *Physics*. Vols. 1–2. Translated by W. Charlton. Oxford: Clarendon, 1970.
Barth, Karl. *Rudolf Bultmann: Ein Versuch, ihn zu verstehen*. Theologische Studien 34. Zürich: Evangelischer Verlag, 1952.
———. *The Epistle to the Romans*. Translated by Edwyn C. Hoskyns. London: Oxford University Press, 1963.
Barth, Karl, and Rudolf Bultmann. *Karl Barth–Rudolf Bultmann: Briefwechsel 1922–1966*. Edited by Bernd Jaspert. Zürich: Theologischer Verlag, 1971. ET = Karl Barth—

Rudolf Bultmann Letters, 1922–1966. Edited by Bernd Jaspert. Translated and edited by G. W. Bromiley. Grand Rapids: Eerdmans, 1981.

Bauckham, Richard, and Trevor Hart. *Hope against Hope: Christian Eschatology at the Turn of the Millennium.* Grand Rapids: Eerdmans, 1999.

Beck, Lewis White. *A Commentary on Kant's Critique of Practical Reason.* Chicago: University of Chicago Press, 1960.

van Belle, Gilbert. "Prolepsis in the Gospel of John." *Novum Testamentum* 43 (2001) 334–47.

Bergson, Henri. *Creative Evolution.* Translated by Arthur Mitchell. New York: Modern Library, 1944.

Blachowicz, James A. "Realism and Idealism in Peirce's Categories." *Trans.* 8 (1972) 199–213.

Bloch, Ernst. *The Principle of Hope.* 3 vols. Translated by Neville Plaice, Stephen Plaice, and Paul Knight. Cambridge: MIT Press, 1995.

Boff, Leonardo. *Liberating Grace.* Translated by John Drury. Maryknoll, NY: Orbis, 1979.

Boler, John. "Habits of Thought." In *Studies in the Philosophy of Charles Sanders Peirce.* Second series. Edited by Edward C. More and Richard S. Robin, 382–400. Amherst: University of Massachusetts Press, 1964.

Bowie, Andrew. *Schelling and Modern European Philosophy: An Introduction.* London: Routledge, 1994.

Braaten, Carl E. "Toward a Theology of Hope." *Theology Today* 24 (1967) 208–26.

———. *The Future of God: The Revolutionary Dynamics of Hope.* New York: Harper & Row, 1969.

———, ed. *The Last Things: Biblical and Theological Perspectives on Eschatology.* Grand Rapids: Eerdmans, 2002.

———, and Robert W. Jenson. *The Futurist Option.* New York: Newman, 1970.

Braude, Stephen E. "Peirce on the Paranormal." *Trans.* 34 (1998) 203–24.

Brent, Joseph. *Charles Sanders Peirce: A Life.* Bloomington: Indiana University Press, 1998.

Brogaard, Berit O. "Peirce on Abduction and Rational Control." *Trans.* 35 (1999) 129–55.

Brown, Robert F. *The Later Philosophy of Schelling: The Influence of Boehme on the Works of 1809–1815.* Cranbury: Associated University Presses, 1977.

Brumbaugh, Robert S. "Applied Metaphysics: Truth and Passing Time." *Review of Metaphysics* 19 (1965) 647–66.

Brunning, Jacqueline, and Paul Forster, eds. *The Rule of Reason.* Toronto: University of Toronto Press, 1997.

Buber, Martin. *Between Man and Man.* Translated by Ronald Gregor Smith. London: Macmillan, 1965.

Buhr, Manfred. "Der religiöse Ursprung und Charakter der Hoffnungsphilosophie Ernst Blochs." *Deutsche Zeitschrift für Philosophie* 6 (1958) 576–98.

———. "Kritische Bemerkungen zu Ernst Bloch's Hauptwerk 'Das Prinzip Hoffnung.'" *Deutsche Zeitschrift für Philosophie* 8 (1960) 365–78.

Burton, Robert G. "The Problem of Control in Abduction." *Trans.* 36 (2000) 149–56.

Buzzelli, Donald E. "The Argument of Peirce's 'New List of Categories.'" *Trans.* 8 (1972) 63–89.

Capps, Walter H. "Mapping the Hope Movement." In *The Future of Hope,* edited by Walter H. Capps, 1–49. Philadelphia: Fortress, 1970.

———. *Time Invades the Cathedral: Tensions in the School of Hope.* Philadelphia: Fortress Press, 1972.

Clayton, Philip. "Anticipation and Theological Method." In *The Theology of Wolfhart Pannenberg,* edited by Carl E. Braaten and Philip Clayton, 122–50. Minneapolis: Augsburg, 1988.

Colapietro, Vincent M. *Peirce's Approach to the Self: A Semiotic Perspective on Human Subjectivity.* New York: State University of New York Press, 1989.

Cone, James H. *A Black Theology of Liberation.* New York: Orbis, 1986.

Corrington, Robert S. *An Introduction to C. S. Peirce: Philosopher, Semiotician, and Ecstatic Naturalist.* Boston: Rowman & Littlefield, 1993.

———. *A Semiotic Theory of Theology and Philosophy.* Cambridge: Cambridge University Press, 2000.

Cousins, Ewert H., ed. *Hope and the Future of Man.* Philadelphia: Fortress, 1972.

Cox, Harvey. "Religion in The Year 2000." In *The Future of Hope,* edited by Walter H. Capps. Philadelphia: Fortress, 1970.

Daniel, Jamie Owen and Tom Moylan, eds. *Not Yet: Reconsidering Ernst Bloch.* London: Verso, 1997.

Deledalle, Gérard. *Charles S. Peirce: An Intellectual Biography.* Translated by Susan Petrillio. Amsterdam: John Benjamins, 1990.

———. *Charles S. Peirce's Philosophy of Signs: Essays in Comparative Semiotics.* Bloomington: Indiana University Press, 2000.

Descartes, René. *Meditations on First Philosophy.* Translated by John Cottingham. New York: Cambridge University Press, 1986.

Deuser, Hermann. *Gott: Geist und Natur: Theologische Konsequenzen aus Charles S. Peirce's Religionsphilosophie.* Berlin: de Gruyter, 1993.

Dewey, John. *Experience and Nature.* 1929. Reprinted, New York: Dover, 1958.

Dinesen, Anne Marie. "Tout signe est une promesse: Note sur l'habitude du croire selon C. S. Peirce." In *Qu'est-ce qu'une promesse?,* edited by Per Aage Brandt and Annie Prassoloff, Peotica et Analytica, Supplément 1. Århus: Aarhus University Press, 1991.

———. *C. S. Peirce: Fænomenologi, Semiotik og Logik.* Århus: Tryk, 1992.

Esposito, Joseph L. "On the Origins and Foundations of Peirce's Semiotic." In *Studies in Peirce's Semiotic,* 19–24. Peirce Studies 1. Lubbock, TX: Institute for Studies in Pragmaticism, 1979.

———. *Evolutionary Metaphysics: The Development of Peirce's Theory of Categories.* Athens: Ohio University Press, 1980.

Fann, K. T. *Peirce's Theory of Abduction.* The Hague: Nijhoff, 1970.

Feibleman, James. *An Introduction to Peirce's Philosophy: Interpreted as a System.* New York: Harper & Brothers, 1946.

Fendt, Gene. *For What May I Hope?: Thinking with Kant and Kierkegaard.* American University Studies, Series 5, 104. New York: Lang, 1990.

Fisch, Max H. *Classic American Philosophers.* Century Philosophy Series. New York: Appleton Century Crofts, Educational Division, 1951. 2d ed., New York: Fordham University Press, 1996.

———. *Peirce, Semeiotic, and Pragmatism: Essays by Max Fisch.* Edited by Kenneth Laine Ketner and Christian Kloesel. Bloomington: Indiana University Press, 1986.

Fitzgerald, John J. *Peirce's Theory of Signs as Foundation for Pragmatism.* The Hague: Mouton, 1966.

Flower, Elizabeth, and Murray G. Murphey. *A History of Philosophy in America*. New York: Capricorn, 1977.
Forster, Paul. "The Logic of Pragmatism: A Neglected Argument for Peirce's Pragmatic Maxim." *Trans.* 39 (2003) 525–54.
Frank, Manfred. *Der unendliche Mangel an Sein: Schellings Hegelkritik und die Anfänge der Marxschen Dialektik*. Munich: Fink, 1992.
Freeman, Eugene, ed. *The Relevance of Charles Peirce*. Monist Library of Philosophers. La Salle: The Hegeler Institute, 1983.
Fuhrmanns, Horst. "Einleitung und Anmerkungen." In *Über das Wesen der menschlichen Freiheit*, by F. W. J. Schelling. Stuttgart: Reclam, 1995.
Gale, Richard M. "The Metaphysics of John Dewey." *Trans.* 38 (2002) 477–519
Gallie, Bryce W. *Peirce and Pragmatism*. Harmondsworth, UK: Penguin, 1952.
Galloway, Allan. *Wolfhart Pannenberg*. London: George Allen & Unwin, 1973.
Godfrey, Joseph J. *A Philosophy of Human Hope*. Dordrecht: Nijhoff, 1987.
Goodman, Russell B. *Pragmatism: A Contemporary Reader*. New York: Routledge, 1995.
Goudge, Thomas A. *The Thought of C. S. Peirce*. Toronto: University of Toronto Press, 1950.
Greer, Rowan A. *Christian Hope and Christian Life: Raids on the Inarticulate*. New York: Crossroad, 2001.
Gutiérrez, Gustavo. *A Theology of Liberation*. Translated and edited by Sister Caridad Inda and John Eagleson. New York: Orbis, 1988.
Habermas, Jürgen. "Das Absolute und die Geschichte: Von der Zwiespältigkeit in Schellings Denken." Ph. D. diss., Rheinischen Friedrich Wilhelms-Universität, Bonn, 1954.
Hanson, Norwood Russell. "The Logic of Discovery." *Journal of Philosophy* 55 (1958) 1073–89.
———. "Is There a Logic of Scientific Discovery?" In *Current Issues in the Philosophy of Science*, edited by Herbert Feigl and Grover Maxwell, 20–35. Symposia of Scientists and Philosophers. New York: Holt Rinehart and Winston, 1959.
Hauge, Hans, ed. *Hvad er metafysik? Hvad er moderne?* Århus: Aarhus Universitetsforlag, 1990.
Hausman, Carl R. *Charles S. Peirce's Evolutionary Philosophy*. Cambridge: Cambridge University Press, 1993.
Heidegger, Martin. *Die Selbstbehauptung der deutschen Universität*. Edited by Hermann Heidegger. Frankfurt: Klostermann, 1983.
Henrich, Dieter. *Identität und Objektivität: Eine Untersuchung über Kants transzendentale Deduktion*. Heidelberg: Winter, 1976.
———. *Selbstverhältnisse: Gedanken und Auslegungen zu den Grundlagen der klassischen deutschen Philosophie*. Stuttgart: Reclam,1982.
———. *Fluchtlinien: Philosophische Essays*. Frankfurt: Suhrkamp, 1982.
Hintikka, Jaakko. "What is Abduction? The Fundamental Problem of Contemporary Epistemology." *Trans.* 34 (1998) 503–33.
Höffe, Otfried. *Immanuel Kant*. Translated by Marshall Farrier. Albany: State University of New York Press, 1994.
Hookway, Christopher. *Peirce. The Arguments of the Philosophers*. London: Routledge & Kegan Paul, 1985.
———. *Truth, Rationality, and Pragmatism: Themes from Peirce*. Oxford: Clarendon, 2000.
Hütter, Reinhard. *Suffering Divine Things: Theology as Church Practice*. Grand Rapids: Eerdmans, 2000.

Kant, Immanuel. *Gesammelte Schriften.* Vols. 1–28. Berlin, 1923.
———. *Kritik der reinen Vernunft* vol. 1–2. Edited by Wilhelm Weischedel. Frankfurt: Suhrkamp, 1974.
———. *Critique of Pure Reason.* Translated by Norman Kemp Smith. New York: St. Martin's Press, 1929.
———. *Briefwechsel.* Hamburg: Meiner, 1986.
———. *Critique of Practical Reason.* Translated and edited by Mary Gregor. Cambridge: Cambridge University Press, 1997.
———. *Religion within the Limits of Reason Alone.* Translated by Theodore M. Greene and Hoyt H. Hudson. New York: Harper & Row, 1934.
Käsemann, Ernst. *New Testament Questions of Today.* Translated by W. J. Montague. Philadelphia: Fortress, 1969.
Kent, Beverly E. *Charles S. Peirce: Logic and the Classification of Science.* Montreal: McGill-Queen's University Press, 1987.
Ketner, Kenneth Laine, ed. *Peirce and Contemporary Thought: Philosophical Inquiries.* American Philosophy Series. New York: Fordham University Press, 1995.
Kierkegaard, Søren. "Breve." In *Breve og Aktstykker vedrørende Søren Kierkegaard I.* Copenhagen: Munksgaard, 1953.
Kloesel, Christian J. W. "Speculative Grammar: From Duns Scotus to Charles Peirce." In *Studies in Peirce's Semiotic,* edited by Kenneth Laine Ketner and Joseph Ransdell. Peirce Studies 1. Bloomington: Indiana University Press, 1979.
Korsch, Dietrich. *Der Grund der Freiheit: Eine Untersuchung zur Problemgeschichte der positiven Philosophie und zur Systemfunktion des Christentums im Spätwerk F. W. J. Schellings.* Munich: Kaiser, 1980.
Krausser, Peter. "The Three Fundamental Structural Categories of Charles S. Peirce." *Trans.* 13 (1977) 189–215.
Kugelman, Lothar. *Antizipation: Eine begriffsgeschichtliche Untersuchung.* Forschungen zur systematischen und ökumenischen Theologie 50. Göttingen: Vandenhoeck & Ruprecht, 1986.
Landsberg, Paul-Luis. *The Experience of Death: The Moral Problem of Suicide.* New York: Arno, 1977.
Lausberg, Heinrich. *Handbook of Literary Rhetoric: A Foundation for Literary Study.* Translated by M. T. Bliss, A Jansen, and D. E. Orton. Edited by D. E. Orton and R. D. Anderson. Leiden: Brill, 1998.
Lopresti, James. "Rituals and Hopes." *Worship* 52 (1978) 347–58.
Löwith, Karl. *Meaning in History: The Theological Implications of the Philosophy of History.* Chicago: University of Chicago Press, 1949.
Macfarlane, Alexander. *Lectures on Ten British Mathematicians of the Nineteenth Century.* Mathematical Monographs 17. New York: Wiley, 1916.
Marcel, Gabriel. *Being and Having.* Translated by Katharine Farrer. Westminster: Dacre, 1949.
———. *Homo Viator: Introduction to a Metaphysics of Hope.* Translated by Emma Craufurd. New York: Harper & Brothers, 1962.
Marsch, Wolf-Dieter. *Hoffen Woraus? Auseinandersetzung mit Ernst Bloch.* Hamburg: Furche, 1963.
———. *Zukunft.* Themen der Theologie 2. Stuttgart: Kreuz, 1969.
———. *Philosophie im Schatten Gottes.* Gütersloh: Gütersloher Verlagshaus Gerd Mohn, 1973.
———, ed. *Diskussion über die "Theologie der Hoffnung."* München: Kaiser, 1967.

Marshall, James D. "On What We May Hope: Rorty on Dewey and Foucault." In *The New Scholarship on Dewey*. Edited by Jim Garrison. Dordrecht: Kluwer Academic, 1995.

Matic, Marko. *Jürgen Moltmanns Theologie in Auseinandersetzung mit Ernst Bloch*. Europäische Hochschulschriften. Reihe 23, Theologie 209. Frankfurt: Lang, 1983.

Meeks, Douglas M. *Origins of the Theology of Hope*. Philadelphia: Fortress, 1974.

Menand, Louis. *The Metaphysical Club: A Story of Ideas in America*. New York: Farrar, Straus and Giroux, 2001.

Metz, Johannes Baptist. "Unbelief as a Theological Problem." *The Church and the World*, 6:59–77. New York: Paulist, 1965.

———. "Creative Hope." *Cross Currents* 27 (1967) 171–79.

———. "Religion and Society in Light of a Political Theology." In *The Future of Hope*, edited by Walter H. Capps. Philadelphia: Fortress, 1970.

Misak, Cheryl, editor. *The Cambridge Companion to Peirce*. Cambridge: Cambridge University Press, 2004.

Moltmann, Jürgen. "Hope without Faith: An Eschatological Humanism without God." *Is God Dead?* Concilium 16, edited by Johannes B. Metz, 14–21. New York: Paulist, 1966.

———. *Theology of Hope: On the Ground and the Implications of a Christian Eschatology*. Translated by J. W. Leitch. New York: Harper & Row, 1967. Reprinted, Minneapolis: Fortress, 1993.

———. "Hope and History." *Theology Today* 25 (1968) 369–86.

———. *Im Gespräch mit Ernst Bloch: Eine theologische Wegbegleitung*. Munich: Kaiser, 1976.

———. *Experiences of God*. Translated by Margaret Kohl. Philadelphia: Fortress, 1980.

Moore, Edward C., and Richard S. Robin, eds. *Studies in the Philosophy of Charles Sanders Peirce*. Second series. Amherst: University of Massachusetts Press, 1964.

Murphey, Murray G. "On Peirce's Metaphysics." *Trans.* 1 (1965) 12–25.

———. "Kant's Children: The Cambridge Pragmatists." *Trans.* 3–4 (1967) 3–33.

———. *The Development of Peirce's Philosophy*. Indianapolis: Hackett, 1993.

Murray, Michael J., ed. *Reason for the Hope Within*. Grand Rapids: Eerdmans, 1999.

Myers, William T. "Pragmatist Metaphysics: A Defense." *Trans.* 40 (2004) 39–52.

Nebe, Gottfried. *'Hoffnung' bei Paulus: Elpis und ihre Synonyme im Zusammenhang der Eschatologie*. Studien zur Umwelt des Neuen Testaments 16. Göttingen: Vandenhoeck & Ruprecht, 1983.

Neiman, Susan. *The Unity of Reason: Rereading Kant*. New York: Oxford University Press, 1994.

Nietzsche, Friedrich. *Thus Spoke Zarathustra*. In *The Portable Nietzsche*. Edited and translated by Walter Kaufmann. New York: Viking, 1954.

Oakes, Edward T. "Discovering the American Aristotle." *First Things* 38 (1993) 24–33.

Olson, Roger E. "The Human Self-Realization of God: Hegelian Elements in Pannenberg's Christology." *Perspectives in Religious Studies* 13 (1986) 207–23.

Orange, Donna M. *Peirce's Conception of God: A Developmental Study*. Peirce Studies 2. Lubbock: Institute for Studies in Pragmaticism, 1984.

Pannenberg, Wolfhart. *Jesus — God and Man*. Translated by Lewis L. Wilkins and Duane A. Priebe. Philadelphia: Westminster, 1968.

———. *The Idea of God and Human Freedom*. Translated by R. A. Wilson. Philadelphia: Westminster, 1973.

———. *Anthropology in Theological Perspective*. Translated by Matthew J. O'Connell. Philadelphia: Westminster, 1985.

―――. *Systematic Theology*. 3 vols. Translated by Geoffrey W. Bromily. Grand Rapids: Eerdmans, 1991–98.

―――. "A Response to My American Friends." In *The Theology of Wolfhart Pannenberg*, edited by Carl E. Braaten and Philip Clayton, 313–36. Minneapolis: Augsburg, 1988.

―――. "An Autobiographical Sketch." In *The Theology of Wolfhart Pannenberg*. Edited by Carl E. Braaten and Philip Clayton, 11–18. Minneapolis: Augsburg, 1988.

―――. *Metaphysics and the Idea of God*. Translated by Philip Clayton. Grand Rapids: Eerdmans, 1990.

―――, editor. *Revelation as History*. Translated by David Granskou. New York: Macmillan, 1968.

Pape, Helmut. "Abduction and the Topology of Human Cognition." *Trans*. 35 (1999) 248–69.

Parker, Kelly A. *The Continuity of Peirce's Thought*. Nashville: Vanderbilt University Press, 1998.

―――. "Peirce's Semeiotic and Ontology." *Trans*. 30 (1994) 51–75.

Pasquariello, Ronald D. "Pannenberg's Philosophical Foundations." *Journal of Religion* 56 (1976) 347–62.

Peters, Curtis H. *Kant's Philosophy of Hope*. American University Studies, Series 5, Philosophy 103. New York: Lang, 1993.

Pfeifer, David E. "Peirce's Application of Semiotic to God." In *Studies in Peirce's Semiotic*, 89–100. Peirce Studies 1. Lubbock: Institute for Studies in Pragmaticism, 1979.

Pieper, Josef. *On Hope*. Translated by Mary Frances McCarthy. San Francisco: Ignatius, 1986.

―――. *An Anthology*. San Francisco: Ignatius, 1989.

―――. *In Defense of Philosophy: Classical Wisdom Stands up to Modern Challenges*. Translated by Lothar Krauth. San Francisco: Ignatius, 1992.

―――. *Hope and History: Five Salzburg Lectures*. San Francisco: Ignatius, 1994.

Plantinga, Alvin. *God and Other Minds: A Study of the Rational Justification of Belief in God*. Ithaca, NY: Cornell University Press, 1967.

―――. *Warranted Christian Belief*. New York: Oxford University Press, 2000.

―――, and Nicholas Wolterstorff, eds. *Faith and Rationality: Reason and Belief in God*. Notre Dame: University of Notre Dame Press, 1983.

Plato. *Complete Works*. Edited by John M. Cooper and D. S. Hutchinton. Indianapolis: Hackett, 1997.

Polkinghorne, John, and Michael Welker. *The End of the World and the Ends of God: Science and Theology on Eschatology*. Harrisburg, PA: Trinity, 2000.

Popper, Karl R. *The Logic of Scientific Discovery*. London: Routledge, 1959.

―――. *Conjectures and Refutations: The Growth of Scientific Knowledge*. London: Routledge, 1963.

―――. *Of Clouds and Clocks: An Approach to the Problem of Rationality and the Freedom of Man*. The Arthur Holly Compton Memorial Lecture. St. Louis: Washington University, 1966.

Potter, Vincent G., SJ. *Charles S. Peirce on Norms and Ideals*. Amherst: University of Massachusetts Press, 1967.

―――. *Peirce's Philosophical Perspectives*. Edited by Vincent M. Colapietro. New York: Fordham University Press, 1996.

Pruyser, Paul W. "Phenomenology and Dynamics of Hoping." *Journal for the Scientific Study of Religion* 3 (1963) 86–96.

von Rad, Gerhard. *Old Testament Theology.* 2 vols. Translated by D. M. G. Stalker. Edinburgh: Oliver and Boyd, 1962–65.

Randall, Albert B. *The Mystery of Hope in the Philosophy of Gabriel Mardel 1888–1973: Hope and Homo Viator.* Problems in Contemporary Philosophy 33. Lewiston, NY: Mellen, 1992.

Ransdell, Joseph. "Some Leading Ideas of Peirce's Semiotic." *Semiotica* 19 (1977) 157–78.

Raposa, Michael L. "Habits and Essences." *Trans.* 20 (1984) 147–67.

———. "Peirce's Theological Semiotic." *Journal of Religion* 67 (1987) 493–509.

———. *Peirce's Philosophy of Religion.* Peirce Studies 5. Bloomington: Indiana University Press, 1989.

———. "The Fuzzy Logic of Religious Discourse." *American Journal of Semiotics* 10 (1993) 101–13.

———. "Self-Control." *American Journal of Theology and Philosophy* 21 (2000) 256–68.

———. Review of *A Semiotic Theory of Theology and Philosophy*, by Robert S. Corrington. *Modern Theology* 18 (2002) 302–4.

Raven, Charles E. *Teilhard de Chardin: Scientist and Seer.* New York: Harper & Row, 1962.

Reilly, Francis E., SJ. *Charles Peirce's Theory of Scientific Method.* New York: Fordham University Press, 1970.

Rescher, Nicholas. *The Coherence Theory of Truth.* Oxford: Clarendon, 1973.

Richter, Ansgar. *Der Begriff der Abduktion bei Charles Sanders Peirce.* Frankfurt: Lang, 1995.

Roberts, David D. *Nothing but History: Reconstruction and Extremity after Metaphysics.* Berkeley: University of California Press, 1995.

Rosenthal, Sandra B. "The 'Would-be' Present of C. S. Peirce." *Trans.* 3–4 (1967) 155–62.

———. *Charles Peirce's Pragmatic Pluralism.* New York: State University of New York Press, 1994.

Roth, Robert J. "Anderson on Peirce's Concept of Abduction: Further Reflections." *Trans.* 24 (1988) 131–39.

Royce, Josiah. *The Religious Aspect of Philosophy: A Critique of the Bases of Conduct and of Faith.* New York: Harper, 1958.

Santoni, Ronald E., ed. *Religious Language and the Problem of Religious Knowledge.* Bloomington: Indiana University Press, 1968.

Savan, David. *An Introduction to C. S. Peirce's Full System Semiotics,* Monograph Series of the TSC. Toronto: Victoria University Press, 1976.

Sayers, Dorothy L. *Busman's Honeymoon.* New York: Harper, 1937.

Scheler, Max. *The Nature of Sympathy.* Translated by Peter Heath. New Haven: Yale University Press, 1954.

Schelling, F. W. J. *Friedrich Wilhelm Joseph von Schellings sämtliche Werke.* Vols. 1–14. Edited by K. F. A. Schelling. Stuttgart: Cotta, 1856–1861.

———. *Über das Wesen der menschlichen Freiheit.* Frankfurt am Main: Suhrkamp, 1967.

Schlemmer, Johannes, ed. *Die Hoffnungen unserer Zeit.* Munich: Piper, 1963.

Schneider, Herbert W. "Fourthness." In *Studies in the Philosophy of Charles Sanders Peirce,* Edited by Philip P. Wiener and Frederich H. Young. Cambridge: Harvard University Press, 1952.

Schulz, Walter. *Die Vollendung des Deutschen Idealismus in der Spätphilosophie Schellings.* Pfullingen: Neske, 1975.

———. *Der Gott Der Neuzeitlichen Metaphysik.* Pfullingen: Neske, 1991.

Schwarz, Hans. *Eschatology*. Grand Rapids: Eerdmans, 2000.
Schweitzer, Albert. *Die Religionsphilosophie Kants in der Kritik der reinen Vernunft bis zur Religion innerhalb der Grenzen der blossen Vernunft*. Freiburg: Mohr/Siebeck, 1899.
Sebeok, Thomas A. *The Play of Musement*. Bloomington: Indiana University Press, 1981.
Seigfried, Charlene Haddock. "Ghosts Walking Underground." *Trans.* 40 (2004) 53–81.
Shade, Patrick: *Habits of Hope: A Pragmatic Theory*. Nashville: Vanderbilt University Press, 2001.
Shanahan, Timothy. "The First Moment of Scientific Inquiry: C. S. Peirce on the Logic of Abduction." *Trans.* 22 (1986) 449–66.
Smith, John E. "Religion and Theology in Peirce." In *Studies in the Philosophy of Charles Sanders Peirce,* edited by Philip P. Wiener and Frederich H. Young, 251–70. Cambridge: Harvard University Press, 1952.
———. *The Spirit of American Philosophy*. New York: Oxford University Press, 1963.
———. "Community and Reality." In *Perspectives on Peirce*. Edited by Richard Bernstein. New Haven: Yale University Press, 1965.
Spera, Salvatora. "La Philosophie de la Religion de Schelling dans son développement et son rejet par Kierkegaard." In *Kierkegaard and Dialectics,* edited by Jørgen K. Bukdahl, 147–90. Aarhus: University of Aarhus, 1979.
Staat, Wim. "On Abduction, Deduction, Induction and the Categories." *Trans.* 29 (1993) 225–37.
Swinburne, Richard G. *The Existence of God*. Oxford: Clarendon, 1979.
———. *The Coherence of Theism*. Oxford: Clarendon, 1993.
Teilhard de Chardin, Pierre. *The Phenomenon of Man*. Translated by Bernard Wall. New York: Harper & Row, 1965.
Theunissen, Michael. "Krise der Macht: Thesen zur Theorie des dialektischen Widerspruchs." *Hegel-Jahrbuch*. Edited by Wilhelm R. Beyer (1974) 318–29.
Thompson, Manley. *The Pragmatic Philosophy of C. S. Peirce*. Chicago: University of Chicago Press, 1953.
Tinder, Glenn. *The Fabric of Hope: An Essay*. Grand Rapids: Eerdmans, 1999.
Trammell, Richard Louis. "Charles S. Peirce's Understanding of Religion." Ph.D. diss., Columbia University, 1971.
———. "Religion, Instinct and Reason in the Thought of Charles S. Peirce." *Trans.* 8 (1972) 3–25.
Turrisi, Patricia Ann, ed. *Pragmatism as a Principle and Method of Right Thinking: The 1903 Harvard "Lectures on Pragmatism."* New York: State University of New York Press, 1997.
Velkley, Richard L. "Unity of Reason as Aporetic Ideal." In *The Unity of Reason: Essays on Kant's Philosophy*, by Dieter Henrich. Edited by Richard L. Velkley. Cambridge: Harvard University Press, 1994.
Ward, Roger. "Experience as Religious Discovery in Edwards and Peirce." *Trans.* 36 (2000) 297–309.
Weiss, Paul. "The Logic of the Creative Process." In *Studies in the Philosophy of Charles Sanders Peirce,* edited by Philip P. Wiener and Frederic H. Young, 166–82. Cambridge: Harvard University Press, 1952.
West, Cornel. *The American Evasion of Philosophy: A Genealogy of Pragmatism*. Wisconsin Project on American Writers. Madison: University of Wisconsin Press, 1989.
White, Alan R. *Methods of Metaphysics*. London: Croom Helm, 1987.
Whitehead, Alfred North. *Process and Reality*. Corrected edition. Edited by David Ray Griffin and Donald W. Sherburne. New York: Free Press, 1978.

Widmann, Peter. "Kants tre spørgsmål" [Kant's Three Questions]. In *Teologi og modernitet*, edited by Peter Thyssen and Anders Moe Rasmussen, 22–33. Århus: Aarhus Universitetsforlag, 1997.

Wiener, Philip P. *Evolution and the Founders of Pragmatism*. New York: Harper, 1949.

Wisdom, John. *Paradox and Discovery*. Oxford: Blackwell, 1965.

Wolstenholme, Gordon, ed. *Man and His Future*. A Ciba Foundation Volume. Boston: Little, Brown and Company, 1963.

Zournazi, Mary. *Hope: New Philosophies for Change*. New York: Routledge, 2002.

www.ingramcontent.com/pod-product-compliance
Lightning Source LLC
Chambersburg PA
CBHW062046220426
43662CB00010B/1676